THE UNITED NATIONS UNIVERSITY/THIRD WORLD FORUM

STUDIES IN AFRICAN POLITICAL ECONOMY

African Diaspora Research Project
Urban Affairs Programs
Michigan State University
East Lansing, MI 48824 -- USA

Adjustment
or Delinking?

THE UNITED NATIONS UNIVERSITY/THIRD WORLD FORUM

STUDIES IN AFRICAN POLITICAL ECONOMY
General Editor: Samir Amin

The United Nations University's Project on Transnationalization or Nation-Building in Africa (1982–1986) was undertaken by a network of African scholars under the co-ordination of Samir Amin. The purpose of the Project was to study the possibilities of and constraints on national autocentric development of African countries in the context of the world-system into which they have been integrated. Since the 1970s the world-system has been in a crisis of a severity and complexity unprecedented since the end of the Second World War; the Project examines the impact of this contemporary crisis on the political, economic and cultural situation of Africa today. Focusing on the complex relationship between transnationalization (namely, the dynamics of the world-system) and nation-building, which is seen as a precondition for national development, the Project explores a wide range of problems besetting Africa today and outlines possible alternatives to the prevailing development models which have proved to be inadequate.

THE UNITED NATIONS UNIVERSITY/THIRD WORLD FORUM

STUDIES IN AFRICAN POLITICAL ECONOMY

D0140298

Adjustment or Delinking?

The African Experience

Edited by Azzam Mahjoub

United Nations University Press
Tokyo

Zed Books Ltd.
London and New Jersey

Adjustment or Delinking? The African Experience
was first published in 1990
by:
Zed Books Ltd., 57 Caledonian Road, London N1 9BU, UK, and
171 First Avenue, Atlantic Highlands, New Jersey 07716, USA
and:
United Nations University Press, Toho Seimei Building,
15–1 Shibuya 2-chome, Shibuya-ku, Tokyo 150, Japan
in co-operation with
The Third World Forum, B.P. 3501, Dakar, Senegal.

Copyright © The United Nations University, 1990.

Translation by A. M. Berrett.
Cover designed by Andrew Corbett.
Typeset by EMS Photosetters, Rochford, Essex.
Printed and bound in the United Kingdom
at Bookcraft (Bath) Ltd, Midsomer Norton.

British Library Cataloguing in Publication Data

Adjustment or delinking? : the African experience.
 – (Studies in African political economy).
 1. Africa. Economic development. Political aspects
 I. Mahjoub, Azzam. II. Series
 330.960328

 ISBN 0-86232-842-X
 ISBN 0-86232-843-8 pbk

Library of Congress Cataloging-in-Publication Data

Adjustment or Delinking? : the African experience/
 edited by Azzam Mahjoub.
  p.   cm. – (Studies in African political economy)
 Translated from the French by A. M. Berrett.
 Bibliography: p.
 Includes index.
 ISBN 0-86232-842-X (Zed Books)
 ISBN 0-86232-843-8 (Zed Books : pbk.)
  1. Africa – Economic policy. 2. Africa – Economic conditions –
 1960– . I. Mahjoub, Azzam. II. United Nations University. III. Series.
 HC800.A5526 1989.   89-9027
  338.96–dc20
                                                              CIP

Contents

Tables

Preface

Samir Amin*

I am pleased to introduce this book in our Third World Forum–United Nations University African series. It is the product of a working group devoted to examining some present or past African attempts (Algeria, Burkina Faso, Egypt, Ethiopia, Ghana, Tanzania, Uganda and Zimbabwe) at a form of development different from that evolved by the world expansion of capitalism.

Africa, of all Third World regions, has seen the largest numbers of such attempts. The governments in twenty of the fifty African states have, at some time, more or less radically, declared the intention to 'break' with the colonial and neocolonial past and embark on a new national and radical path of an independent and socialist development. This socialism is sometimes specifically labelled (Arab or African), at others proclaimed to be scientific, Marxist, or Marxist–Leninist. Depending on the circumstances, this declared break with the past has been made in the heat of the moment, right after the victory of the liberation movement seizing independence: sometimes after a long and bitter war (Algeria, Angola, Cape Verde, Guinea-Bissau, Zimbabwe); soon after the achievement of independence (Nkrumah's Ghana, Guinea, Modibo Keita's Mali, Tanzania); or following major political and social changes (overthrow of the monarchies in Egypt and Libya); or, again, following popular anti-neocolonial movements (Benin, Burkina Faso, Congo, Rawlings's Ghana, Madagascar, Uganda). In most if not all cases, the army played an important role in the political shift under discussion.

But in these experiences Africa also has a high proportion of questionable results: some see them as mediocre, others as little different from those obtained by classic neocolonial development. Neither the goal of economic liberation from dependence on the world capitalist system, completing political liberation, nor that of building a new society in sharp contrast to that of the capitalist Third World seem to have advanced sufficiently to have reached the point of no return. Indeed, an effective reversal of the trend and an often noisy return to 'development' as desired by the Western powers has occurred in a number of these countries, either following *coups d'état* or as a result of a gradual shift. Today, almost all are facing the real threat, augmented by the

* Translated by A. M. Berrett

crisis, of being forced to submit to the *diktat* of the West, operating through its 'international agencies' – the World Bank, the IMF etc.

These two facts are worth looking at more closely.

World capitalist expansion has always had and still has a polarizing effect. From the very beginning it produced and perpetuated, in a variety of forms, a contrast between centre and periphery that was immanent in actually existing capitalism. In this sense then, the development of the periphery has always entailed a never-ending 'adjustment' to the demands and constraints of the dominant capital. The centres are 'restructured', the peripheries are 'adjusted' to these restructurings. Never the reverse.

Nevertheless, the violence of the effects of these successive adjustments is not always the same from one phase to another in the history of capitalism. For this worldwide expansion takes the form of a succession of long cycles (20–50 years) in which A phases of 'prosperity' and accelerated growth alternate with B phases of structural crises of the global system. During the A phases of prosperity 'adjustment' seems to be less difficult, sometimes even easy for some countries: the demand for exports grows at high rates, capital is available and looking for outlets, conflicts are attenuated (the period is often a long period of peace – at least relative peace) etc. This adjustment in general growth is of course unequal, because the periphery fulfils various functions in the global system and there are several peripheries rather than a single periphery. There are the 'rich' peripheries, important for the system at the stage under consideration, which provide products whose marketing worldwide is growing faster than others (because they are associated with the technologies in the van of progress), which offer worthwhile markets for the capital and products of the centre.

The ease with which they 'adjust' leads to many illusions, such as those the World Bank and other ideological supporters of capital have fuelled, especially for the newly industrializing countries (NICs): clearly, the external indebtedness produced by their very success had not been foreseen. But there are also those left aside, ones of no interest in the typical structures of the system of the day. These sometimes fulfilled important functions at an earlier stage in the evolution of the global system, but have now lost their place. They constitute the 'fourth world', those delinked whether they like it or not, who passively suffer the fate that the system dishes out to them. For the countries of the 'fourth world', the 'least developed', regarded as something new, are in reality a permanent product of capitalist expansion. An example of this old fourth world is provided by the regions exploited through the use of slaves in the Americas in the mercantilist period; north-east Brazil and the West Indies (Haiti among others). Once these regions were looked upon as 'prosperous' and they formed the core of the periphery corresponding to the system that existed at the time. Subsequently the new structures of capitalist development marginalized the relative importance of these areas, which are today among the most wretched of the Third World. The history of capitalist expansion is not only that of the 'development' it has occasioned. It is also that of the savage destruction on which it was built. There is in capitalism a destructive aspect, usually glossed over in the flattering image of the system that is produced.

The phases of restructuring (B phases) constitute the moments of truth in the evolution of the system. Illusions vanish. The difficulties – the danger of which had been denied – become the means by which the dominant capital imposes its *diktat*. There is no more any question of dreams of independence; the law of profit reminds the 'underdeveloped' of the fate reserved for them: super-exploitation and subjection. 'Recompradorization' is the order of the day, by all economic and financial means (such as the use made today of the external debt and the food weapon to exert pressure), but also political and military ones (for example, *coups d'état*, or interventions such as that of Zionism in the Middle East etc.).

But in this long succession of misfortunes that is what the history of capitalist expansion is for the peoples of the periphery, Africa occupies a particularly vulnerable place. Whole regions of the continent, laid waste by the slave trade in the service of mercantilist capitalism, have still not recovered from these early ravages. Later, colonization continued the work of destroying the continent. We have two obvious examples.

First, that of settler colonization in North Africa (above all Algeria) and East and Southern Africa (Kenya, South Africa, Zimbabwe). Part of the remote origin of the current difficulties of Algerian agriculture – the 'deruralization' of the country, accelerated by war – is to be sought in this. In Zimbabwe, the highlands seized by the whites – thus forcing the Africans confined in poor and inadequate reserves to provide cheap labour – owed their apparent 'prosperity' only to this workforce that could be made to work and their waste of the country's natural resources. The liberation of the country finally made it possible to shed light on this alleged 'success' of settler agriculture. But it also bequeathed a problem that is not settled.[1]

The second example is that of the rape of the land and the super-exploitation of peasant labour that colonization imposed elsewhere, in the areas of the *économie de traite*. Here, as I have written elsewhere, colonization was able to secure a surplus at zero cost: without investments to improve production methods (control of water, implements and mechanization etc.) or agronomic research (other than research into a few export crops, at the expense of food crops). The surplus was doubtless very limited in absolute terms, but was an onerous burden for the peasantry and for the future of the country, through the soil destruction on which the trade system rested. There, too, the current difficulties of African agriculture, reaching the extreme of famine in the Sahel, have their remote origins.[2]

In reality, Africa, at the height of triumphant colonization, had only a marginal position in the world system. In fact it was its role as a mineral reserve (brought out by the work of our colleague Fayçal Yachir)[3] that was the main justification for most of what it did. Later, with independence and neocolonialism, the pillage of agricultural land and mining rent was not challenged, far from it. Neither the agricultural revolution nor industrialization have yet been tackled on the scale required by the demands of our times.

It is the poor prospect offered to Africa through capitalist expansion that accounts for such frequent rejections and the numerous attempts to 'do something', to escape from the simple logic of capitalism. But simultaneously, the objective conditions created by the legacy of this history make this a peculiarly difficult task. The nature of this difficulty could be formulated by saying that the external factor (here particularly unfavourable) combines with internal factors that themselves are not very favourable because they have been shaped largely by the external factor.

The response to the challenge of our time imposes what I have suggested naming 'delinking'. This concept is, in a way, the other term of the contradiction 'adjustment or delinking'. I shall not here discuss in detail the theory of delinking, which was the subject of a recent work to which the interested reader is referred,[4] but in order to avoid any misunderstanding, simply state that delinking is not synonymous with autarky, but rather with the subordination of external relations to the logic of internal development. (Adjustment consists precisely in grafting internal development on to the possibilities offered by the world system.) More precisely, delinking consists in refusing to submit to the demands of the globalized law of value, that is, to the alleged 'rationality' of the system of world prices that gives concrete form to the requirements of the reproduction of globalized capital. It thus assumes that society has the capacity to define for itself a different range of criteria of rationality of internal economic choices, in short a 'law of value that is national in scope'.

Which social forces might be the historical subject of this option in favour of breaking with the world capitalist system? The answer, so obvious as to be almost tautological, is that these forces cannot be other than those that are the victims of peripheral capitalist development and not those that are its beneficiaries. But actual capitalist development not only has polarizing effects worldwide (deepening the contrast between centre and periphery) but also within societies in the periphery (while it does not within central capitalist societies). In other words, income distribution is more unequal in the periphery than in the centre, and, although in the centre it is relatively stable over time, with the development of the periphery it tends towards growing inequality.[5] The result is that the 'privileged classes' have a real interest in pursuing capitalist expansion such as it is, despite the inferior position assigned to them in the system and perhaps sometimes the 'frustration' of their national ambitions. Of course, there are conflicts between them and the dominant capital, and these classes are sometimes capable of crossing swords with imperialism to better their positions in the system. But only so far. That is, in the last analysis they will judge that there is no 'benefit' (they even say no 'possibility' of) in delinking. This is what they express day in and day out when they declare 'interdependence' to be unavoidable ('we are all in the same boat' etc.). The nature of these privileged classes has of course also evolved historically. Formerly, the dominant element in the local bloc allied to imperialism was often made up of the oligarchies of big landowners (in Latin America, India, China, Egypt etc.) or by the 'chieftaincies' (in Africa). The national independence movement was thus forced to rise up against this bloc and to replace it with a new bloc dominanted by new, bourgeois-type classes, (local industrial and financial, rich peasants, and state, bourgeoisies etc.) generally favouring industrialization. This by no means a negligible change of world social alliances, accompanied the global restructuring of the system. This is because the world social alliances by their nature define the structure suitable to the stage of capitalist development reached.

But it is still true that in the societies in the periphery, the privileged classes in question constitute a minority, ranging from a negligible 1% or 2% of the population to a less negligible 10% to 25%. As for the popular classes that are the victims of capitalist expansion, their status varies, and as a result of the very nature of this expansion, tend not to be homogenized and reduced to a single model. Among them there are poor peasantries (in the plural), working classes, urbanized peasants-cum-unemployed in the shantytowns, old *petit bourgeoisies* (artisans) and new ones (junior employees etc.). If we add that peripheral capitalist development, because of its centrifugal character, constitutes an obstacle to the crystallization of the nation and even tends to break up old nations where they existed, we get some idea of how many further causes of division in the camp of the popular forces there are (for example, ethnicity and language, religion, artificial borders bequeathed by colonization and balkanization – particularly marked in Africa).[6]

Delinking thus implies a 'popular', content anti-capitalist in the sense of being in conflict with the dominant capitalism, but permeated with the multiplicity of divergent interests (over and beyond their anti-systemic convergence) of the various fractions that make up the people in question. That is why I advanced the thesis that 'post-capitalism' remains a very long historical stage shot through with a permanent conflict between three poles that define the internal tendencies of society: local capitalism (which responds to the needs expressed by the development of productive forces); socialism (which reflects the anti-capitalist aspirations of the popular masses); and *étatisme* (produced by the autonomy of power from capitalist and socialist forces, which at the same time reflect the aspirations of the new class that controls the state). The conflict-laden balance among these tendencies is itself, of course, variable, depending on the concrete situations and the particular moment.

A social force is necessary to cement the popular alliance, overcome its internal conflicts, formulate the alternative popular national project, direct the popular bloc to enable it to get itself into power, build the new state and arbitrate the conflicts mentioned above peculiar to the popular national transition. This, in my opinion, is the role proper to the revolutionary intelligentsia, the 'organic intellectual' responding to the objective requirement of our times. This is a category peculiar to the situation of the peripheries of the capitalist system, not in the least analogous to the problematic of the *petit bourgeoisie* (a confused class as ever) or with that of the 'single party' born of national liberation, or again with that of the role of intellectuals as channels of expression of the various social classes. Elsewhere I have developed a few reflections on the intelligentsia of the Third World.[7]

Obviously, in these historical conditions, at least two fundamental questions are posed to the intelligentsia and popular power, that of democracy and that of the cultural content of the societal project. I have also dealt with these questions directly in other writings.[8] As regards the cultural dimension, I would like to specify here that neither the surface Westernization of the comprador classes peddling the consumption model of the developed world (and this transmission of the consumption model is only the visible part of the cultural iceberg), nor its apparent opposite – in reality its twin brother – the cultural nationalisms on which so-called fundamentalist religious currents feed, measure up to the challenge. The double blockage to which both these options lead is there to testify to the real difficulty of the project.[9]

A mere enumeration of the problems that the option for a popular national delinking would have to face in the conditions of contemporary Africa would be enough, either to excuse failures, or to demoralize. For first of all it must, at the level of necessary material achievements – development of productive forces and improvement of the living standards of the broad masses – carry through a double agricultural and industrial revolution for which I have said colonization did not prepare the region.

It is not fully realized that the European agricultural revolution developed in a world where the population explosion that accompanied it had the safety valve of massive emigration; at the time, Europe peopled the whole of the Americas and several other regions of the globe. Without this safety valve Western and central Europe would have had to support almost three times its present population since, added to the 400 million Europeans living today, there would be 800 million across the Atlantic who are the descendants of immigrants. But today, for the Third World, living through its population explosion, there is not this possibility of external expansion. Furthermore, modern industry is not capable of absorbing internal, rural to urban migration at the speed that was possible at the time of the European industrial revolution. This means that for real progress technological and social formulae need to be invented to ensure that the bulk of the population remained in their rural home areas for a long time to come.

Obviously, the national liberation movement centred initially, and rightly, on the prior conquest of simple political independence, lacked either a real awareness or an accurate assessment of the scale of the challenge. We must not criticize it for that. But we must be aware that the fine page of history that it wrote is over and done with. Harping on the past does not legitimize the present. We must know how to be patient. We must be aware that the first wave of national liberation has now run its course, and that the forces bearing the next one – with a popular national content – are not yet crystallized around an adequate alternative project. We are thus living in the trough of the wave, marked for that reason by too much disarray and intellectual and political capitulation.

The studies brought together in this book illustrate both the scale of the problems to be resolved and the limits of the conceptions the radical–national state has had of them. The group co-ordinator, Azzam Mahjoub, has endeavoured – successfully – to ask the relevant questions in such a way as to avoid the problematic peculiar to each concrete case studied that would cause us to lose sight of the general lessons we hope to draw from these experiences.

Doubtless, over the last 30 years, there have been other debates as well as the one undertaken by our working group. At least here we should mention the debate on the 'non-capitalist path' which had its moments of glory in the 1960s, when Nasserism was at its height and Nkrumahist pan-Africanism had not yet exhausted itself against the gradual crystallization of new African states. Mention too should be made of what the jargon of progressive African intellectuals calls the 'Dar es Salaam debate' which, in the early 1970s, endeavoured to sort out the question of building socialism in Africa. This is not the place to reopen these arguments which were never closed. Other debates will follow the one whose results are published here. Our programme, among others, has set itself the task of ensuring this.

This work was carried out in the framework of the African Regional Prospects programme conducted jointly by the United Nations University (UNU) and the Third World Forum (TWF). We would like to thank the UNU, the Swedish agency SAREC and UNRISD whose generous support made this work possible. Of course, the opinions expressed are those of their authors alone and do not commit any of the organizations mentioned. We also thank the Office des Presses Universitaires de l'Algérie which, by publishing the work, testified once again to its sense of active African solidarity.

Notes

1. These particular aspects of the agricultural and agrarian problem, like those mentioned below in our reference to the need for an agricultural revolution, have been the subject of another group in the UNU–TWF programme whose work will also be published.

2. See Samir Amin, 'The interlinkage between agricultural revolution and industrialisation'. Paper presented to the OAU–ECA Conference, Abuja, Nigeria, June 1987.

3. Fayçal Yachir, *Les enjeux miniers en Afrique*, Paris, Karthala, 1987. English edition, *Mining in Africa Today: Strategies and Prospects*, in the UNU–TWF series, London, Zed Books Ltd, 1988.

4. Samir Amin, *La déconnexion*, Paris, La Découverte, 1987. See in particular chapter 2, II ('Le modèle de discussion de la loi de la valeur'). (*Delinking*, London, Zed Books, 1990.)

5. Ibid., chapter 3.

6. Samir Amin, 'Nation, ethnie et minorités dans la crise', *Bulletin du FTM* (Dakar), No. 6, 1986.

7. Samir Amin, 'The role of the intelligentsia in the popular national revolution'. Paper, in Arabic, for Conference on the Role of Arab Intellectuals, Cairo, Egypt, 1987; to be published by the Arab Sociological Association.

8. On the question of democracy, see Samir Amin, 'The democratic question in the Arab nation' (Arabic text, in *Al Moustaqbal al Arabi*, No. 4, 1984); Samir Amin,

'Popular national strategy and the democratic question', *Third World Quarterly*, London, 1987.

9. On the cultural question in the Arabo-Islamic world, see Samir Amin, 'Development and the cultural issue: reflections on Arabo-Islamic thought', *Third World Bulletin* (Dakar), No. 7, 1987.

Samir Amin's more detailed publications, in Arabic, are:
The Crisis of Arab Society, Cairo, Egypt, 1985.
Post-capitalism, Beirut, Lebanon, 1987.
'Reflections on the crisis of Arab–Islamic thought' *Al Fike al-Arabi*, No. 45, 1987.

1. Introduction

This book, the outcome of shared thinking about Africa as a whole, is aimed at an examination of post-colonial African experiences often described as socialist, meaning a more or less explicit ideological reference to socialism under a variety of labels and with varying contents (Arab socialism, African socialism etc.). Over and beyond the underlying rhetoric, these experiences constitute, in varying degrees, attempts – some abortive, others still underway – to challenge the operative principle of adjustment to the capitalist world economic system (CWES), a principle seen as leading to unequal and polarized development worldwide.

Originally, this work belonged in an overall problematic initiated by Samir Amin[1] on the contradictory dynamic of nation-building and subordination to transnationalization, the dynamic at the heart of the evolution of post-colonial Africa. What progress have the new African states been able to make towards nation-building, or are they still subordinated to the imperatives of transnationalization?

The concept of transnationalization here refers to the contemporary form assumed by the process of the globalization of the capitalist system; it expresses the tendency of the CWES to become all-embracing in the direction of the formation of a capitalist world economy governed by the law of value. From this angle, underlying this work is the basic idea that adjustment to the CWES signifies subordination to the logic of the functioning of the law of value worldwide, a logic seen as reproducing unequal development.

Challenging the operative principle of adjustment to the CWES thus leads to the alternative concept of delinking, a key concept of this work to which we shall constantly refer. This topic is highly relevant, especially as the world crisis, particularly as it affects Africa, has given prominence to the operative principle of adjustment to the CWES. Key actors within the CWES, such as the World Bank and the IMF, strongly support the need for permanent adjustment to the CWES. The advocation of the so-called structural adjustment policies is the current expression of this requirement. The dominant tendency today is therefore towards adjustment, especially as the situation in Africa is marked by collapsing economies,[2] a deteriorating ecological environment, worsening

* Translated by A. M. Berrett

social tensions and disintegrating political spaces. There seems to be no future for Africa, at least so it is predicted. Manifestly, Africa is a weak link in the CWES.[3] While its adjustment to the CWES has not led to major economic setbacks, at best, and for a minority, it has made possible perverse growth, resulting in rendering Africa more fragile globally,[4] as it is abruptly called upon to make new adjustments. Were all the various initiatives to challenge this operative principle of adjustment fatally flawed? Does the alternative lie only within the necessary adjustment between perverse growth and economic regression? Rejection of this alternative leads precisely to the central theme of delinking. Looking at the problem in the context of Africa, it is proposed first to describe a number of post-colonial attempts that challenge the principle of adjustment to the CWES. How far certain African states initiated and embarked on processes of nation-building within a delinking perspective will also be examined. How were these states, in greater or lesser detail, able to outline a national project to achieve a relative degree of autonomy, underpinning internal and external adjustments, towards a redistribution or transfer of economic and political power and popular participation, correlated in varying degrees with the achievement of greater independence of the outside world?[5]

What social forces (class alliances) initiated and sustained such attempts? What are the ideological contents of these projects? What are the dynamics at work, politically, socially and economically, leading to positive adjustments in the direction of a redistribution of power to the benefit of the national state and popular classes? What is the real content of the challenge (partial and limited though it may be) to the principle of adjustment to the CWES and subordination to the international division of labour? How and to what extent has it been possible to create, consolidate or lose an area of relative autonomy *vis-à-vis* the CWES? What was the play of local social forces and dominant actors within the CWES to counter, deflect or abort these attempts? What are the underlying reasons for the failures these projects have experienced? Why and how are they historically marked, and have they reached their limit? What prospects are there today for the African experiences currently in progress?

The following African countries have been chosen for examination: Egypt, Algeria, Tanzania, Ethiopia, Zimbabwe, Burkina Faso and Ghana. In the 1960s, 1970s or 1980s each of these countries experienced either a process of change driven by a popular outburst leading, in varying degrees, to internal adjustments that sought to benefit the popular classes and were, or were not, articulated on a redefinition and/or renegotiation of the relationship to the CWES towards achieving an area of relative autonomy. Each case will be set out, and, in broad outline, an attempt made to answer the questions posed above.

The principle upon which it is proposed to elicit the historical significance of these experiences rests on a theoretical construction focused on the concepts of adjustment and delinking. These concepts have already been used in this introduction without any proper explanation. The question of the method of investigation and presentation must be faced here. How are theoretical construct, and ordered, concrete analysis of historical facts to be articulated? No theoretical construct can have meaning or reveal anything of value unless it is combined at the methodological level with the concrete study of facts. Without tools, without some systematic but open theoretical frame of reference it is virtually impossible to understand and identify the essential nature of the facts, and to avoid becoming lost in the diversity and the particular. Thus construction of the historical facts relative to the experiences studied presupposes an intrinsic or explicit theoretical filter. This filter or theoretical frame of reference lies initially in historical materialism; but it is also constructed on the basis of often passionate debates with Africa as the field of investigation, and from this viewpoint it summarizes, in hypotheses or propositions, concrete facts or earlier theoretical constructs. This initially inherent frame of reference enables us to signpost and organize our reading of the historical facts relating to these experiences.[6] What was finally chosen, however, rather than proceeding a priori to a detailed explanation of the theoretical nexus focused on adjustment-delinking, rather than positing and constructing the theoretical framework from the outset in a prior systematic form, it was decided initially to limit ourselves to a few underlying hypotheses and guidelines in order to avoid becoming enclosed in a rigid theoretical model, to which the concrete analyses of African experiences would necessarily have to be adjusted.

To analyse the various concrete cases, a relatively open and non-constraining problematic framework has been established through the questions set out above; but a framework sufficiently intrinsic to bring us back constantly to the theoretical nexus articulated on the concepts of adjustment and delinking. Thus, the concrete analysis is organized on flexible lines with the theoretical discussion developed later when it can be informed by the case studies and attempt to provide an explicit, finished character to the adjustment-delinking problematic. Thus, each experience will first be presented according to a pattern in which the hypotheses and propositions that make up the theoretical framework are inherent. This latter will subsequently be clarified, and reconstructed around the key concepts of adjustment and delinking. The pattern in each exposé for each country will be organized around the opening questions we have posed: it seeks first to set out the historical context in which these experiences unfolded, in order to reveal the pre-existing constraints of adjustment and subordination to the CWES (type of integration into the international division of labour, nature of the dominant class alliances articulated on international capital), the social forces at work, the nature of the political change or revolution produced, the characterization of the project, the dynamics of redistribution and challenge to the relationship to the CWES, and the contradictions, limits or prospects of the experience.

Notes

1. Head of the United Nations University research programme 'African Regional Perspectives'.

2. Africa has one-fifth of the world's population but barely 3% of world income. Its share in world trade is under 5%. Globally, the real per capita growth rate declined over the 1970s. Social inequalities sharpened: two-thirds of incomes were in the urban areas. The gap between food requirements and the available food products is rising by 2% per annum. Droughts have revealed the profound structural crisis at the heart of which is an international division of labour which generates underdevelopment and regression.

3. Africa continues to occupy a strategic position in the CWES especially in relation to Europe which it provides with raw materials.

EEC's dependence on Africa (%)

Tropical woods	46	Iron	4.8
Cocoa	41	Manganese	23.3
Coffee	25	Phosphates	15.2
Cotton	20	Uranium	95
Groundnut oil	49	Copper	17.7
Chrome	41		

All of this is in addition to oil.

4. The bulk of African indebtedness is the result of its subordination to monetary, financial and commercial changes in the international system. According to Cline, as reported by F. Hugon, some four-fifths of the growth in the debt of non oil-producing countries can be explained by international factors (oil price rise above American inflation, higher interest rates, decline in the terms of trade and export volumes.) See F. Hugon, 'La crise fiancière en Afrique sub-saharienne et l'intervention du F.M.I.' *Cahiers du CERNEA*, No. 13.

5. The term initial delinking will be used to describe adjustments and redistribution in favour of the popular classes. External delinking further involves actively challenging the principle of adjustment to the CWES by creating a smaller or larger autonomous space. This distinction will be explained theoretically below.

6. Consider the example of the proposition that articulates adjustment-delinking within the CWES to the law of value such as it operates within that system. Additionally, the proposition that separates and links both internal delinking and external delinking. These propositions provide an outline of a preliminary reference framework.

2. Egypt: From the Free Officers' Coup to the *Infitah*

Azzam Mahjoub and Fawzy Mansour*
(Text prepared by Azzam Mahjoub based on Fawzy Mansour's oral presentation at the workshop in Tunis, 1986)

Before the Free Officers' Revolt

In the aftermath of the Second World War, Egypt went through an acute crisis which had its roots in a historical process many centuries old. The country had been in a state of general decline since the 16th century; vassalized by the Turks, Egypt experienced a brutal awakening at the time of Napoleon's surprise campaign. Mohamed Ali's[1] attempted recovery during the early decades of the 19th century failed, leading to Egypt's forced subjection to the capitalist world economic system (CWES) then in the process of formation, and its colonial subjugation to British imperialism. Despite its failure, the national experience of Mohamed Ali inaugurated the new era of the *Nahda* (Renaissance), a concept used to describe the various cultural and political manifestations of the national and pan-national (Arab–Islamic) awakening. In many ways Egypt was one of the most dynamic centres of the Revival and development of an anti-colonial nationalist movement led mainly by the educated strata in the towns. Opposition to British colonial rule developed in Egypt in the late 19th century and found its dominant expression, notably in the inter-war period, in the Wafd party.

The Wafd party recruited its activists in the ranks of the *petit bourgeoisie* while in fact feeding on the ideology of modernization and reform characteristic of the bourgeoisie.[2] By the 1920s, in the framework of a monarchical regime aligned with British imperialism, the Wafd had, despite a few interludes, secured a monopoly on the exercise of political power.

Economically, especially since colonization, the development of Egypt had essentially been based on the export of cotton (which accounted for four-fifths of exports). The existing social system presupposed an alignment of dominant classes on imperialism: this was the case with a landed bourgeoisie that was in the process of becoming a capitalist one, and an essentially comprador bourgeoisie often of European or naturalized Levantine origin (trade, transport etc.). But the colonial process facilitated the emergence of a productive capitalist sector run by an embryonic bourgeoisie that did, however, display a certain amount of dynamism and national feeling. After the

---

* Translated by A. M. Berrett

Second World War, both politically and economically, Egypt experienced a blocked historical situation. Political stagnation combined with economic deterioration to sharpen acute social disparities.

In the early 1950s, the vast majority of the Egyptian people (almost three-quarters) was made up of proletarianized rural (55%) and urban (17%) masses[3] receiving only one-tenth of total incomes. Two-thirds of Egyptian fellahin possessed less than one feddan! The ruling class (mainly semi-capitalist landowners and the comprador bourgeoisie) 4% of the population received 35% of total income. The gap between average income in the rural and urban areas was 1:4. Within the proletarianized masses[4] the rural–urban gap was 1:6 or 7.

The *petit bourgeoisie* (wage-workers in the tertiary sector, cadres, small producers, traders and peasants) comprising 20% of the population and receiving 40% of total income was a relatively important social force from which most of the active leading governing political personnel was drawn. Finally, the urban proletariat (3%), which was comparatively numerous for a Third World country; but it still suffered from political and organizational immaturity and was in fact incapable of playing a leading role in the national patriotic movement.

At the beginning of the 1950s, the national patriotic movement, strengthened by the sudden appearance of the Zionist colonial state, did experience some growth. But, due to lack of political and ideological coherence, it was quite unable, by direct action, to force through the changes rendered even more necessary by the socio-economic deterioration and the opposition to change or progress displayed by the political class associated with the palace.[5] In this historical context the Free Officers' *coup de force* of 23 July 1952 occurred.

The Free Officers and the spirit of Bandung

The social origins of the Free Officers' group lay essentially in the urban and rural small and middle bourgeoisie. Ideologically, it contained various schools of thought (Wafd-type reformism, *Nahda*-type Islamicism and socialism). This ideological heterogeneity led to the establishment of a political line that was essentially opportunistic, that is, an orientation that changed under the pressure of events.

What held the Free Officers' group together was *nationalism*, the main theme of which was the evacuation of British troops.[6] The ultimate objective was thus to put an end to the imperialist military presence and then create a modernized army (taking up Mohamed Ali's project) capable of restoring national dignity to the Egyptian people, indeed to the Arab peoples, faced with the Zionist–imperialist challenge.

Economically, the aim was to pursue a prudent reformism (a limited agrarian reform) and initiate a liberal-type 'modernizing' development process backed financially by international capital.

This initial view held by the Free Officers' group subsequently underwent a radicalization under the pressure of events consequent upon the tripartite aggression at Suez, especially as the Bandung Conference was opening up a new area of solidarity between the colonial and semi-colonial peoples. The Bandung Conference in fact saw the culmination of the national liberation movement.

Rather than putting forward a project as such, the conference constituted a new political space for the peoples of the Third World. The principles of convergence, solidarity, unity, non-alignment and positive neutralism (notably with regard to imperialism) defined this space and the spirit of Bandung. Bandung was the starting point, marking the political entry on to the world stage of this previously disparate group of countries subjected to a variety of colonial rulers; it opened the way to the formation of an area of autonomy favourable to nation-building.

While it was the principle of national liberation that linked together the various components represented at Bandung, it has to be acknowledged that there were divergences, notably on the articulation to be developed between national and social liberation, between nation-building and disengagement or delinking from the CWES.[7]

There were three opposing tendencies:

The first conceived national liberation as a process leading to a prudent *reformism*, based on the political option that national independence could be achieved in the framework of a compromise respecting the acquired rights and interests of Western imperialism in general, whether strategic, economic or cultural.

The second suggested a more radical reformism initiated by the state, and a so-called positive neutralism, in the sense of a relationship articulating co-operation and conflict with the imperialist powers. It opted for a rather *étatiste*-type development path, with acceptance of the principle of interdependence and hence the logic of the system of international economic relations.

Finally, the third tendency argued the need for a link between national and social liberation with the principle of challenging adjustment to the CWES and hence disengagement: delinking.

The Free Officers' group that seized state power in Egypt belonged historically in this new political space opened up by Bandung. Initially leaning rather towards a prudent reformism but later shifting to a more radical stance under the effects of the Suez crisis; this latter in fact, in the context of the prevailing system of world relations, opened up a relative margin of autonomy and manoeuvre, a margin consolidated by an unchallenged internal legitimacy.

The nation-building project

The bulk of the readjustment occurred in the 1960s. Gradually, a nation-building project began to take shape, founded a populist-type ideology; it was a project for a modernizing development focused on industrialization, initiated by the state (becoming omnipotent) and strongly backed by the USSR (both economically and militarily). The project sought to be an attempt at *renegotiation* of its relationship to the CWES, by challenging the dominant forms of the old colonial-type international division of labour and integration into a new international division of labour, conferring a status that was less inferior but still *de facto* subject to the logic of adjustment to the CWES.

What was the content of the adjustments implied by the project? In terms of the economy, all major financial, industrial and commercial businesses, whether foreign or Egyptian were nationalized – *étatized*, becoming the foundation of a vast state sector that now became the strategic motor of development, structuring all social relations, and from which there gradually emerged a bourgeoisie constituting the hegemonic centre of a new alliance of dominant classes.[8]

The new state power also embarked on an agrarian reform which was to be one of the key mechanisms for social adjustments in the form of a redistribution in favour of the peasantry, the bulk of which was proletarianized. It must be noted, however, that the reform was limited in scope and even had perverse effects. The landed base of the old monarchical power was indeed destroyed, but it is generally agreed that the agrarian bourgeoisie and rural notables consolidated their positions.

Initially the state limited property to 200 feddans, affecting 6% of the cultivated area; only part of this land was redistributed, the rest being absorbed into the state sector. Subsequently (in 1969), the ceiling was reduced to 100 feddans. For the most part the land was allocated the original owners, and the movement affected only 10% of landless families. In addition, the method of fixing rent was institutionalized and this consolidated the permanence of tenants' rights (small peasants, poor peasants) thus limiting the political power of the big landowners. At the same time, a movement to generalize the co-operative system got underway, enabling the state to acquire a leading role in the agricultural sector.

By the end of the 1960s, the redistributive measures had affected about one million feddans, benefiting 342,000 families. One-tenth of big estate land was affected, 13% of the usable agricultural area was transferred from big landowners to rural tenants or permanent owners. Furthermore, through state control, mediated usually by the middle rural bourgeoisie, the mechanisms were put in place whereby a reverse movement was to be effected at the expense of the peasantry and the rural areas in general; thus, pricing policy was at the heart of these mechanisms. The difference between market prices and *official prices* of peasant deliveries to co-operatives constituted a disguised levy on peasant labour, estimated at 5–7% of agricultural income in the second half of the 1960s.

In short, the adjustment in favour of the peasantry, which remained limited by the effects of the agrarian reform, in fact underwent a reverse process. Average rural real income declined relative to average urban real income. The ratio was 61.1% in 1953, 52.4% in 1960 and 38.6% in 1970. In addition, in the countryside, the rich peasantry consolidated its base: since 1952, it had increased its land base by nearly 20%. Broadly speaking, the rural bourgeoisie (middle and rich) secured a dominant position for itself: almost two-thirds of the land (62%) and over four-fifths of total agricultural machinery.

Ultimately, the project aimed at a relative internal delinking, in the form of a partial social adjustment in favour of the poor landless peasantry, turned out to be a failure, which was all the more disappointing because there was a global regression in agriculture that led to even heavier dependence on the external world in the shape of a tenfold rise in cereal imports. The counter-performances of the agricultural sector were not unrelated to the development project giving priority to industry.

The industrial project aimed at challenging the classical pattern of the international division of labour; it involved an accumulation regime, which we shall describe as a deficit and under-indebted one, that is, necessarily involving recourse to external capital. In the first half of the 1960s one-third, and in the second half one-quarter of investments necessitated recourse to external credits and borrowings (USSR, USA and USAID in particular).

How could such a model underpin Egypt's readjustment to the CWES?

Adjustment

The strategy envisaged during the 1960s presupposed a different realignment within the international state system in the shape of a focusing on the alliance with the USSR.

The Arab unity project, focused on Egypt (even at the level of discourse), had the effect of sharpening the conflict with the Zionist–imperialist camp. In addition, the *étatiste* orientation and the reference to socialism increased the imperialist powers' hostility; it was in this context that the new adjustment in favour of the USSR occurred. This adjustment, articulated on active non-alignment, made it possible to secure an area of relative autonomy, not in order to embark on a process of disengagement and delinking from the CWES but to negotiate a new relationship with it, altering the classic principle of specialization. It was on that basis that Egypt's industrial development was embarked upon, necessitating seeking funds from a variety of sources: aid from the USSR for big industrial projects (steel-mill, aluminium, cement, engineering industries) and large-scale water projects, USAID helping with infrastructure and light industries, and the USA providing Egypt with foodstuffs up to 1965.[9]

What were the most significant effects of the industrial effort? Industrial employment increased, rising from 10% to 13% between the beginning of the 1960s and the beginning of the 1970s. Cotton, which accounted for three-quarters of all exports in the 1950s, fell to only two-fifths by the beginning of the 1970s.[10] The proportion of exports of manufactured or semi-industrial products, previously negligible, now reached 30%, while imports of intermediate goods and raw materials (55%) became predominant along with imports of capital goods (20%). The geographical direction of external trade (see Table 2.1) shows a breakthrough by the Eastern bloc (mainly the USSR), especially in exports.[11] The role of the USSR in the external debt also increased; by 1971, the USSR accounted for 28% of this debt followed by the USA (15%), Italy (9%), Germany (8%) and Kuwait (9.6%).

Table 2.1
Exports and imports, East and West
(%)

	Exports		Imports	
	1959–60	*1969–70*	*1959–60*	*1969–70*
West	28	18	50	46
East	49	60	27	34

In broad outline, that is how Egypt, while modifying somewhat its type of integration into the international division of labour, in fact deepened its dependence on the CWES, partly through the medium of the USSR.

The accumulation regime underpinning industrialization created from the beginning a series of structural rigidities involving a process of growing indebtedness. The industrial model, an integral part of the ideology of modernization, involved simply the imitative transfer of the dominant consumption model and the corresponding technologies. The type of industries established (and the associated infrastructures) necessitated a growing inflow of imports, without which the whole process would be blocked. This structural rigidity increased the export orientation of the economy (to the detriment of the internal market) and growing recourse to borrowing. The imbalance between the rate of import growth and against that of export growth increased the structural deficit character of the economy.

It must also be stressed that the blockage, and hence the eventual crisis of the Egyptian model, were precipitated by the suspension of American aid and the military commitment (particularly heavy financially) to the war in Yemen, as well as the Zionist aggression of June 1967 and the ensuing defeat. The effects of all these events combined to put an end to the attempt at nation-building and led to a new course of adjustment to the CWES.

At the socio-political level, the Nasserite project saw itself as based on an original Arab construct, *Arab socialism*, believing in the possibility of resolving class conflicts without recourse to violence.[12] This led gradually to the establishment of a new social system which, *de facto*, excluded the popular masses from political initiative and decision-making.[13] The populist national discourse served to evoke support and loyalty but not popular initiative and participation. Furthermore, growing *étatisme* made possible the emergence of a new class structure in which those running the state apparatus built up a socio-economic base for themselves that enabled it to accede as a class (the state bourgeoisie) to hegemony in the new system of social alliances. In fact only the minority associated with large landholdings linked to the monarchy was actually liquidated. The traditional rural and urban bourgeoisie was able to maintain and consolidate itself on the basis of a complex system of relations with the state sector (and hence the state bourgeoisie). Towards the end of the 1960s, this urban, private bourgeoisie controlled two-thirds of manufacturing industry and four-fifths of wholesale trade. The rural bourgeoisie, as we have seen, definitely became richer.

The new system of alliances articulated the interests of these two bourgeois components, while seeking the support of the middle strata and settled urban wage-earners, a system excluding popular participation and any form of autonomous expression on the part of the popular classes.

Early in the second half of the 1960s, the project that emerged from this system encountered its historical limit; Nasser's death precipitated a new course known as the *infitah*, an expression referring to the ways, means and mechanisms of internal and external political, social, economic adjustment to the CWES.

First, there was a shift in the relations of force within the dominant system of alliances, involving a new relationship between the state and the private sector to the benefit of the latter, and at the international level a realignment on US imperialism. Various measures were adopted to make these adjustments possible economically: in the agricultural sector the ceiling on landholdings was raised, and there was a return to freedom in fixing rents; the state sector was dismantled: by sale to the private sector, while the Central Bank's monopoly was abolished and import–export activities liberalized. In addition, an investment code particularly attractive to foreign capital was drawn up. Development was now to take an extraverted course based on the export sector: this explains the de-industrialization and the central role taken by incomes from rent: oil, the emigrant labour force, transit and tourism.

In summary, Nasser's nation-building project rapidly encountered a historical limit: the combination of internal factors inherent in the project (type of alliance, model of industrialization) and external factors, at the centre of which were the constraints exercised by the CWES, precipitated the failure of the project.

The project took place in a historical context marked by a sustained expansion of world capitalism, creating a relative margin in the shape of concessions to the new post-colonial states to embark on processes of industrialization that would, willy-nilly, modify the old forms of the international division of labour.

The project was borne along on popular enthusiasm which initially gave it a basis of credibility. The political measures to assert national sovereignty (evacuation of colonial troops, nationalization of foreign interests) and promote social redistribution (especially the agrarian reform) set out the national dimension of the project. Tilting external relations in favour of the East, and stressing positive non-alignment gave a certain margin for manoeuvre and autonomy. But the project, as it was historically realized, rested on a social system of alliances giving the state bourgeoisie (allied to the traditional bourgeoisie) a hegemonic role, a system calling for the support of the middle social strata and the urban wage earners in the tertiary sector in particular but excluding, *de facto*, the popular classes, and especially the peasants, thus deepening sectoral and social disparities. The implicit ideology, over and beyond the populist tinge, was one of modernization through the imitative transfer of the dominant model of consumption and the corresponding technologies: an imitative modernization deemed, furthermore, to respect the cultural values of Islam. This modernization ended in failure, especially as the global relationship to the CWES, only slightly modified, placed its own heavy constraints on adjustment.

The failure of the project was the failure of the Egyptian bourgeoisie to carry through the work of nation-building. The readjustments currently underway have a profound historical meaning: they testify to the end of the national aspirations of this bourgeoisie, the *de facto* acknowledgement of the necessity for compradorization and adjustment to the CWES. The rent economy promoted this historic course, and is having perverse effects on the whole social structure (perverse behaviour, atomization of the working class etc.) and on the necessary revival of the national and social liberation movement.

The Nasserite project met its historical limits, given its fragility and ideological incoherence (imitative modernization and Islamic cultural authenticity), given the exclusive nature of the social system that it established, and finally given the *de facto* acceptance of the logic of the CWES. The relative modification of the type of integration into the international division of labour (made possible by the conjuncture of the 1960s) was not the starting point for delinking from the CWES whose constraints, including military and political ones (the war in Yemen and Zionist aggression) precipitated the historical limit of the project.

Notes

1. Mohamed Ali, viceroy of Egypt, aimed to modernize the country by creating a military apparatus and a corresponding industrial infrastructure, designed to enable him to strengthen his independence from European capitalist powers. Due to heavy centralized accumulation (heavy taxation, use of monopoly and pursuit of a strict policy of tariff protection), Mohamed Ali succeeded in establishing an industrial complex (factories producing gun cotton, munitions, gunpowder, iron foundries, small-scale naval metallurgy, forges, workshops for ship repair and construction). Light industries included cotton-based textiles (spinning, weaving, printing, cloth-making), sugar-making, glass-making, tanning and paper-making. In our view, a decisive historical factor made it possible to carry through this programme: taking advantage of Europe's difficulties and contradictions at the beginning of the Egyptian monarch's reign (the historical space of autonomy). That explains why, from the end of the Napoleonic wars, the European capitalist powers worked intensively to destroy the cornerstone of the Egyptian economy (tariff protection and the practice of monopoly) and to re-establish freedom of trade. The Anglo-Turkish commercial convention extended to Egypt in 1840 marked the end of this policy of national development. Given the international context and the global relations of force, the military defeat by Turkey in 1841 led to the Egyptian army being cut by four-fifths, thus wiping out the whole industrial effort.

2. In fact the WAFD lacked political consistency as evidenced by the tendencies towards compromise and prudent reformism and its ideology that combined assertion of Islamic cultural values and the ideology of modernization typical of the European bourgeoisie.

3. Out of a total of 27 million, the proletarianized rural masses accounted for 15 million (55%) and the proletarianized urban masses 4.5 million (about 17%). S. F. M. Hussein, *La Lutte de classe en Egypte*, F. Maspero, 1971.

4. The proletarianized urban masses comprised the unemployed, domestic servants, sub-proletariat and unskilled wage-workers. Proletarianized rural masses included landless peasants and those possessing less than one feddan.

5. The monarchy faced an acute lack of legitimacy. The WAFD and the traditional political class also totally lacked credibility.

6. This nationalism did not originally exclude ties with the USA. In the 1950s US imperialism, which had emerged strengthened from the Second World War, sought to establish and consolidate a hegemonic relationship, extending also to Europe. Various US interventions were designed to channel anti-colonialist (anti-French and anti-British) movements and win over nationalists seeking liberation.

7. This political and ideological heterogeneity is indicative of differences in the class composition of the liberation movements: predominance of the *petit bourgeoisie*, the bourgeoisie or popular forces, notably the proletariat.

8. We shall return to this aspect later.

9. The expropriation without compensation measure adopted in 1965 was in fact the pretext for the USA to suspend its food aid and force the country to pay for them in dollars in future.

10. Note too the tendency towards relative decline of the ratios Exports/GDP and Imports/GDP; the former said to have risen from 11% to 15% and the latter to have fallen from 20% to 16.5% during the 1960s.

11. The remainder of trade is with other Third World countries.

12. Non-recourse to violence is inherent to the whole of Islamic cultural values.

13. The decision to reserve half the seats in various state bodies for peasants and workers was to the credit of the regime. At the same time, state power ensured a state monopoly on the exercise of political power for itself by using violence against any form of popular progressive and autonomous expression.

3. Algeria: The Problem of Nation-building

Rabah Abdoun*

This chapter is an analysis of one experience of nation-building. First the concept of nation-building in the context of development theory will be discussed and assessed, and then an attempt made to identify the main problems confronting a nation-building project through a study of the concrete experience of Algeria over the last twenty years. An analysis of the factors that have led to the crisis of such a project reveals the existence of limits – external as well as internal. Identifying these limits makes it possible to show that the nation-building project is historically dated. The contradictions it contains mean that it must transform itself either into a democratic and popular project (in the framework of a gradual and selective disengagement from the world system) or a non-democratic project of dependent integration into the world system (involving the implementation of an adjustment policy).

The problematic of nation-building

The 1970s saw a crisis of development policies in the Third World in general and Africa in particular. This crisis of development policies was part and parcel of the world crisis, the first warning signs of which appeared in the late 1960s in Europe and the United States. Development policies are nation-building policies in so far as they aim at the establishment of a self-reliant and autonomous productive system. These nation-building experiences pursued in some parts of the Third World in the 1950s and 1960s took place in the context of strong growth in the world economy. The crisis in the world economy brought them to a halt.

The enormous variety of these nation-building experiences means that they cannot be reduced to a single model. Nevertheless, they share a number of features: nationalization/*étatization* of the main means of production and exchange and the bulk of the interests owned by foreign capital; development of a significant state sector; investment priority given to the industrial sector and especially basic industries (essentially intermediate goods); and development of infrastructure (big dams, communication networks etc.).

* Translated by A. M. Berrett.

While at the socio-ideological level these nation-building experiences claim explicitly to be socialist, in the socio-political arena a nationalist and modernist techno-bureaucracy, resting principally on the army, holds power and controls the state and the state apparatuses.

Over and beyond the problem of interpretation, the crisis of nation-building experiences in Africa and the Third World in general raises the question of the relevance of development theories. Before looking at this point, however, what I call the paradox of nation-building will be examined. For, while these experiences were designed to achieve economic liberation through the establishment of a self-reliant and autonomous productive system, simultaneously they create conditions for integration into the world economy that is new in its forms but still dependent.

The paradox of nation-building

The ultimate objective of nation-building is the removal of external domination and economic dependence. The building of a productive system that is 'intraverted' (production is aimed at satisfying internal demand), self-reliant (reproduction of the conditions of production is internalized) and autonomous *vis-à-vis* the dominant centres of the world economic system (transnational firms, imperialist states, international financial agencies) takes place with this objective in view. This development policy has two key features: 1) priority to industry in the allocation of resources; and 2) making the state the prime operator in economic life.

Pursuit of this policy produces the elements of its own negation. For it leads to: a) a process of establishing industrial units which, while being controlled by state-owned enterprises, involve the massive incorporation of technology from abroad; b) a prices and incomes policy that strongly militates against the growth capacities of the agricultural sector and downgrades work on the land; and c) a policy of financing industrialization which tends to have increasing resort to external borrowing.

These features generate a threefold dependence: for food, for technology and for finance. To varying degrees, they reduce the state's capacity to control the process of economic and social reproduction. If it is accepted that the principal functions of the state lie in mastering what is required for the reproduction of the labour force, capital accumulation and finance, then it can be seen that in each of these areas, the thrust of these experiences produces contrary trends. The bases of the reproduction of the labour force become more and more externalized (increased food dependence), the industrial system operates with less and less control, and monetary sovereignty becomes increasingly fragile (large external debt).

The latter feature is of particular importance. Growing external indebtedness means that it is necessary to find resources to finance debt service. This takes the form of an obligation to produce a trade surplus, which can be secured only at the price of a reduction of imports (even where these are vital to continuing accumulation), the growth of exports being relatively inelastic.

In fact, the history of these nation-building experiences shows that they lead

– after a period marked by rapid industrialization in a particular world context – to a process of de-industrialization that varies in scale but is very real. What are the reasons for the crisis of these experiences?

Nation-building policies and the crisis

The nation-building policies pursued (in the 1960s in Egypt and the 1970s in Algeria) quickly ran up against the contradiction between the goals aimed at and the means used to attain them. For, while the goal was to reduce external dependence, the means used paradoxically renewed and strengthened that dependence. Because the nation-building policy rested on a strengthening of commercial, technological and financial ties with the dominant centres, this policy of 'economic liberation' was, in the last analysis, subject to changes in world relations of force. Strong growth in the world economy was reflected in a strengthening of this policy. While the world crisis did not call into question these nation-building experiences, it at least made their achievement, and the progress already made, more problematic.

The vulnerability of these nation-building experiences cannot, of course, be exclusively attributed to external causes – even though their role is important – but also, and above all, it is due to internal factors. It is because the world crisis meets conditions favourable for it to act in the Third World that it becomes manifest. In other words, while the fragility of these experiences is the effect of the integration, on dominated bases, of these social formations into the world system, the foundation of this integration lies in the nature of the internal class alliances that determine specific international alliances.

In fact, the central question of the content of the nation-building policy lies beyond the question of internal and international alliances, and their origin and dynamic. Over and beyond the diversity of experiences, a number of common parameters can be identified. Identifying the various components of this policy will make it possible to explain its failure, that is, the fact of its continued subordination to the logic of the functioning of the world system from which it claims to be freeing itself.

Theoretical foundations of nation-building policies

Nation-building policies are development policies; to examine the former involves examining the theories that underpin the latter.

Development economics, as a specific branch of economics, is a recent creation that emerged with the end of the Second World War and the development of liberation movements among colonized peoples. The early 1950s were marked by the publication of numerous analyses of development. One precursor of this new branch of economics, Albert Hirschman, proposed a typology of development theories.

Hirschman sees the various conceptions of development as resting on two basic ingredients:[1] 1) the mono-economics claim (according to which the laws by which the developed economies function can be transposed, mechanically, to the analysis of underdeveloped economies); and 2) the principle of mutual benefit (which claims that economic relations between developed and underdeveloped countries could be shaped in such a way as to yield gains to both). The two claims can be accepted or rejected. Four basic positions can be identified, to each of which, according to Hirschman, corresponds a family of development theories. These four families are: 1) orthodox economics (which asserts both the mono-economics claim and that of mutual benefit); 2) development economics (which denies mono-economics but asserts the principle of mutual benefit); 3) Marx's position (which asserts the principle of mono-economics and rejects that of mutual benefit); and 4) the neo-Marxists who reject both mono-economics and mutual benefit.

The problematic of nation-building belongs in the field of the theories of development economics in so far as the assertion of the specific character of underdevelopment and its operative laws is accompanied by an acceptance of the principle of mutual benefit in international economic relations. This problematic considers as valid the laws that govern international exchanges and hence the law of international value. Several consequences flow from this: a) the internal price system is closely tied to the world price system; b) the criteria on which state-promoted investment projects are selected pay less attention to the social side-effects than to the economic and financial viability of the investment;[2] c) the rules by which state enterprises function are aligned on those of private enterprises (with the aim of increasing their international competitiveness and exporting).

All these features, which are so many manifestations of the subordination of the nation-building policy to the operating requirements of the international law of value, show the adjustment–integration of the 'emergent' economy into the world economic system.

Because the rationality of the nation-building policy is the same rationality that underpins the world economic system, what happens to one is heavily dependent on what happens to the other. Thus, respect for the principle of mutual benefit involves the subordination of the nation-building policy to the dominant economic rationality and hence its instrumentalization by the dominant forces of the world economic system (transnational firms and banks, imperialist states etc.).

Given that, then 'disadjustment' from the world economic system would be the prerequisite to the pursuit of true nation-building. The central question in these conditions becomes that of defining an alternative rationality that would underpin a concrete dynamic of 'disadjustment'/delinking from the world economic system. Thus, to use Hirschman's typology, the development theory that provides the basis of a true nation-building policy, as part of a dynamic process of delinking, is one that proceeds from the double rejection of mono-economics and the principle of mutual benefit.

The Algerian experience of nation-building

In 1967, a nation-building project, known as the 'Algerian development strategy', was set up with two objectives: to create the economic conditions for the elimination of unemployment; and to meet the needs of the population (which was growing very rapidly, 3.4% per annum). The means to attain these ends were the building of an industrial productive apparatus able to create the conditions for a move from a largely dependent extraverted economy to one more autonomous and self-reliant.

When this experience entered a crisis in the late 1970s, it marked the end of this project and precipitated the formulation of a new economic policy. The socio-political and socio-economic context in which this project was drawn up will first be set out and then examined in broad outline before analysing the economic and social effects of implementing the policy between 1967 and 1980. The crisis of this nation-building policy was the occasion for a redefinition of objectives. Analysis of this question will make it possible to determine the limits of a nation-building project that remains broadly within the logic of the world economic system.

Socio-economic and socio-political context of the early years of independence
The early years of independence were marked by instability among the various social forces. The struggle for power mobilized various fractions of the national liberation movement, the FLN-ALN. Conflicts were less about projects (even though these were not wholly absent) than about personal rivalries. The popular masses, and especially those in the countryside, who had borne the brunt of the struggle for independence, were, if not excluded from the debate, at least mainly used by the actors in the conflict. The army weighed decisively in the outcome of these struggles, both in the crises in the summer of 1962 and 1963 and at the time of the change of regime in June 1965.

A few weeks before the proclamation of independence, a doctrinal project was drawn up (the 'Tripoli Programme' of June 1962) by the ruling bodies of the national liberation movement. In addition, the Evian Agreements, signed a few months earlier, between representatives of the national liberation movement and those of the former colonial power (March 1962) set out the broad outlines of what the new independent state would be and the conditions of its relations with France. The Tripoli Programme called into question the very principle of the Evian Agreements. Those who drafted the programme argued that 'the Evian Agreements constitute a neocolonialist platform which France is preparing to use to establish and organize its new form of domination'. Furthermore, the doctrinal programme was couched in a socialist perspective: 'in order for the development of Algeria to be rapid, harmonious and aimed at satisfying the people's basic economic needs', it asserted, 'it must necessarily be conceived in a socialist perspective in the framework of a collectivization of the principal means of production and rational planning'. In order to do this, two broad principles should guide economic policy: 1) rejection of foreign domination and economic liberalism; and 2) the development of a planning policy with the workers' democratic participation in economic power. According to the Tripoli Programme, the content of this policy would have to be based on the agrarian revolution and industrialization.

As regards the agrarian question, the 'revolution' in the countryside (which has three aspects: agrarian reform; modernization of agriculture; and conservation of the environment) is seen as a priority, since it conditions 'the creation of a domestic market and the beginnings of industrialization'.

The country's industrialization is conceived as the means of development; and industrial policy would pay special attention to 'basic industries' (petroleum and steel). As the Tripoli Programme puts it:

> the country's real long-term development is tied up with the establishment of the basic industries required by a modern agriculture. In this respect, Algeria has great possibilities for petroleum and steel industries. In this area, it is up to the state to bring together the conditions necessary for the creation of heavy industry.

As we shall see below in more detail, the basic principles of the nation-building project that was drawn up in 1967 were already present in the 1962 Tripoli Programme. But before this project came about, a number of struggles, resulting in the political marginalization of the popular masses, marked the years 1962 to 1967. The central question around which these struggles were waged was how the economy should be organized. More precisely, the issue was that of the role of self-management and the state in society.

The continuation of the structures of the colonial state in independent Algeria – in accordance with the spirit (and the letter) of the Evian Agreements – made the new state a centralizing one. It was run by personnel recruited on the basis of criteria that had less to do with commitment in the struggle for independence than with administrative competence, technical skill or, more simply, education in the French language. These criteria, *de facto*, excluded the broad illiterate popular masses from the state apparatus and hence from power. In addition, a system of bureaucratic control of the popular masses was gradually established. Reversing and/or reducing the self-management system completed the state's grip on the country's economic and political life.

Self-management first appeared in agriculture, during the summer of 1962. The abrupt and massive departure of the European community (10% of the population) under pressure from the ultra-colonialist organization, the OAS, left the best lands in the country abandoned (almost three million hectares).[3] In October 1962, agricultural workers spontaneously took over the running of the 'abandoned' estates and organized on self-management lines. In March 1963, decrees regulating self-management were promulgated. In fact, they deprived this system of its content by making provision for the supervising ministry to appoint a director for each self-managed unit. Nevertheless, from this point on, the system developed under the supervision of the state not only in agriculture but also, although more hesitantly, in industry and services. At the same time, from 1963 onwards state enterprises (state-owned companies) were created in industry and services.

The Algiers Charter (issued by the Congress of the FLN, the ruling single party, in April 1964) considered that, 'self-management expresses the desire of the country's labouring classes to emerge on the political and economic stage and make themselves into a leading force'. But the self-managed sector was gradually trimmed back and finally eliminated in industry and services, and transformed into the state sector in agriculture. This new dynamic was the result of a conflict that occurred, in 1967, between differing schools of thought over the question of self-management.

This conflict was between the Ministry of Industry and Energy and the UGTA, the single workers' trade union. The former argued that self-management was a system ill-adapted to Algeria's context of underdevelopment and preferred the system of *sociétés nationales* (state-owned companies), while the latter remained faithful to the principle of self-management and rejected its elimination. The conflict ended in victory for the Ministry. *Étatization* of the economy was now able to move forward rapidly, although an investment code which protected private capital was promulgated at about the same time.

This code (Ordinance of 15 September 1966) was decidedly liberal in inspiration. It guaranteed private capital (both national and foreign) a minimum of ten years without nationalization with, if any nationalization occurred, compensation within nine months to a value 'at least equal to the accounting value on the last balance-sheet' and 'which may be transferred abroad within six months'. Companies set up under this regime had the choice of working alone or in association with the state in the form of mixed state–private companies; additionally, they received big tax concessions. But 'the key sectors of the economy' continued to be excluded from the operation of this code, these sectors being reserved to the state alone.

Overall, the trend towards *étatization* of the major means of production and exchange became sharper in 1966 and 1967. It rested on a set of nationalizations of foreign interests in the mining sector (1966), the industrial sector (1967: the Durafour workshops etc.) and the banking sector (1966–67: this sector was completely reorganized in 1967). This wave of nationalizations culminated with the 24 February 1971 decisions on hydro-carbons (which rendered null and void the Franco-Algerian oil agreements of 20 July 1965, which were then in fact just about to expire).

Hydro-carbons being the country's chief resource, the authorities pay special attention to them. Thus, the responsibilities of a state-owned company, Sonatrach, set up on 31 December 1963 and initially responsible for transporting and marketing, were extended to the exploration, production and processing of hydro-carbons. Oil production grew rapidly, especially after 1966, rising from 20.5 million metric tons in 1962 to 26 million in 1965; 39.1 in 1967; and 42.1 in 1968. Gas production rose from 0.8 billion m³ in 1964 to 2.9 billion m³ in 1966.

Petroleum taxation accounted for only 21% of budgetary receipts in 1966, but this figure grew rapidly in the 1970s. The proportion of hydro-carbons in exports rose rapidly, from 58% in 1963 to 73% in 1967. In the area of employment, out of a total estimated population of 12.5 million in 1967, the potential economically active population, that is, the population of working age (15–65 years of age), totalled 5.85 million and the employed population 1.748 million, or the employment of one economically active person in three. If the figure for the number of people employed is related to the total population, it can be seen that, on average, each employed person supported seven Algerians. The proportion of women in the employed population was extremely low, since only 90,500 women were employed; 5% of the total. In 1966–67, the agricultural sector provided most jobs, with 58% of the total, followed by services with 24%; industry provided 8.2% and construction and public works 5.9%.

In the 1960s Algeria had a relatively low rate of urbanization: in 1960, it was estimated at 30% for a total population of some 10 million, including one million Europeans, these latter concentrated mainly in the large cities.

Following independence, three-quarters of the Algerian population were in the rural areas. With the departure of the settlers, and especially after 1967, when the industrialization policy was launched, a massive drift from the rural areas developed.

The nation-building project (1967–80)

The 'development' or 'nation-building' strategy was spelled out in 'development plans', the function of which was to programme investments and detail priority actions to be undertaken. There were three development plans: the three-year plan (1967–69); the first four-year plan (1970–73); and the second four-year plan (1974–77); the years 1978 and 1979 being covered by annual plans.

The doctrine underlying this strategy was based on four broad principles. The first gave priority to investment over consumption in the distribution of national income. The second gave priority to productive investment in the sectoral distribution of investments. In addition, industry was given priority over agriculture. The third gave priority, within the industrial sector itself, to investment in producer goods industries (capital goods and above all intermediate goods), consumer goods industries being given relatively little encouragement. Finally, the fourth principle laid down that the state, through public enterprises, was the principal, if not the sole, economic operator. This was, in fact, a constraint due to the weakness of national private capital during the 1960s and an effect of the policy of eliminating self-management. These principles made up an *étatist* 'model' of accumulation whose core was the 'industrializing' intermediate goods industries (steel and petrochemicals mainly).

Analysis of public investment policy over the period 1967–80 shows:

– the achievement of a high and rapidly growing rate of investment: 26.8% in 1967–69; 38.7% for 1970–73; 48.5% for 1974–77; 54.4% in 1978; 45% in 1979; (in 1980 and 1981 the rate of accumulation slipped to around 41.6% and 41.1% respectively).

– a clear priority in the sectoral distribution of investments in favour of industry (including hydro-carbons). In terms of credits realized, the proportion going to industry (including hydro-carbons) was: 53.6% of total investment for the period 1967–69; 57.3% for 1970–73; 61.1% for 1974–77; 61.7% in 1978; 62.2% in 1979; (in 1980 and 1981 the proportion going to industry fell back to 56.0% and 45.7% respectively). Conversely, agriculture received only 15.2%, 8.2%, 4.9%, 4.7% and 3.2% respectively (and 3.5% and 4.0% for 1980 and 1981). If to this are added the credits allocated to water projects the proportions are still relatively low with 20.6%, 12.0%, 6.3%, 7.9% and 6.7% respectively (and 8.4% and 6.5% for 1980 and 1981).

From these figures it emerges that the counterpart of the growth in the proportion of investments going to industry was a greater reduction in investments in agriculture (and water projects). This is especially true for the period 1967–79; but it is also clear that after 1979 the reduction in the proportion of investments going to industry was not to the benefit of agriculture.

– finally, there was a distinct shift in the distribution of investments within the industrial sector itself. The hydro-carbon industry took the lion's share of investments in this sector: 51.3% in 1967–69; 47.0% in 1970–73; 48.5% in 1974-77; 45.2% in 1978; 51.4% in 1979; (and 48.5% in 1980 and 42.3% in 1981); whereas plan figures generally gave it a smaller amount with 42.0%, 36.8%, 40.6%, 61.8% and 56.6% respectively (and 42.8% and 40.7% for 1980 and 1981).

Conversely, the intermediate and capital goods industries, the hard core of the strategy, actually, in financial terms, received a smaller volume of investments than that initially provided for in the various plans: 41.2% (as against 49.0% planned) in 1967–69; 46.7% (as against 53.5%) in 1970–73; (44.7% as against 51.0% in 1974–77).

There was thus a significant distortion compared to investment plan figures to the advantage of the hydro-carbons sector whose production was principally destined less for the local market than for export.

This distortion, which calls into question the objective of making the economy self-reliant, reflects the preponderance of the logics of the constituents over the overall logic and thereby reveals the weakness of the planning system.

The striking feature of public investment financing over the period 1967–80 was the small contribution of the local surplus and massive recourse to rent and external borrowing. It has been estimated that the available domestic product accounted for only one-quarter of investment financing during the period 1967–78; the bulk of the financing of accumulation having been covered by the product of the sale of hydro-carbons on the world market (55%) and external borrowing (20%), which is simply a form of 'anticipated' rent.[4]

Recourse to external borrowing to finance accumulation increased greatly during the period, especially with the second four-year plan. Debt, as a percentage of GNP, rose from 20% in 1972 to 25% in 1974 and reached 50% in 1978; it fell back after 1979. Debt service grew as a percentage of GNP even more spectacularly: 2.7% in 1972, 5% on average in 1974–78 and over 9% since 1980.

Debt service constitutes a hidden levy on national wealth by the outside world: it was not only growing but large. In fact, debt service as a percentage of the value of exports rose very rapidly: 4% in 1967; 13% in 1975; 25% in 1978;

and almost 40% in 1979.

It has been calculated that in 1979 debt service absorbed the equivalent of the value added by agriculture.[5] Furthermore, while debt service was absorbing a growing proportion of the value of exports, the structure of exports tended to focus on a single product: hydro-carbons. In 1967–70, hydro-carbons accounted for only 70–75% of merchandise exports, which already showed a clear specialization, their share grew rapidly after 1973 to reach 93% in 1974; 96% in 1977 and 1978; 97.5% in 1979; and 98% since 1980.

With hydro-carbons constituting virtually all exports they also made a large and growing contribution to the financing of the state budget. Revenue from petroleum used to provide only 13.2% of total state receipts, but this figure rose to 22% in 1967, over 35% in 1972 and over 50% between 1974 and 1979 (apart from 1978, when the rate fell slightly to 47.2%). The years 1980 and 1981 saw this upward trend in the proportion of oil revenue in the state budget confirmed, with rates of 63.2% and 64.2% respectively. After 1982, the proportion was relatively reduced, but it still remained large: 55.8% in 1982 and 46.6% in 1983.

The years 1967–80 saw extensive capital accumulation involving mainly the intermediate goods and hydro-carbon industries. This accumulation was financed by rent from the export of hydro-carbons and, to a lesser but still considerable extent, by recourse to borrowing on the international financial market. This process of capital accumulation led to the development of industrial branches, new ones in the majority of cases. Thus steel-making developed with the creation of the El Hadjar complex (Annaba); non-ferrous metals metallurgy with the zinc electrolysis plant (Ghazouet); petrochemicals in the plants at Skikda, Annaba and Arzew; building materials with the creation of a dozen cement-making plants with a million metric tons capacity; engineering industries with the machine tools complex (Constantine *wilaya*); industrial vehicles complex (Rouiba, Algiers); the tractor motor plant (Oued Hamimime, Constantine); the excavator (Ain Smara, Sétif); handling equipment (Côte Rouge, Algiers); and public works equipment plants (El Harrach, Algiers); the crane (Béjaïa) and pipe and pump (Berrouaghia) production plants; agricultural machinery complex (combine harvesters, ploughs etc. at Sidi-Bel-Abbès); electrical and electronic industries with plants producing household electrical goods at Tizi-Ouzou (refrigerators and cookers) and Sidi-Bel-Abbès (radio receivers, television sets); plants producing batteries and battery chargers (Sétif); electrical transformers and motors (Azazga); lamps (Mohammedia); telephone cables and equipment (Tlemcen) and so on.

These industries developed in the framework of companies owned and controlled by the state. Each state-owned company controlled one or more branches. Thus Sonatrach was involved not only in prospecting for, producing, transporting and marketing hydro-carbons, but also in refining, petrochemicals and the plastics industry (Sétif). Another example is the SNS: initially responsible for steel production and the marketing of steel products, this enterprise also became involved in non-ferrous metals metallurgy and the manufacture of a few capital goods.

But there are fewer state-owned companies than there are industrial branches. Furthermore, the state-owned company not only looks after production but also performs other functions such as marketing for which it has a monopoly on imports, the supply of raw materials and even in some cases the training of its staff (Sonatrach with the Algerian Petroleum Institute and other training centres, SNS with its training institutes at El Hadjar etc.). These state-owned companies quickly became very big businesses with large numbers of employees (by 1980 Sonatrach had 100,000 employees, SNS almost 40,000). The giant size of these state-owned companies was to be criticized in the early 1980s in the name of economic efficiency, and a 'restructuring'/dismantling of them was undertaken.

What happened to employment and the structure of employment between 1967 and 1980? Before looking at this issue, it will be useful to point out the high growth rate, rapid urbanization, and large proportion of young people in the Algerian population.

The population increased from 12.5 million in 1967 to 18.6 million in 1980, an average natural growth rate of 3.1% over the period.[6] In 1980, for almost 760,000 births there were slightly more than 142,000 deaths, a net increase of 620,000.

Just under three-quarters of the Algerian population is very young: in 1967, 71.3% were under 30 years of age, and 73.2% in 1980. In 1967 some 7,404,000 people were under 20, and 1,557,000 in the 20–29 age group, by 1980 there were 10,722,000 and 2,942,000 in each of these groups respectively. With almost 60% of the population under 20 and almost 75% under 30, Algeria is faced with the twin problem of massive numbers in school and finding jobs for young people entering the labour market seeking their first job.

Finally, the Algerian population is heavily concentrated in the coastal towns, mainly in the three large cities of Algiers, Oran and Constantine. These conurbations have almost one-fifth of the population, and the capital, Algiers, alone has more than 10%. This urbanization is a recent phenomenon; it began to develop just after independence, and accelerated with the spread of industrialization. During the 1970s, it was estimated that 100,000 people were annually leaving the countryside to seek work in the towns.

Employment increased rapidly between 1967 and 1980, growing faster than population (4.64% as against 3.1%): this meant a fall in unemployment, since the number of people of working age remained more or less constant during that period.

In 1977, the year of the second post-independence national census, the unemployment rate was 22.3%, 670,000 unemployed out of an economically active population (which includes employed people in addition to those without jobs and seeking work) of three million.

By comparing the number of those employed with the total population (17 million) in 1977, as has already been noted, each employed person on average supported more than seven others (actually 7.3). If we consider the working age population or the potential economically active population (15–65, 8.3 million in 1977), we observe that of seven potential economically active people, only two are employed (3.5:1).

Again in 1977, the proportion of women in total employment remained low at 5.9%, virtually the same as in 1966 (when it was 5%).

Table 3.1
Algeria: Economically active population and unemployment rate in 1977

	Men	*Women*	*Total*
No. employed[1]	2,198,738	138,234	2,336,972
Unemployed I[2]	320,901	4,859	325,760
Unemployed II[3]	326,616	16,451	345,067
Total unemployed:	647,517	21,310	670,827
Econ. active pop.[4]	2,846,255	159,544	3,007,799
Unemployment rate	22.8%	13.4%	22.3%
Potential econ. active pop.[5]	4,018,000	4,264,000	8,282,000
Total population:	8,454,000	8,609,000	17,063,000

[1] Persons working at the time of the census or who had worked at least six days during January 1977.
[2] Persons of working age who had no job, who had an occupation at least six days during January 1977 and who were seeking a job.
[3] Persons of working age who had never worked and who were seeking a job.
[4] Total of occupied population and job-seekers I and II.
[5] Population of working age (15–65).

Source: Calculated from *Séries statistiques* 1967–82, Ministry of Planning, Oct. 1984, pp. 7 and 4.

Between 1967 and 1980 the number of jobs rose from 1.7 million in 1967 to over three million in 1980 (a 76% increase) whereas total population rose more slowly, from 12.5 to 18.6 million (a 48% increase).

Between 1969 and 1979, 1,125,000 jobs were created, an annual average of over 110,000 jobs. These were concentrated in the construction and public works sector (almost one-third of new jobs), administration (over a quarter) and industry (including hydro-carbons) with a little over one-fifth of new jobs. Conversely, the numbers employed in agriculture virtually stagnated.

This sectoral distribution of job creation in the 1970s totally transformed the structure of employment. Thus, the share of agriculture in total employment fell from 50% in 1969 to a little over 30% in 1979, while the industry's share (including hydro-carbons), administration and above all construction and public works rose. In 1969, industry (including hydro-carbons) had accounted for 8.5% of jobs and in 1979 13.3%, the share of administration rose from 16.3% to 20.4% and the construction and public works sector from 4.3% to 14.5% of total employment.

The crisis of the nation-building project
The late 1970s saw the beginnings of the crisis of the nation-building project.

Table 3.2
Algeria: Distribution of employment by sector 1969–79
('000)

	1969		*1979*		*Increase*	
	('000)	*%*	*('000)*	*%*	*('000)*	*%*
Agriculture	934	49.4	969	32.1	35	
Industry	161	8.5	401	13.3	240	21.3
Construction &						
public works	82	4.3	437	14.5	355	31.5
Transport	64	3.4	126	4.2	62	5.5
Communications &						
services	334	17.6	470	15.5	136	12.1
Administration	318	16.8	615	20.4	297	26.5
Total	1,893	100	3,018	100	1,125	100

Source: Ministry of Planning statistics.

Poor performances in the publicly-owned productive industrial system, increased dependence in the food, technical and financial sectors as well as the breakdown of the social consensus manifested in the development of labour struggles and social opposition were the main features of this crisis.

The industrial productive system was established on the basis of massive imports of technology. The absence of local competence in these technologies meant: 1) low productivity; and 2) massive and growing recourse to foreign technical assistance.

Thus, the number of people working in the industrial sector (excluding hydro-carbons), which over the period 1967–78 received 53% of total investments (excluding hydro-carbons) rose by a factor of 3.3 and added value by 2.8, but productivity by only 0.8. This points not only to a low level of technological competence in the production apparatus, but also to a lack of commitment, a form of 'resistance' on the part of the labour force to (and in) the factory, given the problems that it was encountering not only inside the factory but outside, in everyday life.

The case of the construction and public works sector is even more striking. The number employed in this sector, which received 17% of investments during the period, rose by a factor of 5.6 and its value added by 2.8, but its average productivity fell by 50%.

Generally speaking, while the total number employed increased by 160% (excluding hydro-carbons), productivity increased by only 38%, meaning a net fall in average productivity per employee between 1967 and 1978.

During the 1970s, the establishment of a publicly-owned industrial apparatus accentuated technical and financial dependence. In the same way, food dependence worsened as agricultural production stagnated at a time when the population's average consumption level was rising. The absence of any increase in agricultural production, despite the implementation of an 'agrarian revolution' in 1971, was the effect of a policy of bureaucratic control of the

Table 3.3
Algeria: Movement of principal indicators of the Algerian economy (excluding hydro-carbons), 1967–78 (1967 = 100)

Branches	Public investment 1967–78 (%)	Employment	Added value	Added value per worker	Purchasing power
Agriculture	14	98	129	131	182
Industry	53	333	281	84	92
Construction & public works	17	561	280	49	73
Transport & communications	13	300	400	173	88
Communications & services	3	133	190	140	132
Total (excluding hydro-carbons)	100	160	220	138	150

Source: S. P. Thiery, 'La crise du système productif algérien', thesis, IREP, Grenoble 1982.

rural areas – a pricing policy that discouraged producers, and the creation, as the sole channel through which the peasantry could express itself, of an organization – the UNPA – subject to the party-state, with the function of exercising political control of the peasantry.

In the field of technology, new industries were largely established by recourse to turnkey or supplier-financed contracts. There was thus resort on a massive scale to foreign companies to set up these factories. Lack of an adequate policy for training groups of Algerian workers who would be able to keep these plants running in accordance with the terms of the contracts is one of the factors explaining the growing resort to foreign technical assistance. A comprehensive study of the El Hadjar steelworks showed that, between 1970 and 1980, the proportion of the cost of foreign technical assistance as a percentage of the total wage bill of Algerian workers in the plant rose from 10% to 30%.[7]

Again, over the 1970s, foreign technical assistance grew very rapidly, much faster, not only than the rate of growth of public industrial investment (including hydro-carbons), but also than the rate of growth of the number of contracts. Between 1973 and 1978, expenditure on technical assistance rose 870%, the total amount of industrial investments rose 510%, and industrial contracts 620%.

Table 3.4 shows how rapidly technical assistance expenditure was increasing; as a percentage of the amount of industrial contracts this expenditure was growing inexorably.

Table 3.4
Algeria: Technical assistance expenditure and amount of contracts 1973–78
(billion AD)

	Public industrial investments[1] %	Amount of contracts %	Technical assistance expenditure %
1973	6.3	3.57	1.0
1978	32.5	22.3	8.7
Average annual growth rate:	31.4	35.7	43.4

[1] Including hydro-carbons.

Source: compiled from various Ministry of Planning documents.

Thus, in 1973, foreign technical assistance involved transfers by Algeria of one billion Algerian Dollars (AD), the equivalent of 28% of the amount of contracts made that year (of which there were 511). In 1974, the amount of the transfer rose to 2,747 billion AD, equal to 36% of the amount of contracts (689 in number). In 1978, technical assistance expenditure reached 8.7 billion AD, 39% of the amount of contracts (946 in number). In total, over the period 1973–78, transfers for foreign technical assistance amounted to 28.8 billion AD, 36.3% of the amount of the 4,912 contracts made over the period (for a total of 79,340 billion AD).

It is also worth noting that the supply of foreign technical assistance was very limited. Thus 63% of transfers for technical assistance over the years 1973–78 went to the firms of four countries: France (with 20% of the total), the USA (17.6%), West Germany (13.9%) and Italy (11.7%).

Compared to the evolution of the amount of public industrial investments (31% annual growth on average between 1973 and 1978) and that of the amount of industrial contracts (36% p.a.), the rise in technical assistance expenditure was, in both cases, markedly higher (43% p.a.). The rapid rise in this expenditure, expressed in current prices, is too high to reflect only the rise in the unit cost of technical assistance on the world market. In fact, this rise reflects a growth in the volume of foreign technical assistance that was proving an increasing burden on the balance of payments.

The growth in the cost, as well as the volume, of foreign technical assistance demonstrates a growing technological dependence. Financial dependence too was increasing.

Growing recourse to external borrowing to finance the investment programme has already been noted. What should be stressed is the overwhelming proportion of private credits in the structure of that debt (over three-quarters). Thus, according to an OECD study in 1982, of US$5.9 billion of borrowing in 1975, 4.7 billion (79.6%) was from private sources. In 1980, out of total borrowing of 17.2 billion, private loans accounted for 12.7 billion (74.1%).

In the area of foodstuffs, dependence was also increasing. Thus, despite serious and lasting shortages of some consumer goods items, imports of agricultural and industrially produced consumer items were very high: 11.9 billion AD in 1978, 28.4% of total imports. Imports of consumer goods represented 45.7% of total exports in 1978, almost half the value of hydro-carbon exports. The rent derived from hydro-carbons (92.3% of exports in 1978) was in fact mainly financing the purchase of consumer goods (45.7% of exports) and debt service (25.3% of exports). This situation was not a one-off matter. It reflected a trend, the development of the country's food dependence. If this dependence is measured by the ratio between exports and imports of foodstuffs (including 'drinks and tobacco'), calculations show a rapid deterioration: 131 in 1966 (positive balance); 98 on average 1967–69; 80 during the first four-year plan; 15 during the second four-year plan; 12 in 1978; seven in 1979. From a situation of relative self-sufficiency in 1967–69, after having earlier been a net exporter, Algeria, by 1979, was importing 14 times more foodstuffs than it was exporting (including drinks and tobacco).

This process of deepening food dependence inevitably affected the conditions of reproduction of the labour force. The gradual reduction and worsening of the country's food cover by locally produced food meant the growing externalization of the conditions of reproduction of the labour force.

Technological dependence, financial dependence and food dependence but also development of resistance and struggles on the part of workers all helped precipitate the crisis of the nation-building project.

Worker resistance was expressed not only in the form of strikes and labour conflicts but also in less immediate forms, such as absenteeism, rapid labour turnover etc. At the very time when an agrarian revolution was being launched (Ordinance 71–73 of 8 November 1971) a document on the Socialist Management of Business Enterprises was promulgated (Ordinance 71–74 of 16 November 1971). The aim of this Ordinance was to regulate relations between the state and workers in publicly-owned enterprises. It seems to have been a provisional compromise between the former and the latter in the phase of extensive capital accumulation in the 1970s.

The workers called this compromise into question just a few years after it had begun to be implemented; they were seeing little in the way of any improvement in either their living conditions (wages, inflation, housing problems, transport problems etc.) or their working conditions: indeed they were getting noticeably worse. This challenge to the consensus, within state-owned enterprises, took the form of an increase in the number of strikes (especially after 1977) and the development of forms of resistance at work (high absenteeism and turnover). By the late 1970s, these struggles had rendered the compromise of the Socialist Management Ordinance null and void. A new method of setting wages was then introduced with the law of 5 August 1978 giving effect to the Labour Code (Statut Général du Travail) whose main feature was the link now established between wages and production, with the possibility of a negative wage in the event of failure to attain set productivity norms. After briefly analysing the evolution of the material fate of the working class over the decade, the intensity and forms of working class struggle in response to the worsening of their living conditions will now be examined.

The increase in the number of jobs over the 1970s led to a significant redistribution of wage income. Household consumption expenditure rose rapidly. Per capita, at current prices, this expenditure rose from 775 AD to 4,956 AD between 1967 and 1983. If this period is examined, a clear increase in per capita consumption expenditure can be observed, rising from an index of 100 to 553. Over the same period, the consumer price index rose less rapidly, reaching 307 in 1981. These data lead one to conclude that there was an improvement in the level of consumption, and even of the standard of living of the population.

The official indices suggest that there was indeed an improvement in the purchasing power and hence the standard of living of workers, since the average hourly wage rose faster than the consumer price index, the former rising from 100 in 1969 to 330 in 1981.

Table 3.5
Algeria: Movement of workers' purchasing power (1969 = 100)

	1969	1979	1981
Consumer prices	100	219	275
Foodstuff prices	100	297	352
Worker's average hourly wage:	100	265	330
of which:			
highly skilled worker	100	196	265
skilled worker	100	288	386
unskilled worker	100	225	291
labourer	100	247	318
Worker's average purchasing			
power:	1	1.2	1.2
highly skilled worker	1	0.9	0.96
skilled worker	1	1.3	1.4
unskilled worker	1	1	1
labourer	1	1.1	1.2

Source: compiled from various Ministry of Planning statistics.

But if the (official) index of food prices (food being the largest item of expenditure in workers' household budgets) is related to the average hourly wage index, a very steep decline in workers' food purchasing power can be observed between 1969 and 1981. Over that period the ratio between the average worker's wage index and the food price index fell from 0.89 in 1979 to 0.93 in 1981.

Distinguishing among the various categories of workers, an even steeper fall in purchasing power (expressed in food consumption terms) can be observed among highly skilled workers (0.66 in 1979, 0.75 in 1981), unskilled workers

(0.75 and 0.82 respectively) and labourers (0.83 and 0.9); skilled workers, on the other hand, slightly improved their situation by the end of the period (0.97 in 1979 and 1.1 in 1981).

In fact, the consumer price rises recorded in the official index are largely underestimated owing to the fact that the range of goods in the index often includes items with the slowest price rises. Nor does it take account of prices on the black market. But there was often a considerable gap between the official price and the real price on the market. This gap was all the greater when, from the mid-1970s, shortages (sporadic or permanent) affected a wide range of items of mass consumption, which led to the development of a 'black' market to which households were forced to turn for their supplies.

The deterioration in workers' living conditions became a matter of concern to the single trade union organization which asserted:

> examination of the movement of prices and wages since 1970 reveals a marked deterioration in workers' purchasing power partly made up in late 1977- early 1978 but aggravated in the second half of 1978 and especially in 1979.[8]

Workers responded to these worsening living conditions by action, in which the strike was the last resort. In 1964 there were 33 strikes, and 72 in 1969, but in 1977 there were 521, and 922 in 1980. In 1981 and 1982 the number of strikes fell slightly.

The number of striking workers rose rapidly, from 4,500 in 1964 to 11,000 in 1969 and 110,000 in 1980. Furthermore, in relative terms, more and more workers were involved in strikes. While in 1964 one in 27 workers was a striker, in 1969 the figure was one in 25, one in 17 in 1972, one in 9 in 1977, and one in 7 in 1980.

Moreover, it is significant that in the early 1970s, strikes mainly affected private firms, while in the second half of the 1970s the trend was reversed: in 1977 36% of strikes were in the state sector, 44% by 1980, and by 1982 63% of the total were in the state sector.

Exercise of the right to strike (illegal in the state sector but tolerated in the private sector) was less a means of challenging working conditions or the way the work process was organized than a protest about workers' living conditions and wage levels. The number of strikes sparked off by wage demands rose sharply. While 36% of strikes were about wages in 1964, in 1969 it was 44%; 64% in 1977; and 71% in 1981.[9]

Similarly, the high rate of labour turnover in industrial enterprises originated in the quest for higher wages. In the industrial vehicles plant at Rouiba the turnover rate reached 22.56% in 1978, equivalent to a complete restaffing every four and a half years. Workers were changing firms (and even trades, in some cases) in the search for higher wages. A recent study[10] clearly shows how absurd were the effects of this turnover. Analysing the case of Rouiba, the author remarks:

French adjusters are recruited whose salary is 15 times that of an Algerian adjuster and could be used to train 94 adjusters at 53,600 AD per trainee. In other words, foreign technical assistants are recruited, as 'workers' or 'technicians', to avoid the drain of Algerian workers who leave because of their low wages.

The crisis of the nation-building project, which was marked by the break-up of the social consensus initiated in the early 1970s, reopened the question of redefining economic and social objectives based on new alliances between social groups and forces.

As the 1980–84 five-year plan was being launched, a deeply critical economic and social survey of the decade 1967–78 was drawn up and published in May 1980.

What new directions would be taken?

The 1980s: towards a policy of adjustment

The beginning of the crisis of the nation-building experiment led to a realignment of social forces within the ruling bloc. In the early 1980s the state's economic rhetoric began to change. Reference to socialism became more and more discreet. Conversely, terms such as 'profitability', 'realistic pricing', 'economic efficiency', 'competition' began to enter the dominant rhetoric.

In 1980, a number of regulations were adopted in various areas of economic life. One by one these measures as a whole outlined a new project, initially implicit, but increasingly overt. This project broke radically with the nation-building project. At the level of economic policy, the approach stressing the establishment of a self-reliant economy was gradually replaced by an attitude sympathetic to adjustment to the world system. Several actions and decisions by the state contributed to the formation of the new project, of which economically, the adjustment policy constituted the concrete manifestation.

In the area of public investment, after 1980 there was a change in priorities in state policy. Thus, the first five-year plan (1980–84) contained no new industrial project on the scale of those initiated during the previous decade. The project to create a capital goods industry, the idea of which goes back to 1975–76 with the CEMEL project (heavy electrical engineering plant), was abandoned. This abandonment was part of the reconsideration of the policy of industrialization. The absence of a local capital goods industry (initially covering a more or less varied range) capable of replacing, at least partly, the industrial production equipment installed during the previous decade meant permanent recourse to foreign firms, and thus went against the objective of economic self-reliance.[11]

The observed halt to public industrial investment led to a process of relative deindustrialization, which did not of course reach the scale of the deindustrialization to be observed in a number of South American countries (associated with external indebtedness), but was no less real.

With regard to the trade balance, this policy led to the emergence of a recurrent surplus after 1979, which was largely a result of the sharp reduction in capital goods imports. This surplus contrasts with the structural deficit in the balance of payments recorded in the 1970s (apart from 1974, when a slight surplus was achieved as a result of the oil price on the world market being quadrupled).

The abandonment of the policy of industrialization occurred at a time when the national economic situation was marked by a sharp reduction in the growth rate and a spurt of inflation. Thus, the growth rate, in real terms, fell from 7.3% on average over the years 1967–78 to 4.7% in 1980–83[12] and the inflation rate (calculated on the basis of official consumer prices) was 11.1% on average over the years 1979–83.[13]

The rapid rise in inflation in the 1980s, which principally affected consumer goods and especially agricultural items, was closely associated with state measures to liberalize the trade in agricultural products. In 1980, the state gave up direct control of the fruits and vegetables trade and public agencies (OFLA at the national level and COFEL in each *wilaya*) were deprived of the monopoly on the wholesale trade in these products.

This measure led immediately to a sudden surge in the prices of mass consumption agricultural products; Table 3.6 gives only an indication of the scale of this increase.

Table 3.6
Algeria: Prices of certain mass consumption agricultural products (in AD/kg)

	Dec. 1969	Dec. 1980	Dec. 1983
Potatoes	0.60	2.90	4.05
Carrots	0.79	2.95	5.25
Tomatoes	1.37	7.05	9.05
Oranges	0.65	2.90	8.55
Beef	11.80	66.45	79.80

Sources: Statistiques, No. 6, first quarter 1985, ONS, Ministry of Planning.

In the early 1980s, in order to minimize the effects of the surge in prices of items of mass consumption, and thus avoid social discontent invading the streets, the government devoted a large and growing share of its expenditure to supporting the prices of basic items. Credits allocated to financing price support funds rose from 900 million AD in 1979 (4.5% of recurrent expenditure in the state budget) to 1,945 million in 1980 (7.3%), 2,325 million in 1981 (6.8%) and 3,850 million in 1982 (10.1% of the state budget).

In the area of land tenure, laws on urban property were promulgated. Thus Law No. 81-01 on 7 February 1981 made it possible for state property to be granted to individuals (so-called 'abandoned property') for accommodation or professional, business, commercial or craft use. In a situation of acute housing crisis, this measure aimed officially to 'clean up' the state housing sector, but ended up in fact making housing a traded commodity; this inevitably affected those on low and medium incomes.

The 'commoditization' of housing was further extended by the promulgation of the law of August 1981 setting out the financial procedures for communes to alienate their property stock and, above all, Decree No. 83-741 of 24 December 1983 on the regulation of private national economic investment in landed property. This decree was the end-product of the process of 'commoditizing' housing, at least in terms of regulations, since, from that date:

> In the framework of the provisions of the above-mentioned law no. 82-11 of 22 August 1982, private national physical or moral persons, may invest in property dealing with a view to renting or selling buildings. (Art. 1, para. 1 of the Decree.)

This liberalization of property dealings led to rapidly rising land prices on the free market, the result of which was a considerable rise in urban rents.

In fact, 'commoditization' of housing and urban land was not an isolated measure, but part of a vast movement to restructure and liberalize the whole economy. This movement, which took off as the 1980s began, can be seen in a new agrarian policy, a policy encouraging private economic investment, and a policy to rationalize state-owned enterprises and make them profitable. This economic liberalism was in stark contrast to the refusal to open up democratically. Viewed from this angle, one manifestation of this was the onslaught against the working class, which was now to be brought under control and exploited to the maximum.

The 'restructuring' of agriculture or the end of the agrarian revolution
The beginning of the 1980s was marked by the introduction of a new policy in agriculture. Liberal in content, this policy represented a radical challenge to the policy pursued during the 1970s of which the law on the agrarian revolution (Ordinance No. 71-73 of 8 November 1971) was the foundation from which everything flowed. Henceforth, the very principle of the agrarian revolution was rejected since Law No. 81-18 of 13 August 1983 on agricultural land (thus implementing the guidelines contained in the resolution of the sixth session of the central committee of the FLN of 24 December 1981 devoted to an examination of the private sector) freed land dealings between individuals (which had been forbidden by the 1971 Ordinance on the agrarian revolution) and thus opened the way to the reconstitution of big landholdings.

In addition, the very existence of the agrarian revolution was challenged since, of the 4,992 CAPRA (Coopératives Agricoles de Production de la Révolution Agraire – Agrarian Revolution Agricultural Production Co-operatives) covering an area of 1,266,554 ha in 1982, only 91, covering an area of 13,119 ha, still existed in 1983; 4,901 CAPRA had thus been dissolved and the lands thereby taken back were either allocated to individuals (453,859 ha) or assigned to the state's 'self-managed' sector to form DAS (Domaines Agricoles Socialistes – Socialist Agricultural Estates).[14]

By liquidating the CAPRA, which were the very substance of the agrarian revolution, the latter was drained of its content and gradually replaced by a new state policy that encouraged the reconstitution of large landholdings. Consequently, ten years later, big landowners whose lands had been nationalized or limited in the framework of the agrarian revolution and whose lands had not been returned began to be compensated. The Decree of 29 January 1983 set out the rules governing compensation for nationalized lands. These were very favourable to the former big landowners as they could now immediately receive the equivalent of 20% of the compensation, the remainder being made up of Treasury bonds redeemable in five years (as against 12 years proposed in the agrarian revolution documents) and paying interest at 6% (as against the 2.5% envisaged previously).

The development of the non-agricultural private sector

In the period 1968–82, in agriculture, the private sector always held a dominant position (despite the nationalization of lands and the increase in the number of co-operatives at the time of the implementation of the agrarian revolution during the 1970s) whereas in the non-agricultural sectors the private sector shrank, relative to the public sector, in varying degrees depending on the branches.

In 1983, the private agriculture sector covered about 60% of the agriculturally useful area and accounted for about 60% of the production of cereals, fruits and vegetables, 90% of meat and 85% of milk. In 1982, the private sector provided employment for 660,000 persons, or 69% of total agricultural employment (as against 628,000 in 1967, which represented almost 72% of agricultural employment).

In the non-agricultural sector, examination of the distribution of global employment between the public and private sectors between 1967 and 1982 shows a marked reduction in the relative share of the private sector. Despite an increase of 76% in the total number of persons employed, the private sector's share fell from 44% in 1967 to 27.5% in 1982. If jobs in the administration are excluded, the fall was even greater, the share of the private sector falling from 67.6% to 39.6% between 1967 and 1982.

Table 3.7 shows that, apart from transport, in which the private sector slightly increased its share (47.7% to 49%, as against a slight reduction in the share of the public sector which fell from 52.3% to 51% between 1967 and 1982), the private sector's share fell, although it remained considerable, especially in commerce and services where it continued to be dominant in terms of the number of jobs it provided.

Despite the fall in its relative share in employment in construction and public works, the private sector retained a significant position, its share being estimated at over 33% (as against, it is true, a majority share in 1967, with over 58%). In addition, between 1967 and 1982, the private sector increased its numbers in construction and public works by over 330%, rising from 71,700 to 180,400 employees.

The reduction in the private sector's share was greatest in the industries: whereas it employed 57.3% of those working in this area in 1967, it employed only 25.8% of them in 1982. But here again, although its relative share fell, the numbers working in the private sector increased, in absolute terms, by 70% over the period, rising from 70,500 to 120,500. Examination of the patterns of

Table 3.7
Algeria: Structure and evolution of employment by form of ownership (%)

	1967		1979		1982	
	public	private	public	private	public	private
Industry	42.7	57.3	70.5	29.5	74.2	25.8
Construction & public						
works	41.3	58.7	63.3	36.7	67.3	32.7
Transport	52.3	47.7	54.0	46.0	51.0	49.0
Commerce & services	20.2	79.8	39.6	60.4	44.0	56.0
Administration	100.0	—	100.0	—	100.0	—
Sub-total:						
non-agricultural	56.1	43.9	69.7	30.3	72.5	27.5
Agriculture	28.2	71.8	57.6	68.1	31.2	68.8
Total	*42.2*	*57.8*	*57.6*	*42.4*	*60.9*	*39.1*
Total in volume						
('000):	736.9	1,011.1	1,737.5	1,280.5	2,085.2	1,336.8

Source: calculated from various Ministry of Planning statistics.

average annual growth in numbers employed in the various sectors of economic activity over the years 1967–82 confirms that for all sectors, except transport, the increase in employment was mainly due to the extension of state control over the economy. The private sector continued to grow, however, more slowly than the public sector (apart from transport), but nevertheless significantly, in industry (over 4%) and especially in construction and public works (over 11% p.a.).

Table 3.8 gives a breakdown of annual growth rates of employment by form of ownership and branch of economic activity in the period 1967–79 and the subsequent period. The shifts brought out in this table show a general slowdown in the employment growth rate after 1979 compared to the earlier period, irrespective of the form of ownership and in every branch of economic activity, except commerce and services in the private sector, and administration.

This decline in employment growth rate is largely traceable to the construction and public works and industry sectors. In the former it fell from 16.3% p.a. between 1967 and 1979 to 8.1% between 1979 and 1982, and in the latter from 10.3% to 5.3%, a reduction of 50% in both cases.

Despite the slowdown in its growth rate since 1979, in terms of jobs, the private sector has developed strongly in industry and construction and public works over the last two decades. With the numbers they employ growing by 11.9% between 1967 and 1979 and 4.0% between 1979 and 1982 for construction and public works, and 4.4% and 1.8% respectively for industry, the private sector grew considerably. In terms of enterprises (five employees and more) the private sector in manufacturing industry grew considerably: between 1969 and 1980 the number of these enterprises rose from 4,000 to 13,500.[15] Despite the reduction in its relative share over the years 1967–82, the non-agricultural private sector nevertheless developed vigorously.

Table 3.8
Algeria: Average annual growth rate of employment by form of ownership
1967–82 (%)

	1967–79			1979–82		
	All sectors	public	private	All sectors	public	private
Total	4.6	7.4	2.0	4.3	6.2	1.4
Agriculture	0.8	1.9	0.4	−0.3	−1.0	0
Industry	10.3	15.1	4.4	5.3	7.1	1.8
Construction & public works	16.3	20.6	11.9	8.1	10.3	4.0
Transport	7.5	5.0	11.7	5.5	3.5	7.7
Commerce & services	3.2	9.2	0.9	4.8	8.6	2.2
Administration	6.0	6.0	—	6.9	6.9	—

Source: calculated from various Ministry of Planning statistics.

What is the situation of private national capital in the industrial sector in the 1980s?

In 1982, according to a survey conducted by the Ministry of Planning,[16] there were 847 private industrial enterprises, each employing 20 wage-earners or more. The number of private industrial enterprises of this size has risen sharply since, in 1981, there were only 710 (an increase of 19% in just one year).

Analysis of the distribution of these enterprises by industrial branch shows the preponderance of textile industries which have 38% (322 enterprises in 1982) of the total number. The food processing, engineering, timber and construction material industries, however, have only 80–100 enterprises in each branch (8% to 12% of the total for each). Mining and quarrying has the least number of enterprises relative to other branches, with only 39 (4.6% of the total).

The number of jobs provided by these 847 enterprises is 32,029. Their average size overall is 38 wage-earners, but, of course, size varies from branch to branch and even within a single branch. Thus, the average size of an enterprise in the foodstuff industry is 46 employees and in engineering 43, whereas in textiles and construction materials the average number is lower, with 35 and 30 employees respectively.

The average size of enterprises is tending to fall, at least from the movement between 1981 and 1982. The number of enterprises rose from 710 to 847 (a rise of 19%), while the increase in number of jobs was less strong, from 30,319 to 32,029 (an increase of 5.6%). This led to a reduction in the overall average number of employees per enterprise, from 43 to 38 between 1981 and 1982.

Examination of the financial results of these enterprises shows clearly how highly profitable they are.[17] While gross output rose by 6.5% between 1981 and 1982 and productive consumption by 5.9%, value added generated in these enterprises rose faster, by 7.4%.

As Table 3.9 shows, added value per worker increased by 1.6% between 1981 and 1982. This rate is, of course, an average which hides gaps that are in some cases quite large. Thus added value per worker in chemicals rose by 17.5% (between 1981 and 1982) and by 13.9% in timber and paper. Conversely, productivity fell in the food processing industries (–4.7%) and textiles (–0.8%).

Table 3.9
Algeria: Movement of certain economic aggregates of private industrial enterprises with 20+ employees (1981 and 1982)

	1981	*1982*	*Increase*
Enterprises	710	847	19%
Employees	30,319	32,029	5.6%
Gross output (10^6 AD)	3,725.3	3,968.7	6.5%
Productive consumption (10^6 AD)	2,237.3	2,370.0	5.9%
Value added (10^6 AD)	1,488	1,598.7	7.4%
GO/employees (10^3 AD)	122.9	123.9	0.8%
VA/employees (10^3 AD)	49.1	49.9	1.6%

In 1982, two legal texts on private investment were issued. The first was concerned with private national economic investment (Law No. 82-11, 21 August 1982, *Journal Officiel de la République Algérienne*, 24 August 1982). The second dealt with the formation and running of companies with both state and foreign capital (Law No. 82-13, 28 August 1982, *Journal Officiel de la République Algérienne*, 31 August 1982). While the latter Law aimed, through the creation of state-owned companies with foreign capital participation, at ensuring 'the transfer of technology', the former contained measures to encourage the private national investor, who was called on to act in areas as varied as industrial sub-contracting, construction and public works, the maintenance and repair of industrial equipment, tourism, services and the transport of travellers and goods.

This Law provided that projects to create or extend a business would be examined, for approval, by a national commission when the investment was more than three million AD and by a *wilaya* commission when the amount was under three million AD. In addition, a public agency, the Office National pour l'Orientation, le Suivi et la Coordination de l'Investissement Privé (OSCIP) under the Ministry of Planning was set up in January 1983 with the aim of: 'guiding private national economic investment towards activities and regions likely to meet the needs for development and ensure that it complements public investment . . .'

A preliminary assessment of the effects of the new Law on investment can be made by using data from the OSCIP. Between May 1983 and September 1985, a period of almost two and a half years, 1,800 private investment projects were recorded and approved. The total amount of investments was 6.2 billion AD and the number of jobs created was estimated at 34,500. Generally, the size of the new enterprises was modest, since the average amount invested was 3.4 million AD for an average of 19 new jobs per enterprise. The cost of creating one job proves to be relatively low, 180,000 AD on average.

As regards the distribution of investment projects, the 'traditional' sectors continued to attract private investors (foodstuffs, textiles, plastics). Projects for sub-contracting machinery or spare parts manufacture continued, still, to be relatively scarce.

Restructuring of public industrial enterprises

In the late 1970s, the public sector was organized into state-owned companies of which many were large (Sonatrach, for example, employed over 90,000 people, the SNS over 30,000 etc.) and responsible for a wide range of activities (production, marketing, maintenance of equipment etc.).

Table 3.10
Algeria: Survey of investment projects by the national private sector (1983–85)

	May 1983 to December 1984	January 1985 to September 1985
No. of projects	1,200	600
Total investment (10^9 AD)	3.7	2.5
Total no. of jobs planned	22,500	12,000
Average investment per project (10^6)	3.1	4.2
Average no. of jobs per project	19	20
Average cost of creating one job (10^3 AD)	164.5	208.3

State economic activity was thus controlled by a few state-owned companies, with *wilaya* enterprises (local public sector) having a relatively marginal role. In the industrial sector, the 19 state-owned companies employed some 360,000 people as against 22,500 in local enterprises (in 1983). The large size of state-owned companies, as well as the wide range of activities in which they were involved, gave the leaders of these enterprises wide and growing economic power.

In 1980, a law (Decree No. 80-242, 4 October 1980) was promulgated providing two justifications for restructuring. The first was to facilitate the management of productive facilities with the aim of improving efficiency through specialization of new enterprises on a single product line and a single function (separating the functions of production, marketing and investments). The size of enterprises would thus be limited. The other was to decentralize the economy and strengthen regional and local management capacities (through increasing the number of head offices of new firms in the country's hinterland).

In fact, the restructuring of state-owned enterprises was pursuing not only an economic objective but also a political one. Economically, by limiting the size of enterprises and making them specialized, the restructuring aimed to rationalize the management of enterprises so as to make them financially profitable (apart from Sonatrach all the state-owned companies were running structural deficits). Politically, restructuring appears to be an attack on the stratum of technocrats whose power is based on control of large state-owned companies.

This process of splitting up big state-owned companies into a large number of smaller enterprises with narrower responsibilities was thus part of a twofold movement: fighting against the state technocracy (the 'builders' of the nation-building project); and imposing economic rationality (the quest for profitability) in public enterprise.

The most powerful state-owned company, Sonatrach, was the first to be restructured. A law (Decree of 6 April 1980) transformed this state-owned company into four new companies: Sonatrach, reduced in size, retained responsibility for prospecting, exploiting and marketing of hydro-carbons; the ERDP (refining and distribution of petroleum products); the ENPC (state-owned plastics and rubber company); the EGTP (large-scale petroleum works). Then, in August 1981, six other enterprises were created out of Sonatrach, each specializing in one area (drilling, well-work, well-servicing, geophysics, civil engineering, pipelines). Finally, since 1983, three other companies have been formed: engineering, national fertilizer and petrochemical company and national maintenance company.

In total, the 70 state-owned enterprises have been restructured into more than 400 new enterprises. The 19 state-owned industrial enterprises before restructuring, became 115 new enterprises after restructuring, distributed as shown in Table 3.11.

Table 3.11
Algeria: Distribution of state-owned industrial enterprises after restructuring

	No. of former enterprises	No. of new enterprises	Employees in 1983
Energy/petrochemicals	2	16	122,990
Heavy industry	5	57	105,840
Light industry	12	52	137,250
Total	*19*	*115*	*366,080*

Restructuring state-owned enterprises led to a drastic reduction in the average number of employees in each enterprise. Whereas, on average, the number of employees of a state-owned industrial enterprise before restructuring was over 19,000, it is now only 3,200 after restructuring. Of course, as Table 3.12 shows, this average conceals great variations; nevertheless restructuring led to a sharp fall in the number of employees per enterprise.

The attack on the working class
The quest for profitability in the state-owned enterprises led the state to establish a new system of regulating labour relations and setting wages. The

Table 3.12
Algeria: Number of employees per enterprise before and after restructuring

Branches	Enterprise before restructuring	No. of employees[1]	No. of enterprises after restructuring	Average no. of employees in each enterprise[2]
Energy/ petrochemicals	SONATRACH	96,460	13	7,420
	SONELGAZ	26,530	3	8,844
Heavy industry	SNS	33,000	17	1,941
	SONACOME	28,720	11	2,611
	SONELEC	15,420	8	1,927
	SONAREM	14,700	6	2,450
	SN METAL	14,000	5	2,800
Light industry	SNMC	26,140	9	2,905
	SONITEX	24,870	6	4,145
	SN SEMPAC	24,070	6	4,012
	SOGEDIA	12,890	3	4,299
	SNLB	10,490	4	2,622
	SNIC	9,590	5	1,918
	SONIPEC	8,510	3	2,837
	SONIC	6,130	1[3]	—
	SNTA	5,600	3	1,867
	SN EMA	4,960	3	1,653
	SNERI	3,230	5	646
	SNAT	770	4	192

[1] Before restructuring (1981 figures).
[2] This is simply an estimate and does not reflect any concrete reality (except by pure chance – which is most unlikely).
[3] Not yet restructured, so far as we are aware.

Source: compiled from various data (Ministry of Planning statistics and articles in the national press).

Labour Code (Statut Général du Travail (SGT), Law of 5 August 1978) implementation of which only began in 1982) replaced the GSE system based on the 'relative' participation of workers in the management of their enterprises in the state sector. It is also surely significant that the questioning of the GSE in the 1980s occurred just as the principles of the agrarian revolution were themselves being challenged.

We have seen that the period 1967–80 was marked by a significant growth in the numbers employed in the various sectors of economic activity (except agriculture). But this growth in employment was accompanied by a decline in productivity which, among other causes, was the result of over-staffing, especially in the industry and construction and public works sectors. It has been calculated that, in 1980, in the light industry sector, out of a total of

186,800 wage employees, 41,800 (30%) were employed outside production units. A survey at the El Hadjar steel plant estimated that in 1980 22% of jobs were unproductive. More generally, it has been estimated that at the beginning of the 1980s, about 10% of employees in the state-owned companies were surplus, which points to the existence of a significant level of 'disguised' unemployment (10% of the numbers employed in the state sector, excluding agriculture).

In the framework of the economic and social policy adopted since 1980, this over-staffing had to be ended, in the name of profitability and economic efficiency. Beginning in 1983, attempts to slim down were undertaken in enterprises, although at present it is not yet possible to assess how far this has gone.

The social protection that workers, and wage-earners in general, had enjoyed since 1973, with free medical care and the social security system, began to be reduced. In the early 1980s, the scope of free medical treatment was reduced and in the same year the revamping of the social security system was a challenge to the rights won by workers. Thus, work stoppages for sickness were now reimbursed to workers by social security on largely disadvantageous terms (only partial reimbursement and stopping it once a certain threshold was reached etc.). This review of the social security system was officially justified by the fight against absenteeism, which certainly is considerable. But it remains the case that this measure is fundamentally repressive.

This policy of gradually eliminating workers' social gains (such as free medical treatment and the old social security system, and also consumer co-operatives within enterprises,[18] staff transport, furnished accommodation enterprises provided to middle management etc.), inaugurated a new form of labour management. The 'Fordist'-type management of the 1970s[19] was replaced by a 'Taylorite' management of the workforce, the shift from the one to the other involving a downgrading of the workforce. This took the form of the elimination of perks and the link, now established with the SGT, between wages and productivity.

Politically, the submission demanded from the workers' trade union (the UGTA) to the single party (the FLN) was part of this attack on the working class. While the UGTA was never really an autonomous body *vis-à-vis* the party and the state, it was now totally subordinated to the party-state. The little autonomy that the UGTA had enjoyed in the appointment of its junior staff was eliminated in 1982 by the application of Article 120 of the 1982 FLN statutes. This Article provides that only activists in the FLN can hold positions of responsibility in the trade union apparatus (which was previously true only for the leading bodies). With this, the UGTA became the instrument through which the party-state controlled the workers.

Conclusion

While it was the reversal of class alliances within the ruling bloc that determined the shifting of the nation-building policy towards an adjustment policy, it was also a sign of the failure of the nation-building project. This failure, as we have seen, resulted mainly from the combination of the domestic economic crisis and the breakdown of the social consensus underpinning the project in the late 1970s. Another factor that also influenced the form and outcome of the Algerian nation-building experience was the external constraint or, in other words, the content of the relationship between the Algerian economy and the world economy and the nature of the international alliances that flowed from it.

After stressing the specificity of the role and status of the state in economic and social affairs in the Third World in general and Algeria in particular, the changes in domestic class alliances during the crisis of the late 1970s will be briefly examined, and the influence of the external constraint on Algeria's economic trajectory in recent decades will be assessed and evaluated.

The role of the state

While the emergence of a nation-building project cannot be dissociated from the nature of the class (or social group) alliances in power, the role of the state which leads the process and attempts (or does not attempt) to carry it through, is absolutely central. But the nature of the state in the Third World is specific.

In Algeria, as in the Third World generally, the state is not the product of civil society, but the reverse. The state is a 'legacy' of the colonial system that continued in its form and essence when the country achieved political independence; it functions as the central instrument for mediating between the outside world, of which it is the product, and 'civil society', which it 'produces'. The Third World nation-state, integrated from its very inception into the international system, develops in mimicry of the states of the centre. It stands thus as the vehicle for transmitting and diffusing within society the values, behaviours and systems of representation dominant on the world level (and which are produced by the states of the centre). But as society resists, the state strengthens itself and the gap between state and society tends to deepen. As the state becomes stronger, society becomes weaker, and the former becomes more autonomous *vis-à-vis* the latter. This growing autonomy of the state makes any compromise on the nation-building project fragile. The breakdown of the domestic consensus is then logically an inevitable part of the dynamic of the experience itself, failing any rejection by the state of the logic of the world system. For rejection of this logic implies a redistribution of power in favour of the workers (the working class and the small peasantry), which signifies the transformation of the nation-building project into a democratic and popular project with a different class content – a rationality distinct from that which dominates worldwide – and gradual disengagement from this system. In short, a different society and state, in which the state is the expression of society and not the reverse.

Changing class alliances

The crisis of the nation-building project in the late 1970s led to the emergence of a new class alliance within the ruling bloc. This alliance was built step by step in the 1980s, through growing exclusion of the popular classes (primarily the working class first).

This new alliance replaced the previous one which included the technocracy, the bureaucracy and the higher stratum of the working class. Based on a compromise sealed by GSE, this class alliance soon proved to be fragile. The economic and social crisis of the late 1970s consummated the breach between those social forces actively committed to the nation-building project. In the late 1970s, the alternative of a democratic opening (through a redistribution of economic and political power in favour of the popular classes) or increased concentration of powers in the hands of the bureaucracy (in alliance with the expanding private bourgeoisie) was now the issue. The solution gradually became clear, as the 1980s advanced, in favour of the second alternative. In this process, the weight of the army has once again been decisive: the sole candidate for the presidency of the Republic in January 1979 was presented as 'the most senior officer in the highest rank'.

During the 1970s, the private bourgeoisie (captains of industry, construction and public works entrepreneurs, big traders) developed rapidly, in close association with the enlargement of the state's economic sector. This bourgeoisie benefited greatly from the development of infrastructure (financed by the state) and public contracting (especially in construction and public works) and also the system of administered prices (low state delivery prices for industrial inputs).

In the early 1980s, the private bourgeoisie, whose economic weight, while far from dominant, was far from negligible, took advantage of the crisis that shook the state economic sector to put forward its own demands and propose its own economic and social project. While this approach was not explicit, it produced results, with several of the private bourgeoisie's demands being met, in the early 1980s (privatization of agricultural land, measures to encourage private economic initiative, liberalization of the trade in fruits and vegetables etc.).

Doctrinally, the basic principles of the nation-building project, enshrined in the 1976 National Charter, were proposed for 'review'. In April 1985, the president of the Republic announced the creation of an *ad hoc* commission to 'enrich' this Charter less than ten years after its adoption. The new National Charter, adopted in 1986, redefined, admittedly timidly and ambiguously, a number of doctrinal principles. Henceforward, economic liberalism is no longer totally opposed to economic *étatisme* ('exploitative' private capital, as a hindrance to national development disappeared between 1976 and 1986!). Similarly, the profitability of an investment is now stressed in contrast to the previous policy for which the immediate profitability of an investment was far from being the key element in making a choice.

The nation-building project thus gradually gave way to a policy of adjustment to the world system, under the leadership of an alliance, still in gestation at the beginning of the 1980s, but whose outlines are becoming increasingly clear: it brings together the state bureaucracy on the one hand, and the private bourgeoisie on the other; the technocracy being relegated to a subordinate position within the ruling bloc.

With the new policy, the working class, called upon to produce the maximum surplus value, suffered a 'Taylorite'-type management in contrast to the 'Fordist' management of the 1970s. The policy of redistributing economic power in its favour in the 1970s was replaced by a policy of complete exclusion.

The influence of external constraints

With political independence won, the popular masses remained mobilized for the struggle for economic independence. The educated *petit bourgeoisie*, in alliance with the organized core of the army, captured this potential for popular mobilization to its own benefit by placing its nation-building project in a problematic of economic liberation. But this project won acceptance only after the system of self-management – a spontaneous mode of economic and social organization on the part of the popular masses in the years immediately following independence – had been eliminated. In a contradictory way, the nation-building project legitimized itself by referring to the aspirations of the popular masses for economic liberation while actually being in competition with the popular self-management project. The need to build a state 'capable of surviving events and men' (declaration of 19 June 1965) was part of this movement to deprive the popular masses of their capacity to intervene politically and economically. The state gradually grew stronger and the nation-building project gradually won out over the popular self-management project.

With the implementation of the nation-building project, starting in the late 1960s, the state's autonomy grew as it became more powerful. 'Civil society', deprived of its sovereignty, fell apart. The implementation of the *étatiste* project led to the formation of new social groups which took the project in hand. In this sense, the state was the 'producer' of social classes. Thus, with *étatiste* industrialization, a layer of technocrats emerged and allied with the state bureaucracy which was itself expanding. The state was thus being strengthened from two directions, and it was this, combined with the industrialization process, that 'produced' the two social groups (bureaucracy and technocracy) which carried the nation-building project. That this alliance lacked a social base was compensated for by the integration into the ruling bloc of the upper layer of the working class. The 1971 GSE was the expression of this compromise. Its fragility has already been noted and, when it entered into crisis, that automatically involved the crisis of the project itself.

But where does this nation-building project belong in the context of the world system and what is the relationship between the former and the dynamic of the latter?

There are three points to consider: 1) the world political situation in the 1950s and 1960s; 2) the world economic context of the 1960s and 1970s (expansion followed by crisis); and 3) the role of profit in the implementation of the nation-building project.

After the end of the Second World War and the Chinese revolution in 1949, the colonial peoples' liberation movement developed rapidly. The Afro-Asian conference at Bandung in 1955 put the issue of the economic liberation of the peoples of the Third World on the agenda, once the national question had been resolved. In this framework, industrialization was seen as the key to economic liberation. The Algerian national movement, which was represented at the conference, adopted this thesis.

Thus the 'Bandung effect' manifested itself during the 1960s in the launching of nation-building projects in Algeria, and elsewhere in Africa (Egypt, Ghana). The Algerian project can thus not be separated from the world context marked by the emergence of the Third World on to the international stage. Its implementation also greatly benefited from the world economic conjuncture of the 1960s and 1970s.

From the end of the Second World War to the mid-1970s, the key feature of the world economy was an unprecedented expansion. Over those three decades, the rate of growth in world production was very high (5–6%) and international exchanges grew at an even higher rate (7–8%). This higher growth rate of international exchanges accentuated the interdependence of economies. Under the impact of technological progress, productivity rose rapidly. These features were manifestations by the countries of the centre adopting a regime of intensive accumulation centred on mass consumption ('Fordism'). This new mode of accumulation produced its own outlets. In that situation, the old international division of labour based on the colonial pact (exporters of raw materials and labour on the one hand and exporters of manufactured goods on the other) became obsolete. Industrialization, in some parts of the Third World, was no longer in such strong competition with the industries of the centre, and a new international division of labour was able to take shape. It was thus in this favourable economic context (combined with the 'Bandung effect') that industrialization projects were initiated in the Third World during the 1960s. The Algerian project was part of this movement to reorder the hierarchy of productive systems. Its existence was dependent on world growth. The world economic crisis of the 1970s contributed to the undermining of the Algerian experience. The way-out opened up by this crisis consisted in the transformation of the nation-building project either into a democratic and popular project or into a policy of adjustment to the world system. As we have seen, the latter carried the day.

Finally, we should reconsider a key feature of Algeria: the availability of energy raw materials (petroleum and gas) in a context of sharp rises in world prices for those basic materials. Thus financing of accumulation during the 1970s was not assured by the mobilization of a domestic surplus (agriculture) but through the rent derived from the export of hydro-carbons. The central role of hydro-carbon-derived rent in accumulation has been stressed above. This role was all the more important as the price of oil rose sharply over the period, leading to a distinct improvement in the country's trade terms.

The price of a barrel of crude oil rose, in constant prices, from $1.9 in 1973, to $11.2 in 1974 (the first 'adjustment' of the price of oil) and from $12.9 in 1978 to

$18.5 in 1979 and $30.5 in 1980 (the second 'adjustment'). But since 1983, the nominal price of a barrel has fallen, and fallen sharply since the end of 1985. Thus, from $34.3 in 1982, the price fell (for the first time) to $29 per barrel in March 1983. In December 1985 the official price was aligned with the spot market price and the price fell below $15 (February 1986). Everything suggests that this downward trend will continue.

The fall in export receipts (hydro-carbons make up 98% of the total), initially attenuated between 1983 and 1985, was amplified from the last quarter of 1985 by the dollar's fluctuations on the international financial market. After appreciating strongly from 1981 onwards, the dollar collapsed in the closing months of 1985.

Rent constituted an essential means of realizing the nation-building project during the 1970s: the reduction in its volume during the 1980s militates against continuation of the experience.

Notes

1. A. Hirschman, 'Rise and decline of development economics', in *Essays in Trespassing*, London, Cambridge University Press, 1981.

2. See Y. Berthelot, 'Développement du tiers monde et méthodes de sélection des projets', *Mondes en développement*, Vol. 9, No. 33, pp. 15–73.

3. On the eve of the launching of the armed struggle for independence, the best lands, 16% of the total, were held by European settlers. These lands, with a total area of 2.7 million ha distributed among 22,000 holdings, produced 55% of total agricultural value added (1954 figures).

4. According to A. Benachenhou, *Planification et développement en Algérie*, CREA, Algiers, 1980, p. 287.

5. Algeria, Ministry of Planning, *Synthèse du bilan économique et social de la décennie 1967–78*, Algiers, May 1980, p. 287.

6. In addition to the Algerian population resident in Algeria, almost one million migrant Algerians were living in Europe, especially in France. According to the 1975 French census, there were 710,690 Algerian migrants, of whom 331,090 were of working age (313,710 of them male).

7. Ali El Kenz, 'Monographie d'une expérience industrielle en Algérie: le complexe sidérurgique d'El Hadjar (Annaba)' Thèse d'Etat, University of Paris VIII, 1983, p. 621.

8. UGTA, 'Propositions de mesures transitoires', July 1979, mimeo., quoted by R. N. Sadi, 'L'entreprise socialiste: essai d'évaluation d'un mode de gestion', *Revue du CENEAP* (Algiers), No. 1, March 1985, p. 40.

9. According to H. Touati, 'La rue, le prolétariat et l'atelier dans l'Algérie d'aujourd'hui', in *Annuaire de l'Afrique du Nord 1982*, CNRS, Paris, 1984, p. 119.

10. S. Chikhi, 'Le travail en usine' forthcoming in *Revue du CREA*, No. 4, 4th quarter 1984, p. 18.

11. See R. Abdoun (ed.), *Biens d'équipement et industrialisation en Algérie*, CREA, Algiers, 1984.

12. According to Lloyds Bank Group, *Algeria: economic report*, August 1984. The real GDP growth rate was 2.4% in 1981, 4.2% in 1982, rising to 7.3% in 1983.

13. According to Lloyds Bank Group, op. cit., the inflation rate rose from 10.2% in 1979 to 13.2% in 1980 and peaked at 14.1% in 1981 and then fell slightly to 8.8% in 1982 and 9.3% in 1983. These rates are calculated on the basis of official prices which do not necessarily reflect actual market prices.

14. Or, in some cases, purely and simply restored to their original owners, previously nationalized at the time of the agrarian revolution in 1972–73.

15. D. Liabès, *Capital privé et patrons d'industrie en Algérie, 1962–1982*, CREA, Algiers, 1984, p. 551.

16. 'Enquête portant sur l'activité industrielle', a few results of which are published in *Statistiques*, No. 7, April–June 1985, ONS, Ministry of Planning, pp. 2–5.

17. This profitability contrasts with the structural deficit of state-owned industrial enterprises (Sonatrach is the exception that proves the rule).

18. In which workers are able to buy consumer items at the official price which is well below the price in the market.

19. We are indebted for this formulation to A. El Kenz. In fact, Fordist management of the workforce in the 1970s was so in part only given the perennial shortage of a wide range of consumer items.

4. Tanzania: The Debate on Delinking

Issa G. Shivji

Introduction

Issues and major controversies surrounding the question of delinking in Tanzania can be best understood in the context of a review of some major theoretical debates at the University of Dar es Salaam. As the only university[1] in the country where the articulators of policy are produced and different ideological trends contend openly, the University has been a crucible of different theoretical premises which have underlined major policy decisions in the country. Indeed, the Dar campus has been one of the few in Africa where debates and discussions have been a hallmark of academic life.

Thus the debate on 'delinking' (or 'disengagement' as it was called) found a place on the Dar campus, located, to be sure, within the general discussion of the 'Development and Underdevelopment Theories'. But this was a development from and in direct confrontation with the then reigning theories associated with modernization school/s. This chapter will first briefly look at the major assumptions and the local manifestations of the modernization school. The second section deals with the 'Development and Underdevelopment Theories'. While the theorization underlying the official ideology of *Ujamaa*, which will be discussed in the third section, was never a direct point of debate on the campus, it is important to note it for the sake of completeness. Section four elucidates the major currents that emerged from the debates and the struggles of the late 1960s and early 1970s. Next the burning questions of the 1980s in the wake of the deep economic crisis that has engulfed the country since about 1979 will be reviewed. Section six briefly identifies some of the problems of the debates of the 1980s, while the conclusion raises some questions on the role of African intellectuals (who *per force* have been the main participants and contenders in these debates) which are beginning to be asked, not only in Tanzania, but in Africa as a whole.

Except in a very broad sense, no attempt will be made to situate these debates in any detail in the political economy of Tanzania. The thrust of this chapter is to elucidate issues connected with and related to the question of 'delinking' or 'disengagement' underlying the debates. But an attempt to contextualize the debates within student and academic struggles which have been the immediate source of ideological struggles on the campus, will be made.

Modernization: 1961–67

The Independence Movement led by the *petit bourgeoisie* lacked a theoretical and ideological vision of the post-independence future. Its main slogan – 'Seek Ye The Political Kingdom . . . !' – was also a declaration of its major limitation. It was a slogan of *struggle* but had no vision of construction. Of course, the class amalgam (for that is what the Independence Movement represented) led by a motley of *petit bourgeoisie* of different social origins and economic interests had very divergent goals. The result, on the attainment of political independence, was two-fold. On the theoretical/ideological level, the theoretical premises and the policies of the colonial period were reinforced, while on the level of the state, the apparatuses of the colonial state were cemented; the initial addition of such paraphernalia as national assemblies and political parties notwithstanding.[2]

Both the continuity and the change that was political independence, found a theoretical expression in modernization theories. This school ruled the discussions and the debates of the earlier 1960s.

The modernization school, of course, was not of local origin, but derived its inspiration and articulation from Western, and in particular North American scholars, such as Rostow and Lewis in economics, Parsons in sociology and Morgenthau and Apter in politics. These metropolitan writers assumed the role of explaining the wave of independence and the tasks ahead for the independent African countries.

They argued that the main characteristic of the colonial economy was its dichotomous or dual nature, the two sectors being 'traditional' and 'modern'; the traditional sector epitomized poverty and backwardness. Its ideology was parochial tribalism while its members related to each other in terms of kinship governed by status. The opposite was the so-called modern sector. Dominated by values of individualism, bound together by contract and producing for the market, it was forward and outward looking and therefore the image of the future, of economic progress and national polity. The large traditional sector weighed down on the modern, and the future lay in modernizing the traditional sector on all levels.

Economically, the subsistence relations of the traditional sector needed to be destroyed by cajoling or forcing peasants into the market, which meant all-round production for export. Further, to lay the infrastructure and build some processing and import-substitution industries, capital was needed. Since this was in short supply while labour was in abundance, foreign capital should be welcomed enthusiastically. In short, the panacea lay in greater and deeper integration into the world capitalist market. The prescriptions of the modernization economists found their policy expression in the IBRD Report[3] that laid the basis of the first five-year development plan.

Politically, the great task was to build a nation. The technical agency for such a task was the state while socially the modernizing elites – bureaucracy, traders, modern farmers, the army etc. – would be the catalyst of change as well as provide the leadership.

The World Bank experts and others provided on technical aid by imperialist states and agencies dispensed these prescriptions as they drew up various plans, programmes and yearly budgets of the country. Meanwhile the local 'elites' in their 'modernizing drives', under the erstwhile ideology of developmentalism[4] (slogan: 'we should run while others walk') eliminated all political obstacles, which meant any organized political opposition, and developed monopolistic state structures whose alpha and omega were the repressive apparatuses.

Be that as it may. As for the theory of modernization, it is interesting that on the local level its most consistent and articulate expression on the Dar campus was in the Department of History. Here, expatriate historians such as Iliffe and Ranger developed, what later came to be called, the Dar es Salaam School of History. The main proposition of this school was that Africans themselves had played a role in their history and that all history was not simply made by the colonialists. Their researchers tried to show the *initiatives* of Africans on various levels – meaning initiatives in the direction of 'modernization'. Thus, commercial farmers, educated civil servants, coffee-growing chiefs and urban African traders were considered 'modernizers' or the embodiment of the African initiative. A volume of biographies of such Tanganyikans edited by Iliffe is significantly entitled *Modern Tanzanians*.

These expatriate historians found some echo in the works of local scholars such as Temu, Kimambo, Gwassa and others. In spite of its basic shortcomings, some valuable research was done under the guidance of this school, yet, of course, it partook of all the limitations of the modernization theories. In its local manifestation it was essentially backward-looking, providing neither any theory as a guide for the future nor an explanation of the present. Its major contribution lay in instilling some pride in the former colonial subjects, while providing the rationale and justification for the modernizing drives of the post-independence rulers.

The modernizing theories had very little staying power; its Tanzanian variant had an even shorter life span. The 'modernizing elites' were pre-occupied with modernizing *themselves* (accumulation of property and indulgence in conspicuous consumption) while the masses sank into even further poverty and backwardness, their greater integration in the world market notwithstanding. The turning point came in late 1966 and early 1967.

Two major events drew the curtain on the first phase and ushered in the next round of even more vigorous and heated debates. The student demonstration against compulsory National Service[5] in October 1966 and the ruling party's adoption of the 'Arusha Declaration'[6] in February 1967, brought into focus two fundamental questions – the role of the university in a backward country and the ideology of socialism (and therefore its converse, imperialism). Both these became important harbingers of the critique of the modernization school which was effectively provided by the underdevelopment theorists.

Development and underdevelopment: 1967–76

The expulsion of over 300 students as a result of the demonstration against compulsory conscription in the National Service was a traumatic experience for the academic community. Hitherto, the University had been nurtured in the image of its Western counterpart and, indeed, the project was financed by Western funding agencies. The students had seen themselves as an elite-in-preparation. The expulsion, followed by the President's public attacks on students as an ungrateful, privileged group, brought forth the question of the place and role of a university in a 'developing' country. While these questions had hardly begun to be answered, the ruling Party, the Tanganyika African National Union (TANU), adopted its famous Declaration proclaiming socialism and self-reliance under its authentic rubric of *Ujamaa* or familyhood. The question was now doubly-compounded. It was not simply one of the role of a university in a developing country, but the role of a university in a developing country aspiring to build socialism. Whatever this socialism meant to different people, including the Party that adopted it, it certainly put the debate about socialism on the agenda. This allowed some young academics and some students on the campus to initiate and participate in vigorous ideological debates. There was begun, for example, what was called the Socialist Club, which grouped together progressive students from Uganda, Ethiopia, Malawi, Kenya and Tanzania, and such lecturers as Walter Rodney. The Socialist Club, with the participation of some of the diasporans who had now been allowed to return, soon became the University Students' African Revolutionary Front or USARF.[7] USARF organized public lectures, inviting such people as Cheddi Jagan of Guyana, Gora Ebrahim of the Pan Africanist Congress of South Africa, Abdulrahman Mohamed Babu (then a Cabinet Minister and a veteran Zanzibari Marxist), Stokeley Carmichael of Black Power fame and so on. It organized Sunday Ideological Classes where discussions were led by students themselves and Marxist, Fanonist and Nkrumahist texts were read, studied and swallowed with great enthusiasm and often religious fervour.

Meanwhile, some academics, for example Sol Piccioto, John Saul, Lionel Cliffe, Walter Rodney and others successfully mounted a course in the Law Faculty called the *Social and Economic Problems of East Africa*.[8] This course, in a sense, was an answer to the question raised as to the relevance of the University or how to make it relevant to a country like Tanzania. It was based on some simple truths but of revolutionary significance at the time. Compartmentalization of knowledge or education into disciplines was a bourgeois approach *par excellence*, which enabled the bourgeois class to exercise ideological hegemony while keeping the ruled and dominated divided and ignorant. The proponents therefore argued for an interdisciplinary approach and the *Social and Economic Problems* course was an experiment in that direction. Hegel's dictum 'The Truth is the Whole' was quoted *ad infinitum* while political economy was offered as a magic wand to facilitate a holistic understanding of society. All students – from engineering to medicine – must, therefore, be exposed to political economy in order to understand their societies better and hopefully serve them with commitment. The launching of the *Social & Economic Problems of East Africa* was the first step. It very quickly evolved into a *Common Course*, compulsory for all students. From then on, through the *East African Society and Environment* offered in the Faculty of Arts and Social Science, the initiative to offer interdisciplinary education culminated in setting up the Institute of Development Studies. This was one side of the story involving questions of committed scholarship and relevant education. But these developments in the academic realm were not isolated, but were inextricably interwoven with practical student struggles,[9] and complemented each other.

Students grouped around USARF not only mounted ideological discussions but also challenged the traditional students' organization, the University Students' Union, Dar es Salaam (USUD). It not only organized public lectures but also condemned the curricula and the syllabi as irrelevant and imperialist-inspired, while expatriate lecturers were branded as 'bourgeois'. In one of their first salvoes, USARF members erected barricades to prevent USUD and WUS (World University Service) membership from descending on the town for their yearly Rag Day to beg for the poor and the needy. In the 1968–69 Faculty of Law crisis, students led by USARF members called for an East African and a people's university and the overthrow of expatriate and imperialist lecturers. The militant mood and commitment of the time is captured in the following excerpt from the second memorandum of the Students' Vigilance Committee which spearheaded and led the Faculty of Law crisis:

> As it was stated in our first memorandum, the real issue at stake is a fundamental one concerning the ownership of this University College, whether the college will ultimately belong to the people of Tanzania and East Africa or to imperialism. The students maintain that at present this University College is controlled by and for the interests of imperialism. The students further maintain that as long as neocolonialist expatriate lecturers constitute a majority of the teaching staff and they are allowed to impose their ideology to the exclusion of socialism, as long as they decide what should be taught and who should teach it, then the University College will remain a dangerous stronghold of counterrevolution and imperialist subversion against socialism in Tanzania ... From this premise it is obvious that the struggle has already outgrown the Faculty of Law where it started, just as it has already outgrown the New Curriculum issue which sparked it off. In short, it is part and parcel of the anti-imperialist struggle.

USARF also produced a cyclostyled Journal *Cheche* (recalling Lenin's *Iskra* and Nkrumah's *Spark*) whose pages abounded with serious and committed writings and whose prestige spread beyond the borders of Tanzania.

It was in this context that the Dar campus received the *dependencia* theories from Latin America *via* Gunder Frank and others; Baran, Sweezy, Samir Amin *et al.* were read intensively. Imperialism was seen as enemy number one and calls were put forth to disengage from the imperialist and world capitalist system. Tanzania's policies were evaluated fearlessly. The debates on 'Tourism and Socialist Development'[10] and the importance of a vanguard party in building socialism were all conducted in this atmosphere both in and outside the classroom. Thus for the first time, the distinction between academics (in the classroom) and politics (outside) began to be seriously challenged. Liberation movements found a forum and an eager ear at the University while some USARF members visited liberated areas in Mozambique.

Underdevelopment theorists took modernization head-on. Backwardness and poverty were not the result of any dual economy, they argued, but rather the result of long-drawn imperialist exploitation, beginning with slavery and now manifesting as neocolonialism. The so-called traditional and modern sectors were two sides of the same coin: underdevelopment. In fact, the traditional sector was a necessary outcome of imperialist domination. Solutions offered by bourgeois theorists would lead only to a greater integration in the world capitalist system and, therefore, to the development of underdevelopment. The solution thus lay in a radical or even a revolutionary disengagement (delinking) from imperialism, and in serious self-reliance. Seminal works were written in this context. Historical research did not look for modernizers – who were now condemned as *petit bourgeois* agents – but concentrated on elucidating various mechanisms of imperialist control during different historical periods.[11] Occasionally these explanations even verged on propounding conspiracy theories. But for all that, underdevelopment theories, for a while, provided a powerful theoretical tool and a biting critique of multinationals, among other things.

The writings of the time delivered a fatal blow to modernization theories. (Even John Iliffe flirted momentarily with the 'development of under-development theory'.[12]) Modernization was buried. Meanwhile, both the practical struggles of the students and the theoretical standpoints of the underdevelopmentalists had begun to move forward, albeit haltingly and confusedly. *Cheche* ran a special issue on class struggles,[13] which attempted to focus on internal relations and on elucidating the props of imperialism within the local state. Shortly afterwards, the Journal was banned and the organization behind it proscribed, on the spurious grounds that the name *Cheche* was foreign and the organization superfluous, since the TYL (the Youth Wing of the ruling Party) could adequately take care of all revolutionary activities on the campus. For a while the radical students continued unperturbed. *Cheche* reappeared under the name *Maji Maji* while the TYL leadership was infiltrated by some former USARF radicals. But only temporarily. Very soon the very basis of student struggles and the inherent limitations of the underdevelopment theories came under serious scrutiny by life itself.

A turning point was the crucial year 1971. The Party adopted one of its most radical documents called *Mwongozo* or the Guidelines which called for workers' participation to advance socialism and people's militia to defend it. It condemned the arrogant, bureaucratic and undemocratic practices of the leadership. The immediate antecedents of the document were the overthrow of Milton Obote in Uganda and the invasion of Guinea Conakry by Portuguese mercenaries. Both had ominous parallels with Tanzania. Like Nyerere, Obote had announced the Move to the Left when he was overthrown and, like Tanzania, Guinea Conakry was the rear base for a liberation movement when it was invaded. Under these circumstances the radical promise of the *Mwongozo* was made. The ink on the document was hardly dry when the workers picked up the cudgels in a spate of wild-cat strikes against their arrogant managers.[14] The movement very quickly moved to the stage of taking over factories. The erstwhile state could tolerate no more. It was one thing to make a promise to gain legitimacy but quite another to perform it. Workers were denounced as unpatriotic, hounded out of their work places, imprisoned and dismissed *en masse*. The notorious FFU (Field Force Unit, a paramilitary force) was often used. The state had shown its teeth. Students, hitherto a protected and pampered minority, also came under the wrath of the state.

The traditional students' body at the University, the Dar es Salaam University Students' Organisation (DUSO), under Akivaga, a former member of USARF, raised some fundamental questions which culminated in what has come to be called the Akivaga Crisis. In 1971, in response to the Vice-Chancellor's graduation-day speech, Akivaga, in an open letter, accused the University administration of bureaucracy, high-handedness and undemocratic behaviour. Students boycotted classes and staged sit-ins. The show of commitment, solidarity and firmness on the part of the student body was unprecedented. Once again the state could not tolerate such 'insolence', particularly when it seemed to have political overtones echoing demands similar to those of workers. The FFU was despatched post-haste to round-up Akivaga and deport him to Kenya, his home country. Parallels between the questions raised by the students and the workers and the way the state responded to both could not be missed. Yet they remained parallels. The two struggles never merged nor even came closer, a reflection of the limitations of both the student struggles and the underdevelopment theories which inspired them. We now turn to these limitations.

Again, it must be emphasized that the underdevelopment theories effectively demolished modernization. They also inspired some useful research, particularly in exposing the role and relations of the multinationals in Tanzania. They even precipitated practical radicalism; but that was about all. Underdevelopment theorists were essentially structuralists. They failed to elucidate processes and therefore failed to integrate their understanding of imperialism into class relations and the character of local states. They did talk about classes, but these classes were imposed on the structuralist framework of underdevelopment. In short, underdevelopment theories could arouse bitterness and inspire rebellion but could not become a guide to revolution, a guide to protracted struggles of the broad masses. This theoretical limitation found its most accurate practical expression in the very nature of student struggles. Student struggles can and do become a catalyst to precipitate a crisis but alone they have little chance of leading a protracted struggle of the people. Student struggles have everywhere revealed the *impatience* and spontaneity of their *petit bourgeois* social base as they, indeed, did in the Akivaga crisis. In that episode, an excellent opportunity to link up with the striking workers was missed – more – never even considered. While a few elements called for a protracted, public debate on the place of the University outside the campus, involving broad sections of the population, the large majority of the student body was interested only in getting Akivaga back on the campus. When the University administration cleverly conceded by flying him back to the Hill, the wind was taken out of their sail. Students returned to classes and settled down to get their certificates, marking the end of an important period in the history of student struggles and ideological debates at the University. There followed a lull in practical struggles as, at the same time, the ideological scene was marked by acrimonious theoretical diatribes which will be discussed in the next section.

Certainly, the lessons of student struggles were not totally lost nor the limitations of underdevelopmentalism, with its mechanistic calls for disengagement, totally ignored. Indeed, from the practical experiences of the late 1960s and early 1970s, particularly the experiences of the post-*Mwongozo* period, a small group of students and teachers began to raise some important questions as to the direction of political struggles and the meaning and character of the African revolution. Gradually, two tendencies began to emerge among those who considered themselves Marxist–Leninist. One argued for concentrating on studying the classical texts, developing theoretical clarity before embarking on any practical activities. In other words, it called for inaction (ironically accompanied by heightened security consciousness bordering on paranoia). The other tendency argued for moving away from the campus, embarking on propaganda in language that people understood, and becoming immersed in the day-to-day struggles of the broad masses. While some discussions on this group of ideas were taking place and making some progress, haltingly though, a new factor intervened.

In the early 1970s a group of Ugandans, exiled following the overthrow of Obote, found refuge at the University of Dar es Salaam. Some of them grouped around Nabudere, who arrived on the campus after doing a stint under Idi Amin, as the Chairman of the Railways Corporation. Nabudere and his colleagues skilfully used the emerging contradiction within the Tanzanian Left on the campus to advance their own ends. Nabudere needed to carve out a niche in the intellectual scene and, at the same time, gain credit with the Tanzanian state, which held a decisive card in political power-brokering in Uganda. What could be more propitious than to mount an attack on the existing Left positions, which had hitherto been the central focus of discussion in intellectual circles and an irritant to the Tanzanian state? That is exactly what he did in a series of vitriolic writings which he and his colleagues were later to dub as the 'Dar Debate'.[15] The debate emerging from the experiences of the earlier period was thus hijacked and put on a fruitless trajectory.

Marxist–Leninist currents

Globalism and broad-frontism

This tendency began and ended with a global analysis of imperialism. It argued that imperialism had entered a new stage after the Second World War which they called 'multilateral imperialism' dominated by such institutions as the World Bank, the IMF, the GATT etc. That the financial oligarchy had now routed and destroyed all bourgeoisies and turned them into *petit bourgeoisies*. Finance capital was the all-pervading dominant capital, therefore, it was erroneous to talk about national or bureaucratic bourgeoisie in the Third World; such simply did not exist. In fact, the so-called states in these countries belonged to the financial oligarchy, which dominated and controlled both politics and economics. This argument was dramatically encapsulated in the title of Tandon's article which rhetorically proclaimed: 'Whose Capital and Whose State?'[16]

Finally, they asserted, there were no ruling classes in these countries. The global ruling class was the financial oligarchy and it also ruled in Africa. The whole argument is put in a nutshell by their main proponent.[17]

> We have already shown that when capitalism enters its monopoly phase it does so with the rise of a financial oligarchy which dispossesses other bourgeoisies and thus turns them into petty-bourgeoisie. Colonialism, which arises with this phase, implies exports of capital.
>
> This capital produces a petty-bourgeoisie in the colonies. It could not reproduce a national bourgeoisie when, in the imperialist country itself, such a bourgeoisie is negated and destroyed, giving rise to a financial oligarchy. In colonies which arose before this phase any national bourgeoisie which might have sprouted was routed by finance capital and was increasingly turned into a petty-bourgeoisie. This petty-bourgeoisie is stratified according to its role in the process of production and distribution. This to us must be the starting point in analysing classes in a particular country.

It followed from the above propositions that: the main contradiction was with imperialism, against which all the people should be mobilized in a broad front; there were only a few agents of imperialism locally. Hence, no class analysis of the local situation nor analysis of the character of the local states was called for. This was automatically derived from the global analysis of imperialism.

Of course, various writings of this tendency tended to vary fairly opportunistically depending on the political atmosphere then existent. Their argument was probably consistent in the labelling of their opponents, or rather those who did not agree with them, as Trotskyists, neo-Marxists etc. It is also important to note that this tendency constantly and incessantly quoted Lenin and Marx as the ultimate scriptures and no argument could be conducted without being backed up by citing chapter and verse.

Imperialism and class struggle

As we said earlier, the experiences of the early period had given rise to some basic questioning on the part of this tendency. This was now accelerated by the questions raised by the Nabudere group. Although accepting the basic Leninist propositions on imperialism, this tendency argued that there was a need to make a concrete analysis of our own social formations and elucidate class relations within, so as to show how these reflected and embedded imperialist domination. And that there was something called local capital, local state and local ruling classes although these classes were in dependent alliance with imperialist bourgeoisies. These alliances had to be concretely understood and identified in the course of struggles. They further argued that new and different forms of capital did arise in the dominated social formations and these could not, for all times and everywhere, be subsumed under finance capital. Further, that the broad front of the people could not possibly include those *classes* (and not simply individual agents!) that directly served as the base of imperialism in our countries. Finally, imperialism was not some external enemy but found concrete and local manifestations in the very social relations and political processes within these countries.[18]

Many other issues arose in the course of these polemics. Suffice it to say that these were some of, what were then considered to be the fundamental questions. Both sides were limited by the style of the so-called debate set by the way the globalist tendency wrote its pieces. The style was to intimidate the opposite side by name-calling and no argument could be made without quoting Lenin or Marx and to quote or cite other writers was considered a *petit bourgeois* heresy. The vitriolic nature of the debate meant that many, otherwise interested persons, were intimidated and stood on the sidelines. Given the nature of the questions raised and the positions taken, it also meant that one tendency was at a disadvantage in that it could not propound all its positions openly.

Finally, it is interesting to note that this so-called debate was totally isolated from any student struggles (unlike the ideological discussions of the previous period). Therefore, the student demonstration of 1978 took the Marxist–Leninist pundits involved in the debate by surprise. The demonstration, for the first time, raised some fundamental *national issues*[19] for which it attracted the wrath of the state for the second time in ten years. Student demonstrators were beaten up and expelled from the University and their organization was banned by the state, never to be revived again. The Nabuderian tendency condemned the demonstration as adventurist and implicitly took the side of the state. Their concern was to wrap up the issues raised by returning to normality. In any case, these positions never worked themselves out as life overtook theory.

This phase came to a dramatic close with the Tanzanian forces' overthrow of Idi Amin. Nabudere and his colleagues rode to power on the backs of the Tanzanian army under the umbrella of the UNLF (Uganda National Liberation Army), an outfit hastily patched up in Arusha to take over power in Kampala as the Tanzanian army was poised just a few kilometres away. In power, some of the theoretical propositions of the Nabuderian tendency were put into practice, a practice politically so opportunist and theoretically so inconsistent, that it knocked the last nails into the coffin of the globalist tendency on the Dar campus. Meanwhile, Nabudere and his friends soon found themselves out of power. This time they took refuge in Nairobi from where they had the audacity to condemn the Tanzanian army as 'occupationist'! Whatever the truth in that condemnation, it came too late, from the wrong mouths and the wrong place. People in glass houses do not throw stones, it is said.

Democratic Socialists

This review would be incomplete without noting another current, which never participated in the debates on the campus but occupied an important place behind the official ideology. This current described itself as 'Democratic Socialist' and provided whatever theorization that there was for the ideology of *Ujamaa*. It was by and large made up of expatriate advisers and experts working in the state, including the state-house and the various ministries. Some of them were close friends of the then President Nyerere and indeed, his admirers. A concise list of the membership of this group is provided by Pratt in the book edited by himself and Mwansasu.[20]

In their ideological persuasions and outlook, democratic socialists were what, in Europe, would be described as social democrats except probably less fervent in their socialism and democracy and more technocratic. As I said, they did not directly participate in the Dar debates and when they did comment on it, in foreign journals, with obvious disdain and resentment. Yet their role cannot be underestimated.

The ideology of *Ujamaa* as pronounced in the Arusha Declaration and related documents had no explicit theory behind it.[21] The ideology was essentially an amalgam of a glorious description of the past (historically flawed, to be sure), a powerful statement of an idealist policy (without a political programme) and a grandiose vision of the future without a grand theory of society. It was the democratic socialists who, in their various writings, acted as publicists and theorists of *Ujamaa*, but more as publicists than theorists. Their theorization was limited to rationalization and justification of the existing policies and a mild critique of the so-called 'mistakes' in their implementation.

They probably considered the campus debates intellectualist, disengagement a pipe dream, and questions of class, state and revolution as outdated Marxist jargon. They pinned their hopes on the great vision and sincere intentions of Nyerere and presumably their own pragmatic approach which, *inter alia*, counselled negotiating better terms of integration in the world capitalist system. In a word, theirs was a trade-unionist vision of reform rather than a socialist programme of revolution.

Issues of the 1980s

The economic crisis: IMF and liberalization

The issues of the 1980s mark, in a sense, the beginnings of a new chapter, if not a new volume, in the debates on the campus. They find their genesis in the economic crisis that has beset the country since about 1979. The 'liberation' of Uganda was a turning point. No doubt, the initial phases of the war, when the task was to throw out the invader, Idi Amin, from the Tanzanian soil, created a moment of great patriotism and national unity, generating enthusiasm and readiness to sacrifice. But this was short-lived and could not be sustained once the Tanzanian army moved into Uganda. Shortages and economic problems emerged with a vengeance and cynicism on the part of the populace overtook initial enthusiasm. The war left the Treasury scraping the last dollar from the foreign exchange kitty and an enormous debt of over US$500 million from which the country has never recovered.

On the official side and in official circles, the discussions since have been dominated by what immediate policies and measures to take for economic recovery; and the terms of these discussions have been set by IMF prescriptions and conditionalities. On the campus, these have had little echo on the public level. But, ironically, the economists of the Economics Department have been drawn into these discussions in a manner and pattern quite distinct from the debates of the earlier period. They consider themselves to be and behave as the think-tank and policy advisers, and their discussions have been characterized by concerns flowing from such self-identification. Their writings and seminars have perforce reflected the attitudes of think-tankers and consultants rather than those of intellectuals–academics with larger visions of national development and the form and character of future society. No wonder, the American trained economists have offered little more than a vulgar endorsement of the IMF prescriptions and a fervent advocacy of economic liberalization (which elsewhere we have termed 'recolonization').[22] Rather than in any public discussion, debates and seminars that have been the hallmark of Dar Debates, the IMF 'debates' have been conducted in an exclusive fashion in luxurious down-town hotels with restricted audiences and official and semi-official participation. Student-body and radical intellectuals have been effectively cut off from these debates. Indeed, any attempt to initiate public debates on the IMF terms have been viewed askance by the powers-that-be and have even received veiled warnings of dire consequences.[23]

The politics of the crisis: anti-imperialism and democracy

This is not to say that public debates have been totally absent on the campus. These have taken place, even if in different forms and fora. Over the 1980s there have been several important seminars, workshops and conferences that have raised some very important issues, which we term the 'Issues of the 1980s', and from which numerous publications emanated. These issues, in their essentials, have revolved around the question of anti-imperialism and democracy, with greater accent on the latter and with an explicit political approach. Below we group together some of these issues for a brief discussion.

Democracy and Constitutionalism: As we noted earlier, the 1980s have been dominated by some very specific issues and concerns revolving around the question of democracy and its legal forms. These issues, to an extent, have arisen from the political developments since the formation of the CCM (*Chama cha Mapinduzi*) which was the result of the merger of the Afro-Shrazi Party in Zanzibar and the Tanganyika African National Union (TANU) in Tanganyika. While the two sovereign states of Tanganyika and Zanzibar formed a union immediately after the Zanzibar Revolution, in 1964, it was really a marriage of convenience and had never been able to take organic root in the popular consciousness. Since then some of the thorny contradictions of the political system have found their expression in, what we call, the Zanzibar Question.

The merger of the Parties and the formation of the CCM itself never really gained the legitimacy of the independence movement that TANU symbolized, nor did it fire the enthusiasm and imagination that the Arusha Declaration had done a decade ago. As for the Zanzibaris, the move was welcomed by a people who hoped that it would open up greater political space and deliver them from what had been a ruthless dictatorship of the Karume era. Yet the move was contradictory. Not long after, the Zanzibaris began to interpret it as an attempt on the part of the mainlanders to usurp their sovereignty, a contention that was to precipitate an open crisis in the constitutional debate.

Meanwhile, on the campus, related though not quite similar issues dominated the scene. While, generally, the questions of democracy and independent organizations of the students and teachers were in the forefront, the Zanzibar Question has never been an open question for debate. Partly, because it is considered sensitive, a political issue that no one would want to touch. But it also reflects the immaturity and timidity of the Tanganyikan Left who never boldly faced this important question in the context of the general issue of democracy and self-determination. For how can one separate the question of democracy in the country from the question of greater autonomy and self-determination for Zanzibar? But to return to the campus.

Since the proscription of their organization following the demonstration of 1978, university students, like all students in the country, came under MUWATA, an organization directly under the Party's Youth Wing. In short, students lost their organizational autonomy. Thus decapitated, organized student politics on the campus have been unable to move beyond mundane issues. But one thing to emerge, was the necessity of forming a teachers' organization. After a long process this was formed in the 1980s under the name of UDASA (University of Dar es Salaam Staff Assembly) which, in spite of ups and downs, has provided an interesting organized forum for some of the issues that have dominated the debate in the 1980s.

Some of the constitutional questions, which later were to occupy central stage, were raised in the Faculty of Law Twentieth Anniversary seminar held in 1982.[24] But these became sharply focused only in the 1983 nation-wide Constitutional Debate. In early 1983 the National Executive Committee of the

Party issued proposals for certain changes in the Union Constitution; the central theme of these proposals was the consolidation of the Union. Presumably, the time was considered ripe for these proposals, following the merger of the Parties in 1977 and a certain amount of democratization in Zanzibar, which in effect had marginalized the former Karume elements (who had been fervently 'nationalist') and brought on to the scene those who were seen as supporters of the Union, or rather a closer union. The Party invited a public debate on its proposals and allowed a period of one year for debate before the finalization of the proposed constitutional amendments.

Admittedly, since independence, this was probably the first and the most important debate to take place in the country as a whole. Many trends emerged in the process and different fora were used. The official media gave official and semi-official views greater prominence, but other alternative views also found some public expression. It seems that two major issues emerged out of this debate: a demand for greater democratization of the political system and a clear demand from Zanzibaris for greater autonomy or, what they called, a federal type Union.

Both these demands were probably most clearly articulated in two seminars, one organized by the Tanganyika Law Society in Dar es Salaam and the other by the University's Institute of Development Studies in Zanzibar.[25] Meanwhile, covert and overt discussions (including distribution of pamphlets) were taking place in Zanzibar, demanding greater autonomy and other paraphernalia of sovereignty. Some of these seemed to be officially sanctioned by Zanzibari authorities. The debate became so intense that the powers-that-be felt it was getting out of hand. The upshot was the hurriedly-called meeting of the National Executive Committee in Dodoma between 24 and 30 January 1984 to discuss, what was picturesquely called, the 'pollution of the political atmosphere'. It was said that some elements in Zanzibar were bent on wrecking the Union and were going outside the terms of the debate set by the NEC Proposals. This is not the place to go into the details of the episode, but suffice to say that the outcome of the Dodoma NEC meeting was the resignation of the then Vice-President of the Union and President of Zanzibar, Aboud Jumbe, who was held responsible for permitting the 'pollution of the atmosphere'; the arrest and detention, among others, of Wolfgang Dourado, who had been one of the most vocal advocates of a 'loose federation', and closing of the constitutional debate.

When the amendments were finally brought to the Parliament, they took very little account of the ideas and proposals emerging in the debate. But one major concession had been made. The original NEC proposals had not included the question of including a Bill of Rights in the Constitution, but the debate, in unmistakable terms, demanded such a bill. In particular, it is believed that the Zanzibaris were adamant about this and included it unreservedly in their own Constitution. Hence, the 1984 Constitutional Amendments included a Bill of Rights, although it was suspended for three years. Since a Bill of Rights is not a Union question, in effect this means that the Bill of Rights operates in Zanzibar under the 1984 Zanzibar Constitution, although it is suspended on the mainland under the Union Constitution.

In short, the debate brought to the fore the general demand for democratization whose exact conception, of course, depended on the different class positions the advocates took. For instance, by and large, the liberal bourgeois notions of democracy predominated – independent legislature, multi-party system, independence of the judiciary, privatization of the economy, sanctity of private property etc. Yet typically in a neo-colony, their liberal form tended to cover compradorial content, representing the interests of the private compradorial bourgeoisie. For, those who argued for an independent legislature, in the same breath advocated a suffrage limited by education; on the one hand they advocated a multi-party system but at the same time exhibited bitter hostility towards the independence of civil organizations, particularly trade unions. They demanded 'liberalization' of the economy but were lukewarm on liberalization of politics.[26]

These forces advocated a freer play of market forces, which in our countries effectively means increased inflow of foreign capital, de-statization of the export and import trade and decontrol of prices. In a word, freer play for the monopolist multinationals! Yet, at the same time, they would oppose any decontrol of wages, which of necessity means freedom of wage-bargaining and freedom to strike, both of which would be impossible without freedom to organize and unionize.

Meanwhile, the state bourgeois component of the comprador bourgeoisie have had little to offer beyond their programme of further statization of the economy under the name of socialism; deeper bureaucratization of the Party under the name of Party supremacy and closer control of the civil society under the name of revolution.[27] This programme has, of course, been largely discredited by the *practice* of the last two decades and with it, unfortunately, their partial anti-imperialist rhetoric has also been discredited. The state bourgeoisie is on the defensive as liberalization marches apace under the IMF tutelage. Nonetheless, it continues with its rhetoric which, combined in practice with economic liberalization, has the danger of producing repressive politics – the intentions and sincerity (if any) of its advocates notwithstanding.

The Struggle for Rights: Some of the debating issues discussed in the preceding section have begun to find practical expression, albeit in a confused and rough form, in what one might sum up as a struggle for rights. That such a struggle is on the agenda is witnessed by the fact that even some official and semi-official organizations have put forward demands for rights.

The concept of rights has come under closer academic scrutiny in various debates on the campus, a recent one being the Faculty of Law 25th Anniversary Seminar on the Bill of Rights.[28] The Legal Aid Committee of the same Faculty has spearheaded, in a practical form, the struggle for legal rights, while the University's Theatre Arts Department has produced some interesting dramatization of current democratic concerns. The weekly History Seminars have provided a useful forum for focusing on some practical forms that the people's struggle takes in various situations, while the UDASA forum has continued to highlight repression and breaches of rights, particularly in neighbouring countries.

The Legal Aid Committee and UDASA were among the first to condemn the killing of some half a dozen sugar-cane cutters at Kilombero in 1986.[29] The workers had gathered together to press their longstanding demands, when the FFU battalion called from Morogoro, 120 kms away, fired on them. The Legal Aid Committee and UDASA called for a judicial, open and impartial Commission of Enquiry. The Commission was eventually appointed although it was not exactly open, neither did its membership reflect concern for impartiality. Its report has yet to be made public. A public UDASA meeting on the campus collected money for the families of the victims while appointing its own committee of enquiry which never visited the scene for lack of official permission and the committee's own laxity in pursuing the matter.

It is significant that even the official trade union, JUWATA, and its leadership came out openly criticizing the killings. The popular trade union weekly *Mfanyakazi* ran interesting and open stories on the issue while the official government and Party papers maintained silence. Some members of Parliament spoke courageously and demanded an explanation while it is rumoured that in some Party meetings, there were heated exchanges. In the course of a public speech in the presence of the President of the Republic the Party Secretary of the Dar es Salaam Region called for one-minute's silence in memory of the Kilombero victims; for this he was severely reprimanded and banished to a remote region of Mtwara.

In short, then, the struggle for rights, inconsistently and incoherently, to be sure, seems to be a practical expression of some of the debating points raised around the question of democratic politics and a liberal constitutional order. As the debate and the struggle proceed, life itself is translating these, what may be called medium-term demands, into immediate demands and tasks.

State, party and people's organizations: It has been argued that, since independence, certain trends can be identified in the development of the state, party and people's organizations in Tanzania.[30] Within the state, power is concentrated in the Executive/Military arm while both the Legislature and the Judiciary have been politically marginalized. The Legislature has been dominated by the Executive while the Judiciary's hands have been tied by restrictive legislation that confers upon the members of the Executive unchallengeable powers. The absence of a Bill of Rights has meant that the Judiciary does not even have residual powers of challenging arbitrariness in the daily operations of the Executive. Furthermore, politically sensitive areas of conflict (for example, trade disputes) are withdrawn from the courts' jurisdiction and vested in the Executive-dominated tribunals.

At the same time, there has been close identification between the Party and the State, both in terms of personnel and in terms of the apparatuses, to an extent that in practice the two cannot be easily separated. Thus the state has borrowed the Party's ideological legitimacy while the Party has made use of the state's repressive apparatus to carry out their respective unpopular tasks.

On the level of civil society, the developments in the organization of the state spelt out above, have been accompanied by suppression of the people's organizational capacity by bringing under the state-party all mass, civil organizations such as students' associations, workers' trade unions, peasants' co-operatives, women's groups, etc. The net result is a development of an authoritarian state, although hitherto under an hegemonic ideology of *Ujamaa*. It is in this context that the demands for greater democratization arising in the midst of a severe economic crisis, on the one hand, and the beginning of a loss of hegemony of the official ideology on the other, can be understood.

While the demand for democratization has tended to take a somewhat abstract form, without clearly spelling out its character, particularly from the stand-point of the people, some shorter-term demands have occasionally found concrete expression. These were expressed in an articulate fashion, for instance, at the Conference held under the auspices of the University of Dar es Salaam to commemorate 20 years of the Arusha Declaration.[31] There it was argued that the first steps towards democratization involved separation of party from state. Further, that the Party should *attain* popularity and supremacy by persuasion and winning the hearts of the people rather than by legislative fiat. And finally, the people's various civil organizations, such as trade unions, student unions, peasant associations etc. should be allowed to be formed freely without party and state domination. By the same token, the affiliation of these organizations with the Party cannot be a matter of legal compulsion but a voluntary decision by the membership and leadership of the respective organizations.

Problems of the 1980s

It has to be emphasized that these debates and discussions have been largely among intellectuals and the intelligentsia; uncoordinated, incoherent, inconsistent and mostly spontaneous. They have lacked any organized form or links with the broad masses of the people. That is precisely why they have taken place in what appears to be a fairly free atmosphere. The unique characteristic of the Tanzanian state has been to allow a fairly free and even critical *intellectual* debate, at the same time, to firmly suppress any *collective* protest or *organized* alternative politics.

Secondly, unlike earlier debates, particularly those of the 1960s and 1970s, the debates of the 1980s have not always been situated firmly within an anti-imperialist ideology nor guided by a grand theory of society. Often, therefore, arguments on democracy and the constitutional order, even among the left, have tended to come close to traditional bourgeois liberal positions. Similarly, demands for rights have tended to be voiced in a manner not very different from those of the imperialist-inspired (especially US) human rights organizations. Certainly, there is some appreciation on the part of a few elements that both the demand for democracy and the struggle for rights must be distanced from the authoritarian state and imperialism respectively. But this appreciation remains peripheral and has yet to attain popular consciousness even among radical intelligentsia.

Thirdly, in our view correctly, the central concern of these debates has been politics. Occasionally this has been to the exclusion of offering tangible economic alternatives to such perspectives as those of the IMF. This has sometimes tended to weaken the national and democratic positions, which today may be considered the cornerstone of people's standpoint. Needless to add that these and other shortcomings are ultimately the expression of an essentially *unorganized* constituency of the oppressed workers, peasants and the lower *petit bourgeois* whose standpoint the radical intellectuals have claimed to espouse.

Conclusion: the crisis of delinking theories

In this broad review of debates and discussions on the Dar campus, there is little doubt that in one way or another various positions have been concerned with delinking, to the extent that they have been concerned with imperialist domination. Yet the theories of delinking, whether in their earlier form of underdevelopment theories or their later forms of delinking and collective self-reliance, have essentially been an intellectualist project. They have failed to translate their theoretical positions into practical politics of the people. In fact, even as a theory or theories, they have proved inadequate to act as a guide to action and to shape the politics of struggle. This is probably best illustrated by the Issues and Debates of the 1980s on the Dar campus, where little is heard of either 'disengagement' or 'delinking'. This is not, we suggest, simply a reflection of the inadequacy of the theories but also an astute, practical comment on the role of African intellectuals today. Since independence, African intellectuals have by and large been successfully absorbed and co-opted into the authoritarian state structures as, at the same time, their intellectual projects have been financed by imperialist aid agencies. This has meant that intellectuals have been among the first to be linked to the imperialist state system. Their calls for delinking therefore, *a fortiori*, have sounded hollow, if not hypocritical. Few, if any, intellectuals have managed to *delink* themselves from the state and imperialism and *link* with the daily struggles of the people.

The current crisis of the neo-colonial states in Africa is, therefore, also the crisis of the role of intellectuals and their theories. This has begun to find expression in the recent seminars of African intellectuals.[32] Recently, both on individual and collective levels, the role of the African intellectual has been receiving serious attention and scrutiny. This time around, it is to be hoped that there will be a sincere auto-critique and not further indulgence in another *intellectualist* project.

Notes

1. The second university was opened only two years ago. This chapter refers only to the debates at the University of Dar es Salaam, here called the Dar campus or the Hill.

2. For a detailed study of the development of the state and its apparatuses in Tanzania see Shivji, 1986a.

3. See IBRD, 1961.

4. For this concept see Shivji (ed.) *The State and the Working People in Tanzania*, Codesria, Dakar, 1986, Introduction.

5. This paramilitary organ was started by the Israelis and drew its recruits from the village youth. Around 1966 the government proposed to make it compulsory for all young people who had attended institutions of higher learning to do two years of national service which was divided into two components: six months of military training and production work in camps and 18 months of normal civilian work, but 60% of a recruit's salary would go into national coffers. The students considered this an unfair imposition when the 'leaders' were enjoying the fruits of independence.

6. The Arusha Declaration is Tanzania's blue-print for Socialism, Self-reliance and Rural development, none of which exist in practice.

7. USARF was, incidentally, led by Yoweri Museveni, the present President of Uganda who came to power through a guerrilla movement.

8. For aspects of ideological and student struggles in the Faculty of Law see generally Mahalu, Tenga, Piccioto and Paliwala in Shivji (ed.) *Limits of Legal Radicalism*, Faculty of Law, Dar es Salaam, 1986, and Kanywanyi, J. L. K., 'The Struggle to Decolonise and Demystify University Education'; Paper presented to Silver Jubilee Seminar, 1986.

9. For a comprehensive account of the student movement and struggles, see Mvungi and Peter in Shivji, op. cit.

10. See Shivji (ed.) *The Silent Class Struggle*, Tanzania Publishing House, Dar es Salaam, 1972.

11. Walter Rodney's seminal work *How Europe Underdeveloped Africa* (1972) was one famous product.

12. See Iliffe, J. *Agricultural Change in Modern Tanzania*, East African Publishing House, Nairobi, 1971.

13. This debate is now published in Shivji (ed.) *Tourism and Socialist Development*, Tanzania Publishing House, 1973.

14. This movement is dealt with by Mihyo P., 'The Struggle for Worker Control in Tanzania', in *Review of African Political Economy*, 4, 1975, pp. 62–85; Shivji, *Class Struggles in Tanzania*, Tanzania Publishing House, 1975, and Mapolu H., and Shivji, *Vugu Vugu la Wafanyakazi Nchini Tanzania*, Urban Rural Mission, Kampala, 1984.

15. This is reproduced in Tandon (ed.) *Debate on Class, State and Imperialism*, Tanzania Publishing House, 1982.

16. Ibid.

17. Nabudere, D. W. 'Imperialism, State, Class and Race: A Critique of Issa Shivji's Class Struggles in Tanzania' in Tandon, op. cit., p. 58.

18. A number of Tanzanians and Ugandans subscribing to this tendency came together to develop a collective response to the questions raised by Nabudere. The first product of this is now published as *Imperialism To-day*, 1981, under the

pen-name, Lucas Khamis. Other planned works included 'The Agrarian Question', 'The National Democratic Revolution' and 'State and Class'. These had to be abandoned at various stages as events overtook with the 'liberation' of Uganda.

19. Among other things, the student memorandum questioned the increase in the privileges granted to the Members of Parliament and Ministers when the country was suffering from a cholera epidemic and chronic economic crisis. It demanded that the Party should not interfere in the revolutionary activities of the students; that the prices of peasants' crops be raised and wages should also be revised upwards. The memorandum is reproduced in the *Review of African Political Economy*, 1977, No. 10, pp. 101–5.

20. Mwansasu, B., and Pratt, C. (eds) *Towards Socialism in Tanzania*, University of Toronto Press, 1979.

21. In a moment of his 'black nationalism' Rodney once tried to produce a theorization which argued that *Ujamaa* could be shown to be scientific socialism. But he never returned to the subject. (See Rodney, W. *Ujamaa as Scientific Socialism*.)

22. See the special issue of the *Eastern Africa Social Science Review* on 'Aspects of the Agrarian Question in Tanzania' (forthcoming).

23. It is believed, although not confirmed, that Dr Horace Campbell's (a teacher in the Political Science Department of the University) contract was not renewed due, among other things, to his open anti-IMF lectures and writings.

24. Some papers from this seminar are published in the special issue of the *Eastern Africa Law Review*, 1978–81, Nos. 11–14.

25. These took place between 27 to 29 July 1983, and 19 to 20 January 1984 respectively.

26. Some of these positions were relatively freely articulated at the Tanganyika Law Society Seminar which, unfortunately, was not recorded anywhere except on the tapes of Radio Tanzania.

27. These positions emerge in the Party *Mwongozo* (or Guidelines) of 1981.

28. This debate took place between 20 and 25 October 1986. The papers and proceedings remain unpublished.

29. See *Africa Events*, September 1986, Vol. 2, No. 9.

30. See generally essays in Shivji, 1986a, the Special Issue of the *Eastern Africa Law Review*, op. cit., and *Essays in Law and Society*, published by the Legal Aid Committee (1985).

31. In December 1986. Papers and proceedings are scheduled to be published.

32. See the papers presented at the Arusha Seminar organized by the African Academy of Sciences. The UDASA Newsletter has also carried write-ups on the role of intellectuals by, among others, Wamba-dia-Wamba.

5. Ethiopia: The Debate on Delinking

Peter Anyang' Nyong'o

Introduction

The overthrow of Emperor Haile Selassie in the latter half of the 1970s marked an important landmark in Ethiopia's history: an old order was eliminated and a new era was born. The new military regime, led first by an elusive core of revolutionaries called the Dergue, declared that it would build a socialist Ethiopia by first going through a national democratic revolution. It indicted the *ancien regime* of several crimes, the most heinous being that it had presided over the backwardness of Ethiopia while the ruling class and the aristocracy wallowed in splendour and wealth. While this backwardness led to the inability of the people to defend themselves against the vicissitudes of nature, such as drought, the feudal ruling class exacerbated matters by not even being aware of these natural conditions and the limitations they imposed on social progress.[1] In fact, it was the famine of the early 1970s, triggered, no doubt, by drought, and the manner in which the Emperor tried to hide the facts from the world, that immediately led to the revolutionary events of 1974.

Another important feature of the Haile Selassie regime was its policy on nationalities. Ethiopia, as a feudal empire, brought under its domination nationalities that otherwise would have been independent nation-states. By the force of arms and tight political and cultural control, these nationalities were compelled to accept the Amharic rule from Addis Ababa. Amharic became the dominant language, and Amhara culture was assumed to be synonymous with Ethiopian culture. In the case of Eritrea – an Italian colony incorporated into Ethiopia through a collusion between Haile Selassie and the United Nations Organization after World War II – this imperial domination led to an armed rebellion by the Eritreans against the Addis Ababa regime. From 1962 to 1974, Haile Selassie's army tried to subdue the Eritreans militarily; as time went by, and without a decisive success on the part of the Ethiopian army, the latter lost confidence in itself and conviction in its mission. Haile Selassie was finally overthrown with part of the army believing that his absence would create an atmosphere within which the Eritrean question – if not the whole nationalities question – would be resolved without resort to arms.[2] To date, this has not happened.

After more than ten years since the overthrow of Haile Selassie, it is appropriate to ask how much has been achieved in 'the new society' created by the Dergue, in 1987, under the name of the People's Democratic Republic of Ethiopia (PDRE). This question should not be asked with the view of cataloguing the 'achievements' of the post-Selassie government(s), but with the aim of analysing the extent to which there has been a break with the past, a new orientation in national development as well as international relations, and the potentiality of providing society with a dynamism for self-regeneration and development qualitatively different from what was known in the *ancien regime*. For, behind the idea of delinking in the Third World is the belief that past ties with the dominant world economies have led to the degeneration of Third World societies in the ways in which they shape and condition internal (or national) developments. This degeneration – or underdevelopment – is due not only to such factors as unequal exchange, decapitalization, etc. on which so much scholarly ink has been spilled,[3] but also the fact that the dominant local social forces are not capable of pursuing (nor do they have the interest to pursue) public policies that will lead to the type of social transformation which will improve the quality of life in their societies and create the potential for a self-centred development in such societies.

Delinking, therefore, must be viewed neither as autarky nor purely in terms of changing relations with the outside world in favour of the 'delinker' in the Third World. Since internal development in the latter is a function of both internal and external relations, and since it is the dialectics of these relations that shape the political economy of a Third World society, delinking must necessarily mean a revolutionary change that makes it possible for these relations to favour a more dynamic and self-centred development or, in our context, industrialization.

In a recent essay on Ethiopia, much in keeping with the methodology of David Landes[4] and Tom Kemp[5], Eshetu Chole[6] argued that, on at least five counts, Ethiopia has not, since the revolution, laid down a sound basis for industrialization. In a keynote address to a conference on 'Conflicts in the Horn of Africa' organized by the Canadian Council for International Cooperation, I have also argued that, in its nationalities policies and search to solve the conflicts between the Ethiopian state and the nationalities, the revolutionary regime has done no better than its predecessors.[7] On successful industrialization, Eshetu went on to note, lies the key to the ability of a 20th-century society to sustain itself. And for Ethiopia to embark on the process of successful industrialization, it must pay particular attention to five key areas: industrial investment; agricultural productivity; technological progress; a leading social force committed to industrialization and capable of carrying society with it; and the growth of a home market as a recipient of, and receptacle for, industrialization. As long as the revolutionary regime engages in military adventures to quell the rebellious nationalities it will have neither the necessary resources for industrial production and agricultural productivity, nor will it develop the authority and capacity to carry the people with it (that is, be legitimate) in this process of industrialization or delinking from the past.[8]

Feudal heritage

The society that the new regime inherited was by and large a feudal one. Its major characteristics were: low productivity in agriculture and poverty of the peasantry due to the feudal relations of production; backwardness in technological development and industrial production; absence of a home market; a disintegrated and disjointed polity held together by an autocratic centre; and a political leadership that had increasingly alienated itself from society.

Nonetheless, there were seeds of change in the old society on which the new one could cultivate. In agriculture, for example, Haile Selassie had initiated some commercial capitalist farming which had the potential of breaking the stranglehold of feudal agriculture on society in the long run. But the emphasis that was placed on coffee production for export, and the hunger for imported manufactures that the foreign exchange so earned helped to kindle, did not augur well for indigenous industrialization. As usual, it heralded the beginnings of import-substitution industries characterized by foreign owner-ship, technological dependence, the predominance of consumer goods with virtually no room for capital goods, and a highly unbalanced pattern of regional distribution of industrial production and infrastructural development. The major 'artery' of industrial production lay within the 'catchment area' of the Djibouti–Addis Ababa railroad, constructed during the Menelik era. None of these has changed much since the revolution.

Haile Selassie's 'modernization projects' had achieved a great deal in the realm of education, and in the promotion of small-scale indigenous entrepreneurs within the major cities in areas of trade and manufacture supportive of, or complementary to, import-substitution. The products of modern education provided the catalyst that alerted Ethiopia to the needs of a new society. From the products of this modern education came advocates of democracy, social progress, socialism and revolutionary change. Their ideas were not necessarily antithetical to the interests of the urban *petit bourgeois* trader and manufacturer who, by their very position in the economy, were enmeshed between the aristocracy and foreign capital. The politics of the former inhibited the development of a capitalist society; the economics of the latter dominated import-substitution and structurally limited the prosperity of the indigenous manufacturer. It is, therefore, rather doubtful whether any new society could have been built without the participation and ideas of significant elements from these social strata unleashed on society by Haile Selassie's modernization projects.

The Dergue's first significant political project was to declare war on these elements. Enough has now been written on both the red and white terrors of the 1975–77 period and how the Dergue crushed all 'its enemies' to emerge supreme as the only revolutionary force in society.[9] Suffice it to say that the major outcome of this 'victory' was the silencing of all open discourse on which the direction and form this new society would take and how a Marxist world view would rationally influence such shape and direction. For all intents and purposes, the official ideology, in Marxist phrases, words and language, became a 'forced orthodoxy' whose tenets were to be dogmatically accepted not debated, bureaucratically implemented and not democratically applied in the process of social transformation.

An analysis of how the revolutionary regime has attempted to detach society from the past – internally and externally – must be undertaken with the above in mind as an essential background. We shall proceed by delineating the five areas referred to earlier and seeing to what extent the process of qualitative social transformation has been initiated as a result of delinking from, or continuity with, the past. This analysis will, of necessity, be brief; an attempt will be made to highlight main features rather than go into elaborate empirical details.

Agriculture, productivity and the home market

Since the revolution, two significant studies of Ethiopian agriculture and agrarian reforms have been undertaken by the post-Selassie regime: one, by Dessalegn Rahmato[10] and the other, by Mesfin Wolde Mariam.[11] Rahmato's thesis is that, contrary to some naive critics of Mengistu's regime, there was a profound agrarian revolution in Ethiopia as a result of the Land Reform Decree of 1975. This Decree redistributed land to the peasants in a way that completely abolished feudal relations of production and, for the first time, 'enfranchized' the peasantry with regard to their collective right to own land as part of 'the Ethiopian people'. This marked a major delinking process from the land tenure system in feudal society, as it gave the self-labouring peasantry the possessory or usufructuary right over the land they cultivate.

But mere individual right to land by the peasantry does not necessarily lead to the productive use of this land, nor does it automatically lead to the generation of the critical mass of surplus needed for industrialization. All this depends on the new relations of production determining the use to which the peasantry puts its labour power. Since the revolution, argues Dessalegn, the independent smallholder has not become the major force in rural production; if anything, the 'intermediary organizations', such as Peasant Associations, play critical roles in how production is organized and surplus extracted from the peasantry by the state. The result is, that the peasant begins to calculate very carefully how much energy he will spend on self-subsistence and how much he will 'give up' to supporting the lives of other people who add more to his misery than to his well-being. Thus, agricultural productivity from peasant smallholders has generally decreased, which partly explains why Ethiopia has been so vulnerable to famine during the past decade . . . and hence increasingly dependent on international charity.

Mesfin Wolde Mariam[12] argues that famine is centrally a product of an entire social system constituted by relations of extraction and exploitation; in short, rural producers – what he refers to as 'subsistence producers' – are milked without replenishing the peasant's capacity to produce. The syphoning of 'surplus' from subsistence producers has two critical but related effects. First, it perpetuates the backwardness of the forces of agricultural production and, therefore, maintains or exacerbates nature's dominance over the producer. Second, the portion of household production retained by the peasant is barely sufficient to cover immediate reproductive needs, that is to say, directly subject to the vagaries of climate. With the unrelenting demands of these claimants, an aberration in the expected rural environment, for example, extended short-fall of rain, can spell disaster for those peasants without reserve grain stocks. The peasantry, in other words, is continuously vulnerable to famine, but this is due less to natural calamities, such as drought, than to its subjugation to other predatory social classes (landlords, the government) whose interests lie in surplus extraction from peasants even when this kills the goose that lays the golden egg. The social edifice, which Mesfin calls the 'subsistence production system', victimizes the rural producer who is fixed in backwardness. According to Mesfin, this system is constituted by three basic aspects: the peasant world, natural forces, and the prevailing socio-economic and political forces. Peasants and pastoralists, who are the bedrock of the peasant world, are trapped in seamless webs of natural and socio-economic forces over which they have no control. It is the supra-exploitative nature of these socio-economic and political forces, the irreducible claims of outsiders, that stunts the productive capacity of the producer and which is ultimately responsible for systematic vulnerability to prolonged reproductive crises. There is no doubt that Mesfin marshalls sufficient historical evidence and data from Ethiopia to prove his points.

Watts and Samatar,[13] however, have taken Mesfin to task on a few main issues in explaining the famine in Ethiopia. First, the two critiques take issues with Mesfin's theorization and empirical description of Ethiopian political economy. There are a few key aspects of this criticism which interest us here, and they are to do with three issues: 1) the theorization of the Ethiopian state and the contours of its social classes; 2) the role of international forces in Ethiopian accumulation and stagnation; and 3) the question of the scale of production in agriculture and its purported benefits.

The Ethiopian state is a militarist 'dirigist' state; it is highly centralized, very dependent on maximum extraction of resources from direct producers for its own upkeep, and dominated by a bureaucratic–military elite that monopolizes decision-making and determines, for the most part, public policy. At the centre of this military–bureaucracy is the Presidency, whose epicentre is the President. In so far as there is no viable organization of other social classes outside the state, representatives of social forces and classes seek to realize their interests by direct representation within the state. In seeking to make such representation effective, they must either stand in awe of the Presidency and seek to win its favours, or servilely serve it and accept its own interpretation of their interests. The peasantry is no exception, and its acceptance of the status quo may be both calculated as well as passive. Where rebellion has been the peasant mode of resisting this extractive and authoritarian state, the state's response in its own defence has been brutal and even more extractive: hence an increasingly intense exploitation of the peasantry in general.

It must be remembered that militarism and militaristic political control is an expensive affair. The Ethiopian state has developed a militaristic state and military forms of political control that cannot be supported by the resources extracted from the peasantry; hence, the continuation of this form of government must, of necessity, mean intensified depression of standards of living in the countryside. Attempts to solve this problem by creating commercial state farms has met with total failure, and the state has had to turn to the smallholder as the source of its fiscal base.

The internal military campaigns also explain the increasing external dependence of the Ethiopian state on its 'military godfathers'. There is no doubt that the Ethiopian state has had to mortgage its coffee exports to the purchase of Soviet arms and Eastern-bloc military services in order to carry out its military campaigns in Eritrea, Tigray and the Ogaden. Were it not for these campaigns, foreign exchange from coffee exports could perhaps be used for more productive investment, either in agriculture or industry.

According to Watts and Samatar, Mesfin strongly insists that the development of large-scale agricultural production is a necessary precondition to solving African poverty and famine. The underlying assumption being that peasant production has not changed over the centuries and is therefore quite incapable of providing surplus necessary for capital accumulation and growth. Suffice it to say that both large- and small-scale farming have been the basis of capitalist accumulation in diverse societies. In the USA, large-scale commercial agriculture is the basis of the success of capitalist farming; in Kenya, the success of the Kenya Tea Development Authority (KTDA) is based on the smallholder tea farmer. The Soviet Union knows of the problems that state farms experienced and how socialism has had to reckon with the inefficiencies of large-scale state farms versus the efficiency of the small farmer 'with capitalist hangovers'.

What is at stake is not really the size of the farm, but the relations of production that are engendered by the size or within which size is exploited for purposes of surplus extraction and accumulation. Once the peasant begins using advanced forces of production, or once the peasant farm is industrialized (à la KTDA), the peasant begins to disappear 'as a social type' and a contract farmer, or a proletariat working at home, emerges. The extractable surplus or the accumulable surplus, of necessity, increases. The extent to which the process of accumulation will lead towards industrialization will again depend on class relations and nature of the state.

Resettlement, productivity and accumulation

We can travel along the same road of argument in reviewing Ethiopia's resettlement or collectivization programmes initiated after the 1974 Revolution. The official assumption has been that resettlement should lead to better production methods by peasants, higher productivity in agriculture, and improved standards of living in the rural areas. Critiques have, however, argued that resettlement cannot have such outcomes: peasants resist resettlement, and the state cannot marshall the capital investment necessary to make it a success. For the moment, the validity of either side of the argument will not be assumed.

Soon after the revolution, the Ethiopian government's investigations into the underlying problems of production were assisted by a World Bank mission, which concluded that if major resettlement and land-use improvement programmes were not implemented within the next decade, increasingly severe famines and further deterioration of living standards would follow.[14] By the end of the 1970s, some 46,000 families, comprising 142,000 people, had been resettled on 88 sites in eleven regions at a cost of approximately US$3,532 per family or US$785 per person. This represented a mere 0.64% of the total rural households. A number of policies, including the use of coercion, the resettlement of urban unemployed, and the settling of single heads of household without their families, proved unpopular, and explain the lack of success of a number of early sites.[15]

The 1984–86 resettlement initiative was the response to, and outcome of, an emergency situation. Resettlement accounted for a quarter of the expenditure in the emergency plan to combat famine set up by the Workers' Party of Ethiopia. Within two years, 300,000 families were to be resettled at a cost of approximately US$61,720 million; 540 tractors and 150,000 oxen were to be provided to cultivate 300,000 hectares, with an estimated yield of 5.34 million quintals (one quintal = 100 kg.) mainly maize and sorghum. In one and a half years two-thirds of the target figure were resettled from five regions in the north (over 90% from Wello, Shewa and Tigray) to five regions in the west (over 90% to Wallegga, Illubabor, Gojjam and Kefa).[16]

The balance sheet of this resettlement programme two years later, revealed that it has been riddled with problems and not, at that time, led to an improvement in agricultural productivity. Perhaps it was even too early to expect such results. What, however, is the likelihood that resettlement will lead to improved methods of production and better living standards for the resettled? To what extent will the resettled generate sufficient surpluses to nurture a dynamic accumulation process? As long as the Ethiopian state is engaged in civil wars with nationalities in Eritrea and Tigray, it is difficult to answer these questions, because the disruption in national life puts a heavy strain on what resettlement schemes could achieve were the state to devote sufficient resources to them. Any analysis aimed at answering these questions would mainly concentrate on certain short-term 'achievements'. Evaluating the self-sufficiency and sustainability of the resettlement exercise in the Wallegga Region, Alula Pankhurst, for example, writes:

> After two and a half years the settlers have obtained their second harvest and most of the new settlements are moving towards short-term agricultural self-sufficiency. In some areas water-logging has caused problems, while in others insufficient water was found when bore-wells were dug. As a result a

number of sites have had to be relocated. In many areas further land needs to be cleared since the hectarage per family has not reached the 0.9 minimum required. Despite such problems, the short-term survival of what were hopeless famine victims has been assured and the settlers have enough to eat. However, a number of longer-term issues need to be addressed and policy choices need to be made.[17]

It is to these longer-term issues and policy choices that Alula Pankhurst does not devote much of his analysis, and on these will depend the extent to which the post-Selassie regime effectively delinks from its past. So far, the history of resettlement is too recent for us to make any conclusive judgement; the content and context of resettlement, however, does not give us much hope that agricultural productivity will increase to the level that will make the rural world of Ethiopia qualitatively very different from the past.

Industry

What has taken place since 1974, Dessalegn Rahmato writes,[18] has been that the state's dominance in the economy has been enlarged in all sectors. By extending the frontiers of public ownership far and wide, and dislodging private enterprise from all areas except small-scale production and petty trade, the military government has succeeded in establishing what may be termed a full-fledged state economy. The previous economic system, it should be noted, was also dominated by the state,[19] but the critical difference now is that while this is a state economy, its predecessor was an open economy in which the state sector was predominant.

The fact that the official ideology of the state argues that there is a 'transition to socialism' should not make us, by dint of that claim, analyse this economy with the yardstick of socialist economics. Thus, the modest programmes of development to which the Ethiopian government has committed itself during this so-called period of transition have been mainly social democratic in content and 'basic needs' in approach.

The state has committed itself to public expenditures aimed at improving food production and attaining self-sufficiency, ameliorating the housing shortage, providing clean water for the rural population and expanding the social and physical infrastructure.[20] Agriculture and the infrastructural sector, within such a programme, of necessity preoccupy the state's attention. The small- and medium-scale enterprises, though largely in state hands, cannot receive as much attention given the scarcity of surplus available to the state. Thus the real growth in the industrial sector has been negligible, if not totally negative, since the revolution. The structure of industrial production has not changed either: like in pre-revolutionary times, manufacturing industry still produces, almost exclusively, light goods for primary consumption, and still relies heavily on foreign sources for machinery and raw materials.

Foreign Trade

Ethiopia's 'trading partners'[21] have changed to some extent, but the structure of foreign trade has not changed substantially since the revolution. Ethiopia remains an exporter of – mainly agricultural – raw materials and an importer of technology and manufactured goods. Within this framework, in common with most other poor, African countries, Ethiopia has had a tremendous increase in its trade deficit over the last decade, largely as a result of the decline in the value of its major export, coffee, in the international market since the end of the 1970s.

Political leadership

We have argued earlier that, for a society to qualitatively change its pattern of development and improve on its past, it must have, among other things, a political leadership committed to this change and one that can carry society with it. Lenin, writing on socialist revolutions, devoted much attention to this, and emphasized the critical role of a clear intellectual ability to analyse and understand (theory) social conditions as a means to changing them and the commitment of such change agents (revolutionary party vanguards) to their mission.[22] But Lenin emphasized that such vanguards acquired the legitimacy to act on behalf of society precisely as a result of rising to such positions through revolutionary struggle and maintaining such leadership positions through undiluted democratic consultation and accountability. At no time did he envisage revolutionaries who could rise to the position of vanguards by 'shooting their way into power' and claiming legitimacy because they said or believed 'the right things' on behalf of the popular masses.

One of the greatest crises of attempts to build socialism in Africa is to be found at the political level; this has to do with the belief, by those who wield political power on behalf of socialism, that building socialism is a missionary affair. Those who are converted come first, they proselytize, gain believers among 'the broad masses' and conduct a jihad among the infidels, by the sword if need be. Without sounding too harsh, such attempts at 'socialist transition' begin on the wrong foot politically and, given the difficult economic environments in which they have to operate, they cannot succeed in delinking any Third World society from its past. Ethiopia is no exception.

This scenario makes it difficult to see the Ethiopian regime as any other than a military authoritarian one seeking to legitimize itself on socialist rhetoric. Its achievements at democratizing society, like those of improving productive forces for socialist development, can be seen only in the context of using democratic discourse as a legitimizing force without necessarily building democratic institutions to empower the citizenry politically and increase state accountability.

Conclusion

Delinking should not be discussed in the abstract, nor should it be viewed mainly in terms of foreign relations. Delinking is a process of social change that involves qualitative departure from a society's mode of life in the past, always aiming for the better. In analysing the changes that have occurred in Ethiopia since 1974, we have seen certain qualitative changes, but the overall structural change in society, such that society will progressively gain the ability for self-regeneration, does not seem to have occurred. If anything, we discover some heightened forms of external dependency and an increasing internal inertia to develop, notwithstanding the revolutionary rhetoric. This is what creates some strong similarity, not difference, with the past.

Notes

1. For a further discussion on how natural conditions and social relations of production interact to impede social progress see Mesfin Wolde Mariam, *Rural Vulnerability to Famine in Ethiopia, 1958–1977*, Addis Ababa; Addis Ababa University Press, 1984.
2. For a more detailed analysis of this see Anyang' Nyong'o, 'Crises et Conflits dans la Vallee Superieure du Nil,' Ramses, 1988/89, Institut Francais de Relations Internationales, Paris.
3. The literature on this needs no reciting; whether from the point of view of the dependency school or the now re-emerging neo-classical school, there seems to be a consensus that both colonialism and independence have given Africa 'raw deals'. The fact that there is a re-emergence of popular struggles in the continent to create better societies is testimony to the fact that people want better societies in which 'to feel at home'. For more discussion on this, see *Popular Struggles for Democracy in Africa*, London and Tokyo: Zed Books and United Nations University, 1987.
4. David Landes, *The Unbound Prometheus: Technological Change and Industrial Development in Western Europe from 1750 to the Present*, Cambridge, Cambridge University Press, 1969.
5. Tom Kemp, *Industrialization in the Non-Western World*, London and New York, Longman, 1983.
6. Eshetu Chole, 'Constraints to Industrial Development in Ethiopia', Paper presented at the Second Triennial Congress of OSSREA, Eldoret, July 1986.
7. Anyang' Nyong'o, 'Conflicts and Crises in the Horn of Africa', Canadian Council for International Cooperation, Ottawa, Canada, April 1988.
8. Ibid.
9. See F. Halliday and M. Molyneux, *The Ethiopian Revolution*, London, Verso, 1981; R. Lefort, *Ethiopia: An Heretical Revolution?*, London, Zed Press, 1983; John Markakis, 'The Military State and Ethiopia's Path to "Garrison Socialism"', *Review of African Political Economy*, No. 21, 1981; John Markakis and Nega Ayele, *Class and Revolution in Ethiopia*, Nottingham, Spokesman, 1978. Michael Chege, 'A Revolution Betrayed', *Journal of Modern African Studies*, 1978.
10. Dessalegn Rahmato, *Agrarian Reform in Ethiopia*, Trenton, The Red Sea Press, 1985.

11. Mesfin Wolde Mariam, op. cit.

12. For an able summary and critique of Mesfin's thesis see Michael J. Watts and Abdi I. Samatar, 'Cultures of Hunger, Spaces and Death: A Review of Mesfin Wolde Mariam . . .' *Eastern Africa Social Science Research Review*, Vol. 1, No. 2, June 1985: 103–14. My summary is taken from this review – with which, for the most part, I agree.

13. Ibid.

14. World Bank, 'Appraisal of Drought and Rehabilitation Project in Ethiopia', Washington: World Bank, General Agriculture Division, East Africa, 1974, Report No. 444a OT.

15. See Alula Pankhurst, 'Resettlement in Ethiopia: A Background Paper', Mimeo, 1987.

16. Ibid.

17. Ibid.

18. Dessalegn Rahmato, 'The Political Economy of Development in Ethiopia,' Paper presented to the Conference on Ideology and Policy in Afro-Marxist States, University of California, Santa Barbara, 6–8 December 1985.

19. See, for a further analysis of this, Dessalegn Rahmato, 'Political Power and Social Formation in Ethiopia Under the Old Regime: Notes on Marxist Theory,' Paper presented at the Eighth International Conference of Ethiopian Studies, Addis Ababa, 26–30 November, 1984.

20. Dessalegn, 1985.

21. Dessalegn (1985) argues that the shift has been in the direction, and to the benefit, of the Soviet bloc countries which now export far more, and import far less than they did earlier.

22. V. I. Lenin in 'What is to be Done?' and 'Better Fewer, But Better', *Collected Works*, Moscow, Progress Publishers, 1952.

6. Zimbabwe and Uganda: A Contrasting Record

Yash Tandon

The experience of the USSR and China

What are the implications of the Soviet and, in particular, the Chinese experience for the theory of delinking? The conclusion to be drawn is that delinking is not such an easy affair as some theorists make it out. Under commodity production, the law of value is a powerful determining force which can be ignored only at the risk of dislocating the entire price system, and therefore the allocation of resources between different branches of consumption and production. For the law of value to be limited during the transitional phase of socialism, the class struggle between the directly producing classes, especially their lower ranks, and the appropriating classes has to be not reduced but intensified.

But at the same time the producing classes must have a scientific understanding of how the law of value operates in commodity production and how it can be regulated to serve the broader interest of the society without creating the kind of dislocation in the economy that China suffered during the Cultural Revolution. The lessons to be drawn from the mistakes of that period are not, however, those drawn by the present Chinese leadership, for clearly China is drifting back into free commodity production. In other words, China is becoming 'linked' again.

Zimbabwe and Uganda: general observations

Although Zimbabwe and Uganda are selected arbitrarily as case studies of the delinking process in Africa, they provide interesting subject matter for study. Unlike the Soviet Union and China, they are not only small physically and in their economies but, in relation to the international capitalist system, in a very different kind of situation.

In short, in so far as delinking is concerned, Zimbabwe and Uganda face a different order of problems from those confronting the Soviet Union and China. The two latter have experienced socialist revolution: their problem is to consolidate their socialist gains and prevent a possible reversion to the capitalist relation of production. For Zimbabwe and Uganda, having just acquired the independence, their problem is primarily to consolidate their national independence. For them socialism is still a distant goal.

Unlike the Soviet Union and China, the economies of Zimbabwe and Uganda are entirely within the international capitalist relations of production. For them, it is still a question of securing a measure of national control over their economies which are still by and large controlled by multinational finance capital.

While Zimbabwe and Uganda have in common that they have recently emerged from direct colonial rule, there are significant differences between them which make them interesting case studies in so far as the process of delinking is concerned.

Uganda attained independence in 1962, 18 years before Zimbabwe. But over the last 23 years Uganda has slid backwards both in terms of political stability and of economic performance. Today, the country is ravaged by civil strife that seems likely to persist for many years to come. At the economic level there is an almost total breakdown of industrial manufacturing as well as a total dislocation of agricultural production and of transport network and marketing infrastructure.

Zimbabwe, by contrast, is a newer country, but relatively stable politically, although not without its own internal contradictions which occasionally break into violence. It has inherited a reasonably well-developed economic infrastructure, and is able to provide the basic essential commodities through well-developed agricultural and manufacturing industries.

In Uganda the state has lost its credibility in the eyes of the masses as a custodian of their basic human rights and democratic freedoms. The state machinery, especially the army, has been the greatest threat to the rights and freedoms of the people. The people of Uganda have been ravaged by a rapacious army for almost two decades. It is estimated that approximately half a million people were killed during Idi Amin's rule (1971 to 1979), and 300,000 during Milton Obote's last rule (1980 to 1985). Practically every household in Uganda has been brutalized by the army including, ironically, the families of the armed forces themselves since they have been victims of one another.

Zimbabwe is a populist state that brought independence to the people of Zimbabwe following a mass-based guerrilla warfare. Thus, whereas in Uganda the people are generally alienated from the state, in Zimbabwe the people look upon the state as the provider of their security and material well-being. Indeed, some critics have remarked that in Zimbabwe there may be a tendency on the part of the people to excessive dependence on the state, as for example, the expectation by agricultural co-operatives that the state would plough their lands before they plant their seeds.

In terms of delinking, the different circumstances of Zimbabwe and Uganda provide interesting and contrasting case material. In Uganda the people have tried, over the last almost two decades, to provide for themselves alternative means of securing their interests and, as far as possible, outside the purview of the state. (For example, black marketing (called *magendo*) as well as cross-border smuggling are a way of life with people of Uganda.) In Zimbabwe, the official marketing channels still dominate the exchange of commodities, although some black marketing and smuggling does exist on the margin of official exchange.

In Uganda, the people are trying to delink themselves from state structures and official channels of commodity exchange, whereas in Zimbabwe the masses of people who by and large were marginalized during the minority white regime are trying to get into the system of state assistance in various areas of economic production and social services.

Paradoxically, however, Zimbabwe not Uganda is usually presented as almost a textbook case study of a country able to develop an 'independent' agricultural and industrial base during its years of isolation from the international community. It is argued that the white minority regime was able to take advantage of its being involuntarily 'delinked' by the international community, and build a substantial industrial and agricultural infrastructure. The independent government of Zimbabwe inherited this relatively developed industrial structure. This popular view of Zimbabwe is fundamentally at variance with our understanding of delinking, but this is a subject we shall discuss later.

Uganda, however, has never been involuntarily delinked by the international community, as Rhodesia was. Even in the worst days of Idi Amin when the country passed through periods of semi-anarchy and lawlessness, the economy continued to offer opportunities for trade and investment to international capitalism.

Zimbabwe's role in the international economic division of labour

Zimbabwe was colonized in the 1890s as part of the thrust of British imperialism to control Southern Africa. The British arch-imperialist Rhodes had at the time thought that the country would yield a 'Second Rand' of gold. Gold was indeed found but not in quantities to be compared with that more easily available in South Africa. (Attention was then shifted to agriculture as the mainstay of the proposed economy, and settlers encouraged to purchase land on the cheap to develop agriculture, a move that will be discussed later.) Nevertheless, the supply of gold and other minerals to the world market still formed a significant part of Zimbabwe's role in the world capitalist economy. In addition to gold, finance capital soon discovered that they could mine asbestos, coal, nickel, copper and chrome ore. There were also quantities of bauxite, iron, limestone, mica, magnesite, tin, tungsten, kaoline, phosphate, feldspar, and precious and semi-stones, especially emeralds and aquamarines. These all provided profitable areas of investment for some major multinational mining companies such as Anglo-American, Rio Tinto, Lonrho, Messina, Transvaal, Johannesburg Consolidated Investment, Union Carbide, and Turner and Newall.

With mining came the major imperialist banking and financing houses, first, in 1895, The Standard Bank followed by Barclays and Grindlays, and large merchant houses such as Rothschilds and Lazard Brothers. But the colony could not be held without white settlement. Settlers were encouraged from Britain and South Africa to take advantage of the bountiful land, with the promise of cheap labour and cheap credit.

Both tobacco and cotton, which the people of Zimbabwe cultivated before the advent of imperialism, were taken over by the settlers as well as the production of maize and dairy products, and while the settlers received massive state subsidies, the native producers suffered discrimination. For example, the Maize Control Amendment Act of 1934 guaranteed higher prices to whites than to blacks; and state marketing boards were set up to market settler products.

White liberal (and anti-settler) historians have tended to exaggerate settlers' economic power during the colonial period. Wittingly or unwittingly they gloss over the fact that the settlers were really stooges in the control of big finance capital. They could not have survived without massive doses of investment poured into their enterprises by finance capital. According to one estimate (Stoneman, 1981, p. 139) short-term credit advanced to some 6,200 white farmers in 1975 amounted to $111 million; by early 1980 it had reached $153 million.

Not only did big international capital finance settler agriculture, but was itself involved directly in production, as well as in having a monopoly of marketing products, whether produced by itself or by the settlers. Thus, in tobacco, there were big names, such as the British American Tobacco and Imperial Tobacco Ltd., (both British) and the Rupert Tobacco Corporation (South African). The largest cotton and maize estate plantations are owned, directly or indirectly, by Triangle Ltd. and the Anglo-American Corporation. The largest sugar company is the South African (in fact, British) Triangle Ltd., a wholly-owned subsidiary of Huletts Corporation Ltd. of South Africa, which owns over one million acres of estate land for sugar and ranching. The second largest sugar company is Hippo Valley Ltd., a subsidiary of the Anglo-American Corporation. The bulk of the sugar is processed by Zimbabwe Sugar Refineries Ltd. which is controlled 50.1% by the British multinational Tate and Lyle.

Ranching, which in Zimbabwe is a large industry, is also controlled mainly by multinationals, of which the biggest are Liebigs Ltd. of the UK, and Nuanetsi Ranch Ltd., a subsidiary of the Imperial Cold Storage and Supply Co. Ltd., incorporated in South Africa, but probably still controlled by British finance capital. Each of them owns over one million acres of ranching land, with cattle herds upwards of at least 50,000 each. Lonrho, too, owns one million acres of ranching land, with over 60,000 head of cattle. Between them, foreign corporations' investment in ranching is over Z$25 million.

The manufacturing sector (discussed later) now forms a significant sector of the economy, but it developed only relatively recently. From the perspective of Zimbabwe's role in the international division of labour, manufacturing was not significant. Throughout the colonial period and much later afterwards, this role has been primarily that of supplying minerals and agricultural raw materials to the manufacturers in imperialist countries. Maize became an important product during the Second World War in response to the imperialist country's need to feed its armies to fight the war.

Colonial Rhodesia: political and social structure

Clearly, economic power was firmly in the hands of imperialist monopoly capital; so, too, was political power.

Both the economic and political power of the settler bourgeoisie was derivative. In fact, power is a wrong concept in relation to the settler bourgeoisie. All they had was a degree of influence, limited by the extent to which the colonial state permitted them to exercise it. It suited colonial interest to grant 'concessions' to the settlers in the economic and political fields in so far as it was necessary to humour them, given the fact that the international imperialist bourgeoisie could not run the country directly and had to depend on a local and dependable intermediary class to do that for them. In class terms, therefore, the dominant class in colonial Rhodesia was the international financial oligarchy, led by British capital. Just below this class, and subservient to it, was a small, settler bourgeoisie located mainly in agriculture and later in small-time manufacturing and tertiary services.

Of the indigenous people, some 80% constituted the peasantry, reduced from a state of pre-colonial economic and political independence to a reserve of cheap labour. In 1930, however, the colonial state introduced the 'Native Purchase Areas' allowing a tiny minority of Africans to purchase pieces of land large enough to enable them to become capitalist farmers. The rest of the peasantry was herded into marginal land; over 75% could only be described as very poor, while about 25% consisted of largely poor to middle peasantry, from whom emerged the ranks of a thin veneer of capitalist farmers in the so-called Tribal Trust Lands (now called communal lands).

The impoverished peasantry drifted from land to mining and to urban centres in search of work. By independence, there were approximately one million workers, of whom about half constituted the agricultural proletariat, whilst the rest provided labour for mines, a small emerging manufacturing sector, and in domestic service in the households of the bourgeoisie.

An African *petit bourgeoisie* emerged over time, mostly as 'progressive' farmers, small-time traders, teachers, priests and a few professionals and intellectuals. Though small in number, they were the carriers of the ideas of revolt against the colonial system, and were in time to lead the struggle to independence with the peasants acting as the shock guerrilla troops against the colonial army.

UDI: was Rhodesia 'delinked'?

It has been argued in some quarters that the internationally imposed sanctions, instead of damaging Rhodesia's economy, helped it not only to build a strong, diversified economy, but even enabled the settler bourgeoisie to sever itself from the control of the international bourgeoisie. It has even been suggested as a generalization following from Rhodesia's experience that Third World countries should similarly 'delink' themselves from the international economic system as a deliberate strategy. If it is indeed true that Zimbabwe's relative industrial growth can be credited to its years of isolation, then why should independent Zimbabwe not continue to perpetuate this isolation in order to grow further? In other words, should it try *not* to 're-link' itself with the international system and thus negate the 'good work' of the settler bourgeoisie during the period of UDI? But, in fact, during the years of so-called isolation Rhodesia was even more firmly linked to the international economic system than before. In other words, rather than delinking, the links between Rhodesia's economy and the world economy became stronger and more extensive. The UN sanctions were a mere formality; trade and investments flowed into Rhodesia like water through a sieve. Circuitous routes were discovered to channel commodities and capital to Rhodesia, and although this might have meant an additional cost to Rhodesian entrepreneurs, in the form of commissions, the flow of commodities, including oil, never ceased. Furthermore, South Africa existed as a wide open door through which to direct all international connections. The notion that Rhodesia was isolated during the years of the UDI is one completely divorced from reality.

Even more significant, from the perspective of the delinking debate, is the fact that instead of developing an 'independent' industrial base, Rhodesia's economic growth in the UDI years was financed and controlled by multinational corporate interests. A Rhodesian economist, D. G. Clarke, bears this out:

> Foreign investment has always been important in the economy of twentieth-century Zimbabwe. Indeed, despite the application of sanctions following UDI in late 1965 and the theoretical blockage to capital flows thereby induced, the stock of external investments in the economy has risen substantially in real asset value. Foreign asset ownership has even become relatively more important in certain productive sectors.[1]

According to Stoneman, out of a total capital stock of $2,250–2,750 million (crude calculation) in 1979, at the end of the UDI years, some $1,500–2,000 million was foreign owned, and of this the bulk belonged to either British companies ($815 million), or South African companies ($583 million).[2] If these so-called 'South African' companies were to be further analysed in terms of their capital ownership and/or control, many of them, such as the giant Anglo-American, would in fact turn out to be really British or US companies. The so-called 'South African capital' is mainly a geographical concept, though indeed it is possible that some investments in Zimbabwe are held by South African nationals without any international finance capital interest, but these are likely to be small, relatively insignificant ventures.

The continued dominance of imperialist finance capital is acknowledged even by the representative spokesmen of the international bourgeoisie themselves. According to a Special Report prepared by the London-based Economic Intelligence Unit, 'In 1979, it was estimated that upwards of 70 per cent of the country's capital stock was foreign owned, rising to over 90 per cent in the mining.'[3] This is corroborated by the Rhodesian economist, D. G. Clarke, according to whom 'foreign owned mining companies account for between 73 and 95 per cent of total output in the industry. A reasonable estimate would put the figure at around 85 per cent.'[4]

Above all, the manufacturing sector claims pride of place as the major 'growth industry' during the UDI years. In 1981, for example, manufacturing contributed Z$1,098 million to the GDP compared to agriculture's Z$738 million and mining's Z$217 million. In terms of composition, manufacturing has steadily shifted from traditional processing industries such as food, beverages, textiles and tobacco towards such technologically heavier industries as metals, metal products and chemicals. But a careful study of the manufacturing industry, sector by sector, shows that although the settler bourgeoisie provided some of the managerial cadres for the manufacturing industries, these industries were firmly within the control of the international financial oligarchy through the provision of capital, machinery, technical know-how, and marketing arrangements.

Specifically: Lyons (UK), Brooke Bond (UK), Liebigs (UK), Lever Brothers (UK), Delta Corporation (UK-SAf), National Canners (UK) and Heinz (USA) dominated the food and beverages industry; David Whitehead (owned 65% by Lonrho) and Consolidated Textiles (UK) textiles; Salisbury Portland Cement Co (S.Af), Ceramic Holdings (S.Af), IPCORN (UK–S.Af), Tanganyika Concessions Ltd. (UK), the Rhodesian Pulp and Paper Co (S.Af), Umtali Board and Paper Mills Ltd. (UK) and the Lion Match Co (UK), among others, dominated the production of commodities such as cement, tiles, glass, timber, paper, matches, etc.

Industry by industry it can be shown that foreign companies, mostly British (due to historical and political circumstances), dominate most of these industries. Only in chemicals, telecommunications, metal and metal products can be found a little more diversification of ownership and/or control. For example, a subsidiary of Höchst (FRG) produces chemical dyestuffs, plastics, mining and agricultural chemicals and pharmaceuticals. The US company, Johnson and Johnson, is also in chemicals and allied products. The Swiss Company, Hendelgesellschaft, was involved in mobilizing capital for the Zimbabwe Iron and Steel Corporation. Other US companies operating in Zimbabwe include the International Telephones and Telegraph Corporation, Union Carbide American Metal Climax, Burroughs Corporation, Ford Motor Co., Goodyear Tyre and Rubber Co., International Harvester Co., Hoover Co. and Eastman Kodak. A number of Canadian multinationals also operate in Zimbabwe, prominent among which are Falconbridge Nickel Mines Ltd., and Massey Ferguson.

In banking and finance, The Standard Bank and Barclays Bank, between them, still hold two-thirds of the deposits and continue to act as principal channels for mobilizing international finance credit for agricultural and industrial development in Zimbabwe. The third British bank in Zimbabwe, Grindlays, which until recently was largely controlled by another British bank, Lloyds, was, in August 1983, taken over by the Citibank, one of the biggest US banking groups. Among merchant banks the largest still are the Merchant Bank of Central Africa Limited, followed by the Rothschilds group (of London), and the Rhodesian Acceptances Limited (RAL), then the Lazard Brothers (also of London) and the Anglo-American Corporation; two smaller ones are the Syfrets Merchant Bank Ltd. (now part of Zimbank), and the Accepting Bank of Zimbabwe (part of the Standard Bank group).

There are also numerous discount houses, insurance companies, development corporations, credit companies and trust companies, the bulk of which are directly or indirectly (that is, through South Africa) owned and controlled by British finance capital.

Thus, the idea of Rhodesia 'delinking' itself from the international system is purely notional. What has happened, certainly, is a diversification of Rhodesia's economy during the UDI years. But that diversification has taken place not despite the international financial oligarchy, but at the latter's behest and control.

Independence: elimination of settler political power, continuation of imperialist domination

With the domination by international finance capital, led by British capital, it is clear that the struggle to be rid of the Smith regime and the so-called 'settler capital' (which, in fact, was part of international finance capital) was aimed at eliminating a mere intermediary between international capital and the exploited and oppressed people of Zimbabwe.

The liberation war years, especially between 1977 and 1979, created more serious problems for the Rhodesian regime. First, because the state's defence expenditure increased enormously, thus adversely affecting its ability to provide the infrastructural support necessary for capital to make profits. Secondly, as the Smith government began to lose the war, the political security it had initially provided for international capital could no longer be guaranteed.

It became evident to imperialist capital that they had to compromise with nationalism, and they made overtures to what they thought was a more moderate national leader in the person of Joshua Nkomo. When Nkomo made common cause with the more radical wing of the nationalist movement led by Mugabe, they turned to Muzorewa in the name of 'internal settlement'. Imperialist capital, operating mainly from South Africa, spent vast sums of money to buttress Nkomo, and there were large 'slush funds' to back the Muzorewa faction of the nationalist movement.

In view of the dominance of British capital in Rhodesia, the task fell on Margaret Thatcher's Conservative government to effect changes in the state and polity of Rhodesia that would, while passing political power to the hands of the nationalists, ensure conditions for the continued operation of British (and by extension, other foreign) capital in independent Zimbabwe. The result was the Lancaster House Agreement, with all its limiting conditions imposed on the independence and sovereignty of Zimbabwe.

Since independence, two contradictory views on the character of post-independent Zimbabwe have surfaced. One, that might be regarded as a *petit bourgeois* nationalist viewpoint, holds that Zimbabwe is now in a position to control its own economy. The second view, which may be regarded as a neo-Trotskyist position, argues that by signing the Lancaster House Agreement the political leadership betrayed the people's revolution.

The second view is the easier to dispose of. In a book entitled *Zimbabwe: A Revolution That Lost Its Way?* André Astrow wrote:

> When the details of the final Agreement were disclosed there was little doubt which side had made the bulk of the concessions. Carrington had what he wanted out of the negotiations. The PF leaders finally conceded to virtually every point of the plans he placed on the table at the beginning of the Conference. Under pressure from Britain, the Rhodesian army and the Presidents of the Frontline states, the PF made a series of compromises which guaranteed the status of the leadership of the new Zimbabwe but represented a set-back for Zimbabwean workers and peasants.[5]

It has been suggested that if the guerrilla struggle had been extended, and fought on the basis of an anti-capitalist programme (rather than limited to eliminating the discriminatory structures of settler society), the revolution might have continued until socialism was achieved.[6]

The problem with this kind of argument is that it expects history to move forward in big leaps, and conceives of workers' struggle in a unilinear undialectical manner. Astrow's complaint is that the independent government of Zimbabwe has not brought about a fundamental change in the capitalist relations of production:

> Yet after several years after independence, little meaningful change has actually taken place, . . . Today the state apparatus has remained virtually intact and the basic economic structure of the country unchanged . . . the ex-guerrillas of ZANLA and ZIPRA who sought to actively participate in the radical transformation of Zimbabwean society have seen their efforts frustrated by the petty bourgeois nationalist leadership . . . Moreover, not only has the Government failed to promote socialism in Zimbabwe, but on the contrary, has successfully worked to strengthen its economic ties with imperialist countries, placing Zimbabwe firmly in the Western camp.[7]

Delinking is not a simple matter, nor is it a one-shot event. The struggle of the working peoples to assume control over their means of production passes through many phases, each of which has its own dynamism and its own contradictions. The people of Zimbabwe's struggle for national independence was a major political step forward; if it has not proceeded in a 'continuous revolution', that is not the end of the line, but only the beginning of another phase. We have demonstrated how Zimbabwe's economy is part and parcel of the international capitalist system, and to imagine that the ZANLA and ZIPRA guerrilla fighters would have led the struggle to the point of socialism's victory in Zimbabwe is to engage in fanciful abstraction.

Who controls Zimbabwe's economy?

The opposite viewpoint, that with independence Zimbabwe is now in a position to control its own economy, is 'politicist' in that it does not take into account the hard economic fact that the Zimbabwean economy is still very much part of the international capitalist economy, and nothing can easily be done to change this.

Essentially, the argument that it is the government which sets the policy framework within which the private sector operates is purely formalistic. The government controls monetary and fiscal policy, and thus theoretically sets limits to private companies' profitability. It allocates foreign exchange, and lays down policy on imports and exports incentives, and thus theoretically regulates Zimbabwe's foreign trade. Through its control over interest rates and credit policy, it can theoretically regulate investment in the private sector; through its control over wages and prices, it can theoretically regulate the entire economy.

At least one Zimbabwean economist, Roger Riddell, one-time Chief Economist of the Confederation of Zimbabwe Industries, was so impressed by the array of tools the government possesses to regulate the economy, that he regarded the state as an equal, if not dominant partner with the private sector. Riddell saw in Zimbabwe 'what in Africa is perhaps a unique relationship between the private and public sectors'.[8] There is nothing unique about this relationship, and, furthermore, the government does not really have as much power over the economy as might at first sight and formalistically appear.

The government does not make policy in a power vacuum. Its hands are tied by a complex of historical circumstances. For example, much as it would like to take back the land from former white settlers and give it to the people from whose forefathers it was appropriated, the government cannot do so. The implications of such a move could be violently destabilizing. Reaction in Britain and the United States, and in finance and the banking circles generally, including the IMF and the World Bank, could be so hostile that Zimbabwe could find itself in an extremely unpleasant situation with representatives of finance capital.

Now the Zimbabwean government can perhaps risk offending finance-capital, but then it must feel it has the entire masses behind it to launch into an alternative programme of action. In fact, the initiative has to come from the people themselves to take on imperialism head-on. Any attempt to carry forward the revolution from 'on top' is likely to flounder in any case.

Short of revolution from below, the Zimbabwe government can function only within the parameters set for it by the international capitalist system. Its monetary policy, for example the bank rate, and the rate at which the Zimbabwe dollar exchanges in the world currency market, are not matters decided by the government as if it were acting in isolation from the world economic forces. But these points are so obvious it is futile to labour the argument that the government in Zimbabwe (and this is generally true of practically all Third World countries) is much weaker than would appear once it is viewed formalistically.

In an article examining Zimbabwe's monetary policy and planning process, Theresa Chimombe analysed the use of monetary policy to manage economic crisis, and concluded:

> The experience of Zimbabwe, like many other developing countries with a predominant market sector, shows the failure of monetary policy as an effective tool to attain given macro-economic objectives. Monetary policy becomes an active but indirect rule. It is meant to induce the economy to higher growth rates, employment, and stability but fails to exercise any direct control or to ensure that the economic units behave in the desired manner.[9]

It is more accurate to state that the Zimbabwe government's economic policies are set within a certain framework defined by the international capitalist system than to state that the government sets a policy framework within which the private sector operates. It is important to bear this in mind, especially for critics from the left who sometimes too glibly assume they can offer better alternatives to the government's policies.

This is not to say that the people of Zimbabwe have no option at all, and that everything is predetermined. Political independence does offer people an opportunity to organize their struggle against imperialism in a broader, more democratic manner than before independence. But a radical break from the system (delinking) presupposes more than the people acquiring formal decision-making structures. Tanzanians, for example, have discovered that they cannot change the fundamental aspect of the system simply because they have acquired formal control over state institutions.

Independence has also opened up the system to the demands of the people from below, which even a neo-colonial state cannot entirely ignore. Independence has brought some substantial gains to the people of Zimbabwe, mainly in the field of social services and especially in the area of education. Primary student intake increased by 268% between 1979 and 1984 and today over 93% of this age group are in school compared to 40% at independence. Secondary school intake has increased by 638% over the same period, so that today over 83% of grade seven pupils proceed to Form One compared to 18% at Independence.[10]

The health programme is now more broadly based and more widely distributed. Since independence the government has shifted emphasis to favour preventive rural health care through the establishment of Rural Health Centres and the Village Health Worker Programme. Furthermore, considerable resources have been diverted to the rural areas in the form of, for example, water pumps and dip-tanks, which enable the rural people to increase their productive activity.

It must, however, be recognized that Zimbabwe is nowhere near delinking from the international capitalist system. If anything, the looser links that hitherto bound some sectors of the economy to the international system are now being tightened. For example, during the 1984–85 agricultural season the Zimbabwean peasantry delivered a bumper maize harvest, much beyond official expectations. Zimbabwe has thus been hailed as providing the model for African agriculture. In an analysis of who got what out of this increased production, and from official statistics, we concluded that on average the peasants secured only 18% of the final returns, and about 10% was for transport costs and government levy. The remaining 72% went to agro-chemical companies supplying hybrid seeds, fertilizers, insecticides and herbicides. In 1984 the price of fertilizers increased by an average of 50% and again in 1985 by another 45%. We calculated that a peasant would need to produce a minimum of eight to nine bags of maize per hectare (about one tonne) in order to meet input costs and interest on credit raised from the Agricultural Finance Corporation. The bulk of the peasantry, working on poorer soils, are barely able to produce this minimum necessary to pay for costs incurred and, therefore, despite the bumper harvest many ran into debt.

Since independence, the government has taken over some industrial and financial enterprises. For example: substantial holdings in a pharmaceutical company, CAPS Holdings; 40% shares in the Wankie Colliery Company; and 49% in Olivine Industries. The CAPS shares were paid for with hard currency, outside Zimbabwe. The Wankie Colliery is 62% owned by the Anglo-American Corporation and the Union Minière, and Olivine is 51% owned by the American multinational, Heinz. The government has also taken majority shareholding in the Zimbabwe Banking Corporation (formerly Rhobank), and a minority shareholding in the Bank of Credit and Commerce of Zimbabwe.

All this, however, has had very little impact on the basic structure of the economy. We know from other examples in Africa that formal state ownership of industrial enterprises, rather than facilitating national control over the economy, has further entrenched it within the international capitalist system.

Conclusion

Far from Zimbabwe delinking from the international system, the economy has been even more firmly integrated into that system. Colonialism saw the entry of international finance capital to organize agricultural and mineral production to meet certain demands of international accumulation on a world scale. That process has since intensified and, no matter to what extent political changes take place, this fundamental fact remains unchanged.

The penetration of finance capital has, inevitably, set into motion in its wake the opposite movement which, in time, threatens to bring about the demise of imperialism in all its phases. But that movement itself develops through many phases, of which political independence is only one.

Zimbabwe's political independence has certainly created some space for its people to demand their economic and political rights. Imperialism has conceded some of these rights, though not without a fight. In the meantime, imperialism continues to encircle the Zimbabwean peasantry and the workers in a tighter embrace. The exploitative relationship between imperialism and the people of Zimbabwe is deepening. This, in turn, creates its own contradictions that can be resolved only at a political level.

Uganda: general observations

Uganda, as stated earlier, secured its independence almost a generation (18 years) ahead of Zimbabwe. And yet in practically every aspect of its development it is now far behind Zimbabwe. Imperialist ideologists may be tempted to argue that this is because Uganda's independence was granted prematurely, or that Zimbabwe was fortunate in that colonialism stayed there as long as it did.

It is not even worth arguing against such propositions because from the point of view of the oppressed peoples there was never any justification for colonialism. That a million people have lost their lives since independence in fratricidal warfare in Uganda is no reason to have wished for a prolonged period of colonialism, and in any case, as we shall see, these conflicts were themselves fuelled by imperialism.

Uganda's role in the international economic division of labour

The need for imperialism to export capital to involve directly in the production of cheap raw materials for metropolitan manufacturing industries was essentially what lay behind the 'scramble for Africa'.[11] Uganda's place was defined in this scheme of things by the increasing difficulties faced by British monopolies in securing good quality, cheap cotton from the United States (which was using the cotton for its own industries), and rubber. Early attempts to grow rubber in Uganda failed, however, as a result of drastically falling prices. But cotton thrived, soon to be joined in the 1920s by coffee. Native robusta coffee was grown in pre-colonial Buganda, but it was imperialism that made it an export crop.

In 1902, a section of British textile monopolies based in Lancashire formed the British Cotton Growing Association (BCGA) to encourage the production of cotton in Uganda. The Church Missionary Society, very active in Uganda, formed the Uganda Company to teach the natives the value of 'industry' and 'trade'. These monopolies were behind the construction of the East African Railways, significantly called the 'Uganda Railway', because its main function was to carry cotton, and later coffee, to the port for shipment to Britain.

Tea was also introduced in the 1920s to counter higher production costs in India, Ceylon and the Dutch East Indies, and some sugar production also began in the same decade. But Uganda's role in the international division of labour was to produce primarily cotton and coffee for the British and other imperialist monopolies. Sugar and tea, amply produced in other areas of the empire, were relatively less important.

Copper was known to exist in the Ruwenzori Mountains, but it was Zambia and Zaire (among others) which were to provide these to the monopolies; only after the Second World War did copper mining begin in Uganda. This is also true of industries which were actively discouraged by the colonial power since the monopolies would brook neither competitor users of the much-needed raw materials, nor a reduction of the colonial market through local production. But colonial policy shifted post-1945. A much-weakened Britain, trying to protect its colonies against threats from the US, other European, and later, Japanese monopolies, encouraged British monopolies to transfer capital and technical know-how for industrial production to the colonies, thus encouraging a limited amount of industrialization in those countries.

In Uganda, a state body, the Uganda Development Corporation (UDC) was created that rapidly established joint ventures with many British monopolies to produce a variety of products and services, including cement, textiles, grain milling, hotels and housing. In addition, there was massive investment in the development of the hydro-electric plant at Jinja, whose first user was the Uganda Cement Industry.

The state-owned UDC's centrality in industrialization, and direct state investment in the provision of hydro-electric power, underscores the relative importance of state capital in Uganda. This needs to be stated because state-controlled enterprises are frequently and incorrectly associated with 'socialism'. State enterprises in Uganda began not with Obote's so-called 'Move to the Left', but with British colonialism. Unlike Rhodesia and Kenya, where after the Second World War a settler community was encouraged to participate in a certain amount of industrialization, in Uganda the colonial power had to use the state apparatus directly to set up industrial enterprises, in conjunction with British monopolies.

What is true of state enterprises is also true of the co-operatives. During the colonial period (and, indeed, even afterwards) co-operatives were not 'socialist' instruments of production and distribution. After the Second World War, the British used the co-operatives to transfer processing and marketing of basic agricultural commodities from the hands of individual middlemen directly to the state. Similarly, state credit institutions were created to exercise direct control over production. For example, the Uganda Credit and Savings Bank (UCSB) was created in 1950 to facilitate control over the production of the rich peasantry. It also served the function of divorcing them from the political struggles of the peasantry in general.

Finally, it is not enough to say that the main function of Uganda in the international division of labour was to provide the two main agricultural commodities to the international market (cotton and coffee). One must go beyond that, and recognize that *all* production in the colony – primarily agricultural, later extended to processing industries – was, directly or indirectly, controlled by mainly British capital, and provided the basis for the export of British capital. It is important to remember this when we come to analyse classes in Uganda, and relate this to the delinking debate.

Political and social structure

Because of the peculiarities of pre-colonial society in Uganda, and the manner of British entry into it, the social structure that emerged there was very different from that which emerged in colonial Rhodesia.

The main, significant historical fact in Uganda was that the inter-imperialist rivalry in late 1880s for control of the source of the river Nile found the various societies in Uganda in the throes of rapid, even revolutionary, changes. Buganda was central to these changes, and thus central to this inter-imperialist rivalry. As a result, the feudal-type ruling class in Buganda was split between the *Ingeleza* faction, backed by the British monopolies, and the *Fransa* faction, backed by French, German and Belgian monopolies. In the event, the British faction triumphed and, in return for services rendered, the British recognized the right of over 4,000 Baganda chiefs to what came to be known as *mailo* land. These chiefs became the landed aristocracy of Buganda.

A number of consequences followed from the Buganda (Uganda) Agreement of 1900. The constraints on space make it impossible to analyse the significance of this Agreement here, but so profound were its effects both on Baganda society and the rest of Uganda that much of what has since happened in Uganda cannot be understood without reference to the consequences of this Agreement.

First, it resulted in the effective dispossession of the Baganda peasantry and clan lands, as well as the emasculation of the Kabaka's (King's) power. In the 1920s the dispossessed *bakopi* formed the 'Bataka movement' to challenge the landed aristocracy's domination and found in the Kabaka an ally against the Chiefs. To this day, the Bataka movement, although one does not hear about it, remains the Buganda people's main movement against imperialism.

Secondly, the defeated *Wafransa* factions could never be fully accommodated within the political system created after the 1900 Agreement. As a recent history of the Democratic Party of Uganda puts it:

> The Protestant chiefs, led by Kaggwa had their hour of glory and the Catholics emerged as political underdogs in the colonial regime, a position they maintained throughout the colonial era. Unfortunately, the second class citizenship of the Catholics was not confined to Buganda, where the big battles between Protestants and Catholics were fought in the 1890s. It spread throughout the Uganda Protectorate. While the Catholics were second class citizens, the Muslims were virtually regarded as aliens and had minimal political influence.[12]

The inter-imperialist rivalry between the British and other continental monopolies continues to this day, still using more or less the same local allies as in the early colonial period. When Amin came to power, he was backed by a number of Muslim countries, and this too is related to Uganda's early history.

Thirdly, the British used the *Ingeleza* agents to take over and pacify the rest of Uganda.

And finally, since the Baganda and other chiefly hierarchies provided a dependable intermediary, the British did not need a settler class to act as their local agents as they did in Kenya and Rhodesia. A few settlers did in fact try, in the first decade after the 1900 Agreement, to establish large plantations. Backed by a few monopolies, they went into rubber production, but were soon bankrupt. Textile and coffee monopolies discovered that the peasant producers were much cheaper than capitalist settler farmers, because peasants used mostly family labour, and the low level of their subsistence requirements was easily fulfilled in Buganda, in terms of basic food, by the perennial *matoke* (plantain).

Other consequences followed from the way the British imperialists organized production. Due to labour shortage, only some areas (mainly in the south and west) were encouraged to grow cotton and coffee, while other areas (mainly in the north and west) were designated labour-supply areas. Even today, the bulk of Uganda's industrial and agricultural proletariat comes from the north and the north-west. The poorest among the rural communities in Buganda, for example, are 'immigrants' either from the other areas of Uganda or from Rwanda and Zaire.

The already confused social structure in colonial Uganda was further complicated by the imperialists' encouragement of Indians' immigration from India, first to build the railways, then to act as a trading intermediary between the direct producers and the British monopolies.

The social structure of present-day Uganda was thus more or less defined by British imperialism within a couple of decades of its penetration of the country. This is not to say that it has remained frozen since those early days. For example: after 1927, as a result of pressure from the Bataka movement, the colonial government had to intervene to decrease the power of the chiefly landlord class in Buganda, Bunyoro, Busoga, Ankole and Toro, by reducing them to salaried colonial bureaucrats; after the end of the Second World War, policy shifted to encourage 'progressive' capitalist farmers, thus creating the basis for export of British capital into Uganda in the form of fertilizers and tractors; and the state itself became the bulk seller and purchaser of cotton and coffee on behalf of the monopolies. Previously, this function had been performed for them, much more cheaply, by the Indian middlemen, using their own labour-intensive resources and small capital borrowed from the banks. As a result, the former buying and ginning companies became state agents now working on commission basis.

The imperialist bourgeoisie constitute the ruling class in Uganda, as indeed in Zimbabwe and all colonies and neo-colonies. Below this, and subservient to it, is a class of bourgeoisie whom, in the context of Zimbabwe, we have described as 'comprador', meaning their interests are best served by advancing the interests of imperialism. Since inter-imperialist contradictions continue to bedevil Uganda, these compradors are also divided as between the various monopolies. A small layer of what we call 'national' bourgeoisie constitute the next class. They oppose the dominance of imperialist capital, and seek to control production and market for themselves. But they are weak and vacillating, and constitute a diminishing breed.

At the other extreme are the poor peasants, comprising the bulk of the rural community which constitutes some 90% of the total population; and the violently exploited small and (since the Amin regime) much reduced industrial proletariat. Between these, is a relatively large heterogeneous class of *petit bourgeoisie*, including rural peasantry (some rich, but mostly middle peasantry), the traders, both urban and rural, the professionals, the intellectuals, etc.

State power therefore lies squarely in the hands of the international financial oligarchy. This is as true after independence as before. In other words, state power represents the objectified power of capital, not unified by any means since international capital has its own contradictions between different monopolies, but in overall command nonetheless of the economy and state of Uganda.

Considered from the perspective of the delinking debate, the moment of political independence was an important step forwards in the long struggle towards delinking from the international capitalist system, but it left intact (as it did in Zimbabwe) the structural dominance of imperialism, described above, over Uganda's economy.

Considered from the perspective of imperialism, the only change at independence was that British imperialism's monopoly hold over Uganda was broken, giving way to multilateral imperialism in which many imperialist countries now participated in the loot of the country's resources and the exploitation of its people.

The last 23 years have been years of bitter struggles by the people of Uganda to liberate themselves from exploitation by imperialist finance capital. But these struggles have been marred by intra-class conflicts within the intermediary *petit bourgeois* classes which imperialism left at the helm of state power at independence. The petty contradictions amongst them were utilized by imperialism to further their continued and intensified exploitation of Uganda's working classes. The following section examines the efforts made by the people of Uganda to 'delink' themselves from imperialism.

Obote's first government: efforts to delink

There are many who have tried to analyse Uganda's post-independence history purely in terms of the tribal conflicts between the various peoples of Uganda. I would argue that although these ethnic differences do indeed exist, they are utilized by imperialist forces to divide the people of Uganda in order to perpetuate conditions of their continued exploitation.

Uganda, like Zimbabwe, had its own Lancaster. During the Lancaster House Constitutional talks in 1962, the British played upon the religious differences amongst the Baganda. At the independence talks, the predominantly Catholic Democratic Party was isolated, and an alliance was struck between Obote's Uganda Peoples' Congress (mainly Protestant) and the Kabaka Yekka (wholly Protestant) of King Mutesa of Buganda (the Kabaka). This alliance was backed by the Archbishop of Canterbury representing the Church of England, and some of the large British monopolies operating in Uganda, such as the Unilever Group and Gailey and Roberts Ltd. The international agencies of multilateral imperialism – the World Bank, the IMF, and GATT – were quick to enter Uganda, even before independence, to chart out an economic development strategy for the new nation.

A World Bank mission came to Uganda in 1960 (one year before independence) and presented its analysis of Uganda's economy as a basis for its development programme for the period 1961–66. The Bank proposed, among other things, that agriculture should be the key link in Uganda's economic development, and that manufacturing should concentrate on minor processing industries. The programme it laid out for the first five years provided for a development expenditure of 52 million East African (EA) shillings, 48% of which was to come from 'internal' sources, and the rest in the form of British aid from the Exchequer and the Colonial Development and Welfare Grant.

In his foreword to Uganda's First Five Year Development Plan (1961/62–1965/66), Prime Minister Milton Obote referred to the World Bank mission and stated: 'My Government broadly accepts the recommendations in the report and has produced a development plan closely modelled on . . . the mission's findings, particularly in that it accepts the strategy of development recommended.'[13]

In view of the Plan's emphasis on agriculture, the peasants were encouraged to grow cash crops for export, and to this end were provided with credit facilities to purchase seeds, hoes, and fertilizers. For industry, the plan projected an investment of 7.1 million EA shillings over the plan period mostly concentrated in primary processing and assembly.

Clearly, the objective of the exercise was to further integrate the Ugandan peasantry into commodity production, mainly as suppliers of raw materials (primarily coffee and cotton) for imperialist industries. The manufacturing side was limited to the production of certain commodities with the help of imperialist finance capital.

The Second Five Year Plan (1966–71), was also based on the recommendations of a World Bank mission. This time it reversed the order of priorities. Whereas the First Plan justified the emphasis on agriculture by arguing that as a peasant country this was Uganda's best strategy, the Second Plan now argued that it was the absence of 'a sizeable industrial sector' that rendered the country's economy so vulnerable to fluctuations in the world commodity markets. The new strategy was to make the industrial sector the 'primary basis' for growth and stability, so that Uganda transformed itself into a 'predominantly industrial economy'. Thus began the import-substitution industrialization strategy in Uganda.

To emphasize that international finance capital was the key to this industrialization strategy, the Second Plan stated:

> Although it is intended that an increasing part of the industrial and commercial activity of the country should be under the control of Uganda-owned enterprises, foreign investment has a key role to play. In the future, as in the past, Uganda will welcome investment from foreign enterprises. There is a healthy record of good relations and mutual benefit. The guarantee that foreign businesses can continue to play a creative role and will be well received is not only the specific assurance given in the Industrial Charter and the Foreign Investment Protection Act; it is also in the beneficial contribution of foreign businesses to a diversified industrial development.[14]

The next few years saw remarkable growth in Uganda's industrial development, but it was carried out entirely by international finance capital, using whatever 'local resources' could be mobilized. The British company, Duncan, Gilby, Mathieson Ltd came to manufacture 'local' brands of brandy, gin, whisky, and the banana-flavoured *Waragi*. Another British company, the Chillington Tool Co. of Wolverhampton, came to manufacture hoes for the East African market. The British monopoly ICI came to produce chemicals and fertilizers, while the Unilever Group and Baumans entered the field of food processing and agricultural products. Another British monopoly, Gailey and Roberts Ltd., which was established in Uganda during the colonial period and supplied machinery and equipment, now entered the field of metal furniture manufacture.

In accord with the new phase of multilateral imperialism: the Japanese entered the garment industry through Yamato Shirts Ltd. and Marubeni-Ida Co. Ltd., and the fishnet industry through Nippon Rayon Co. Ltd. The Italian monopolies Societa in Accomandita Luigi Pomini and Societa per Azioni Fratelli Orsenigo came in with their equity and technical expertise to assist the Madhvani Steel Corporation. The Canadian monopoly, Falconbridge Nickel Mines Ltd., brought their equity and machinery to exploit copper and cobalt in the Kilembe Mines located in western Uganda.

These are just a few of the industries that started as 'joint ventures' between foreign capital and the state-owned UDC as well as 'local' entrepreneurs, such as the Madhvanis and the Mehtas.

Most of the funds for industrial development were from external sources. By the end of the First Plan period 29 million EA shillings came from outside, of which 14 million was carried over to the Second Plan period, during which a further 48 million came in, mainly in the form of machinery, intermediate products and technical know-how.

The, mostly British, banks within Uganda concentrated on financing the commercial sector, mainly the purchase of coffee and cotton, the two major cash crops; and also the export–import trade, principally of goods supplied from Europe, the United States and Japan.

The banks were not generally interested in financing the development of either agriculture or industry. The former was funded largely out of state institutions such as the Cotton and Coffee Price Assistance Fund, the Co-operative Credit Scheme, the Progressive Farmers Scheme and the Uganda Credit and Savings Bank.

An American economist, I. Gershenberg, who studied the Ugandan banking scene of this period, observed that between 1960 and 1966 the proportion of bank finance going to the industrial sector declined by 40%, and between 1960 and 1969 the bank finance to agricultural production declined by 50%.[15]

The banks' low investment in agricultural and industrial production became a cause of concern to the government, which issued a directive to them to channel their loans and advances to 'essentials' and away from 'non-essentials.'

> In spite of this directive, the two sectors [agriculture and industry] taken together only accounted for 25 percent of the increase in essential loans. Furthermore, within the agricultural sector, loans for agricultural production actually declined by 12.7 million shillings while loans for agricultural marketing, a traditional outlet for the commercial bank lending to this sector, increased by 35.3 million shillings.[16]

The above, somewhat detailed account, demonstrates that the neo-colonial financial structures inherited by the independent Uganda could not be directed by the government to proceed along the lines it decreed. The banks were behaving perfectly 'normally' in performing their functions according to a certain division of labour within the system of international financing of commodity production and exchange.

Uganda's 'own' bank, the Uganda Commercial Bank, controlled only 14% of the deposits, which made no material difference since it operated within a system that channelled finance only in a particular way determined by the objective conditions of production and marketing.

In fact, the monopoly banks were involved in a massive siphoning-off of investible surpluses created by the peasant sector, and the government and industrial private sector were forced to borrow in the international market for industrial development.

The 1969 crisis and the 'Move to the Left' strategy

By 1969 Uganda's economy was in a serious crisis, due to both political and economic causes. At the economic level it was related to intensified exploitation of the people on the basis of what were presented as 'national' strategies but which, as we saw above, in essence were neo-colonial strategies.

The import-substitution strategy inaugurated by the Second Five-Year Plan laid the basis for a few secondary industries, but they were built on a small local market and an assumed regional East African market that never materialized, because Kenya and Tanzania were following precisely the same strategy backed by competing monopolies. Furthermore, production costs in Uganda, in, for example, the textile industry, were 20–25% higher than cif prices of imported materials from Japan, Hong Kong and India. There was, therefore, no possibility of finding an export market.

Above all, input costs of these industries for machinery, intermediate products and fuel, were continually increasing year after year, so that instead of generating foreign currency they became net users of foreign exchange generated by the traditional exports of cotton and coffee. In other words, the peasants paid for the expensive exercise of ill thought-out industrialization that served mainly to provide channels for monopolies to export their capital, and to earn their super-profits from Uganda.

In 1969 Obote announced the so-called 'Move to the Left' strategy. The main document elaborating on this strategy, 'The Common Man's Charter', declared that the country must follow a strategy to realize 'the real meaning of independence' and to ensure that its resources were exploited for the benefit of the people of Uganda 'in accordance with the principles of socialism'.[17]

While expressing these commendable democratic sentiments, however, the author of the Charter had no idea of how to go about realizing them. For example, in regard to the role that foreign capital was to play in Uganda, the Charter declared: 'In future we would wish to see foreign investments coming into Uganda . . . engaging in priority projects and not projects solely on the basis of profitability.'[18] This is clear evidence that Obote had no understanding of the operation of international finance capital.

In the same year, as part of the 'Move to the Left' strategy, the government announced that all banks incorporated in Uganda should have a paid-up capital of two million EA shillings in cash. Foreign banks were required to have 10 million in cash in Uganda plus, out of their own funds, assets amounting to at least 2% of total deposit liabilities in Uganda. The objective of this measure, it was announced, was to increase development funds, to increase the supply of foreign currency, and to reduce the outflow of foreign exchange through payments made by foreign banks to their head offices overseas.

In May 1970, Obote further shocked the world by announcing that 'with immediate effect' the government was assuming 60% control of 84 major companies, including the oil companies, some industries, the Kilembe Mines, banks, plantations, insurance and credit institutions and the Kampala and District bus services. Compensation was to be paid over a 15-year period out of the earnings of the government's 60% shares in these enterprises.

We shall not record details of the negotiations, and the compromises that ensued, with the banks and the enterprises that were to be taken over. In any case, whatever finally existed on paper made very little material difference on the ground. Furthermore, within less than eighteeen months, Obote was overthrown.

The final denouement of the 'Move to the Left' strategy and the 'Common Man's Charter' was that their author, Milton Obote, when he returned to power in 1980, disowned the strategy, together with its high-sounding sentiments expressed on behalf of the people, and declared that he was now ready to work closely with the World Bank, the IMF and capitalists everywhere if only they could rescue Uganda's economy and help him to stay in power – an illusory dream, as we shall see.

When Obote was no longer serving the interest of imperialism he was removed from power by Amin's imperialist-backed military coup in January 1971. By this time Obote's *petit bourgeois* politics, and his use of the military force to try to settle his political problems, had already created enough internal enemies to be preyed upon by imperialist forces to support the coup. Imperialism and large sections of Uganda's population saw Amin as a 'solution' to the problems created by Obote. Britain was the first country to formally recognize Amin's government.

Idi Amin's 'Economic War'

From the viewpoint of the delinking debate, the only aspect of the Amin period in Uganda of interest is that during which he launched the so-called 'economic war' against 'foreigners' in the country. At the time, many misguided observers, both Ugandans and outsiders, hailed Amin's actions as initiating a process of delinking Uganda from the international capitalist system and establishing a genuine national economy.

There were two phases to the 'economic war'. In the first, launched at the beginning of August 1972, Amin expelled the entire Asian population in Uganda, numbering about 45,000. The Ugandan *petit bourgeoisie* rejoiced at the prospect of taking over the Asians' businesses and properties.

Very soon, however, they were disillusioned, for they discovered that the prosperity they dreamed of was not to be theirs.[19] The businesses and properties were allocated at Amin's whim, and those who managed to acquire these sooner or later became the envy of the soldiers who were quick to use force to snatch these assets. Furthermore, throughout Amin's rule the economic conditions were never propitious for engaging in legitimate business. Many did make a lot of money, mainly by smuggling coffee across the border into Kenya and other illegitimate transactions, and by foreign exchange dealings involving bribery and corruption of government officials. But the masses soon discovered they were worse off than before.

The second phase of Amin's economic war was against British companies in Uganda which, like his predecessor, Amin threatened to take over. But as before this proved to be an insubstantial threat. Only certain companies lost some assets by Amin's actions, but overall imperialism's control of the economy remained intact.

As a result of the anarchy in production and distribution that Amin brought about through his whimsical 'economic war', the economy was so badly run down that by 1977 he was appealing to international finance capital to return to Uganda. In a so-called 'Action Programme' launched in that year, he made extremely liberal provisions, in terms of tax rebates and repatriation of profits, for foreign companies bringing new capital into the country. The 'Action

Programme' provided for rehabilitation of the economy involving an expenditure of 500 million EA shillings over the three years, 1977–80. But before these ambitious plans could materialize Amin was overthrown. But throughout his rule British finance capital never ceased to trade with Uganda. As the British newspaper, *Daily Mail*, put it: 'Despite the cutting of diplomatic relations [with Uganda] and continuing reports of brutality, the campaign to ban trade is likely to prove a difficult one . . . Government policy is not to interfere in commerce.'[20]

Indeed, the British state institutions, the Crown Agents, continued to handle millions of pounds-worth of business with Uganda on behalf of British monopolies. Nor was it only the British who continued to profit from trade with Uganda: other EEC countries (especially France and Germany), the United States and Japan – all found Uganda's anarchy favourable for making super-profits out of the increasing impoverishment of the people.

The contemporary period

Amin was dislodged in March 1979 through the combined efforts of the people of Uganda struggling inside the country, some exile organizations operating from outside, and Tanzanian military forces. At the Moshi Conference, which combined this unity of the various forces, the hand of the British operated discreetly behind the scenes to influence the outcome of the conference.

Britain's favourite, Y. K. Lule, was elected to lead the new government, and within days of his coming to power, the British, in the form of a Commonwealth mission led by a British economist, Dudley Seers, were invited to analyse the state of Uganda's economy, and to propose a strategy for its development. Under this programme, the way was again open for British monopolies to re-enter the Ugandan investment field. Negotiations began with a number of British companies, such as Mitchell Cotts, to restore the properties expropriated from them by Amin, in return for bringing in capital equipment and managerial know-how.

Meantime, Obote was waiting in Dar-es-Salaam to stage a coup to come back to power. As once more Uganda drifted into semi-anarchy, partly instigated by Obote's soldiers in the Uganda army and partly as a result of contradictions within the various government factions, the British sent their agents to Dar-es-Salaam to confer with Obote and test out his views.

It became apparent to the British that the same Obote, whom they had helped dislodge in 1971, was now the only 'strong man' who could hold Uganda together. Obote, they found, had learnt his lessons in exile, and was no longer talking about socialism or nationalization of foreign enterprises. A tacit understanding was reached that the British would help restore him to power and in return, he would facilitate the re-entry of British companies into Uganda, and for Ugandan Asians, now resident in the UK, to return to Uganda and reclaim their properties which had been appropriated by Amin.

Tanzania, whose forces were maintaining peace in Uganda, was also coming round to the view that only Obote could stabilize Uganda. The Tanzanian forces thus stood aside as the military, for the second time in Uganda's history, staged a coup against the civilian government of the Uganda National Liberation Front. Within months the 'strong man' Obote was back in Uganda.

In December 1980, in fraudulently conducted elections, Obote was restored to power, and acknowledged by the British-supported Commonwealth Observer Group. This 'legitimized' Obote in the eyes of imperialism, whilst the people, frustrated in their efforts to exercise their democratic right freely to elect a government of their choice, took to various measures of resistance against Obote's neo-colonial regime.

Imperialism's theory was that if Obote was supported both at the military level in the form of assistance to discipline the army, and at the economic level by 'flooding the shops with commodities' to satisfy the basic material needs of the people, Uganda would be restored to its past glory as 'the pearl of Africa'. To this end the British provided military officers to train Uganda's army, and persuaded Canada, Australia and India, as Commonwealth partners, to also supply officers.

In the economic field Obote now opened the gates to foreign investments with liberal inducements, and invited the IMF to design an appropriate fiscal, monetary and foreign exchange policy for the government. IMF officials actually sat within the Central Bank making policy in the government's name.

This imperialist strategy was, however, bound to fail. For as long as the peoples' democratic rights were daily trampled upon, neither military coercion nor material inducements in the form of commodities in the shops could placate them.

The commodities, in any case, were soon reserved for the few who could afford them. Hyper-inflation put these commodities beyond the pockets of the ordinary people. The business of export–import, carried out on behalf of imperialist monopolies, was reserved for certain commercial groups which had links with the ruling party and the army. For example, the Army Chief of Staff was, at the same time, Chairman of the Uganda Coffee Board which handled the most important, and indeed the only remaining, export commodity of Uganda.

The rank and file of the army, on the other hand, became increasingly undisciplined and increasingly violent in their oppression of the people. The Canadian, Australian and Indian officers soon discovered that discipline in the Ugandan army was not simply a matter of 'training', and they withdrew. Only the British remained until Obote's last days.

As the rural areas were continually ravaged by armed soldiers who found their guns a more reliable means to their livelihood than the meagre wages they received, the people in turn joined the resistance in their hundreds. Very soon there were several guerrilla movements in the bush, the most prominent being the National Resistance Movement, led by Yoweri Museveni.

The five years of Obote's 'second coming' were a nightmare for the people, described by many as more horrific than Amin's eight years. In July 1985, Obote was overthrown by his own army, a section of which was conspiring clandestinely with the National Resistance Movement.

After Obote's overthrow, however, the conspirators fell apart, and occupied whatever territory they could grab. In August 1985, the various factions tried, under Kenya's mediation, to form a government of national unity. But, being militaristic and undemocratic, they were unlikely to agree to share power. For them the issue could only be decided by who was stronger militarily on the ground. In the meantime, the various factions of monopoly capitals were busy behind the scenes to influence the outcome of the negotiations in order to protect their imperialist interests. Museveni, for example, was flown around by the British monopoly, Lonrho.

By January 1986, it became clear that the fledgling army in power under Brigadier Okello was in disarray, mainly because of its own internal contradictions. It was simply a matter of time for Museveni to take over the country with the assistance of his better organized guerrilla forces.

How 'delinked' is Uganda?

During both Amin's rule and Obote's second government, large areas, especially of rural Uganda, were more or less cut-off from the centre. The state was no longer able to provide for the people elementary security of life and property. On the contrary, over the last two decades the state itself had unleashed a bandit army to pillage and brutalize them.

At the economic level, the people had to survive with whatever means were available to them. In a curious way they were 'delinked' from the formal economy. The people became ingenious in inventing alternative products and means of production, as well as alternative channels of exchange (including barter) and distribution (including smuggling across the borders). That is why the World Bank/IMF strategy to control Uganda's economy failed. This strategy, by its nature, was applicable only to the formal economy, whereas much of the economy was underground. The IMF did try, through its 'double window' foreign exchange strategy, to soak up the underground liquid money, only to find itself defeated by the much more resilient, and under the circumstances rational, system of the alternative *magendo* economy.

Did this involuntary 'delinking' open the prospect for the people of Uganda to establish a self-reliant economy independent of imperialism? Unfortunately not. The more likely immediate scenario is that imperialism will try to make the best it can out of a bad situation, impose some kind of order through a populist regime, and once again penetrate the rural economy to bring it to the rule of capital.

Alternatively, if imperialist interests are best defended by fragmenting Uganda, then they would do this, arming rival military factions on the one hand, while entering into separate deals with them on the other, as far as their economic interests are concerned.

Such are the options open to the people of Uganda in the short and medium run. Imperialism has always taken advantage of the fratricidal conflict amongst the people of Uganda, which itself has colonial origins. Uganda's history shows that imperialism was always present, monitoring and manipulating the situation in its favour whenever there was a major crisis within Ugandan politics. This is as true today as it has been throughout Uganda's entire tumultuous post-independence history.

Conclusions

Some general conclusions on the delinking debate may now be drawn, both at the theoretical and the practical level.

At the theoretical level there is much confusion, partly because the contenders in the debate are often talking about different things when they refer to delinking, and partly because scientific, objective analysis is often sacrificed in the interest of wishful thinking. Quite often delinking is made to mean the same as development. Contenders of this confusion rest their case on the basic assumption that the goal of all economic activity is the greater exploitation of the natural and human resources of the country. It follows, therefore, that if a country is able to develop these resources, it has, to that extent, become 'delinked' from underdevelopment and backwardness.

From this perspective, issues such as 'exploitation' or 'self-reliance' are extraneous to the issue of development. What does it matter, they argue, whether development takes place within a capitalist or socialist framework, as long as at the end of the day people have more to eat, better clothes, improved housing and other amenities for a better life? Raising issues of 'exploitation' or 'self-reliance', they contend, simply injects emotive and therefore essentially diversionary elements into a discussion that should be confined to the development of the people's material well-being.

South Korea, Taiwan and Singapore are often cited as evidence to show that their industries are better developed than those of many other Third World countries. The burden of these examples is to prove that, as a result of working within the existing international capitalist system, these countries have managed to develop their economies such that they are less dependent than before on the international system. Development is thus seen as bringing about a measure of 'delinking'.

Put differently, the proponents of this viewpoint argue that there is ample scope for every country to develop within the system of international capitalism. The system offers both resources and guidelines on how development could be achieved, and to the extent that some countries have failed to achieve development, this is primarily because they have not utilized the resources available to them from the international system, either because they have diverted their efforts to some misguided strategies (usually meaning socialism), thus scaring away the much needed capital from outside, or because they are caught up in 'tribal' or other kinds of internal conflicts.

It is economic backwardness, they argue, that creates dependency on the international system: the more backward the economy, the less is it able to look after itself, and the more dependent, therefore, it is on the international system. The extreme and tragic manifestation of this is drought, such as that which hit the Sahel in 1975 and Ethiopia in 1984, compelling these countries to depend on international relief organizations to feed their populations. In the long run, what is needed in these countries is a massive investment of capital for irrigation so that they are not dependent on the rains for food production, and are to that extent able to look after themselves. What is required, they conclude, is 'delinking' from backwardness and dependence. Development is, therefore, another word for delinking.

The proponents of this viewpoint fall into two groups: the conventional supply/demand analysts for whom development is a product of incremental deployment of capital to exploit the physical and human resources available to a country; and the 'Marxist' analysts belonging to a particular tendency, historically associated with the Mensheviks in Russia, for whom there is a logic in capitalism which must first be exhausted before society can move to a higher stage of civilization. This conception of 'delinking' I regard as a total reversal of the scientific meaning of the concept.

Admittedly, economic backwardness does have the effect of making countries vulnerable to natural disasters such as droughts. To that extent the argument that economic development would make such countries better able to look after themselves, and therefore less dependent on the outside world, is valid. But the problem about the present international system is not its susceptibility to droughts (after all, droughts have occurred since the beginning of recorded history) but the inherent tendency within the system to favour those who are owners of capital. The logic of capital accumulation creates a class of owners of capital who, in our own day and age, are the large transnational corporations that operate globally and monopolize all technical and production expertise. On the basis of this monopoly, they extract a price from all who utilize their capital and their know-how.

Admittedly, some development of the productive forces does take place when this capital is combined with the natural resources and labour power in Third World countries, it could not be otherwise. But, as illustrated above, the return to labour is extremely low compared to the return to capital. For example, in the case of maize production in Zimbabwe we saw that the peasants who put their labour into production receive barely 18% of the total value produced, while the bulk goes to the providers of capital.

It is in the nature of the system that, in order to secure a greater share in the total value created, the owners of labour-power have to wage intense class struggle against the owners of capital. In Europe and the United States, the working classes have been able to raise their standard of living only through bitter struggles against capital.

With the beginning of the era of export of capital, we enter the imperialist epoch and with it the era of the struggle of the colonized (the now so-called Third World) peoples to liberate themselves from imperialism. Thus, the class struggle between capital and labour and the nationalist struggle between the oppressed peoples and imperialism, both influence and co-determine the nature of politics and economics in the Third World countries.

It is within the context of these struggles that the issue of 'delinking' has come to the fore. It is a recognition of the fact that within the existing world order dominated by imperialist finance capital there is 'neither peace nor bread' for the bulk of humanity. The famine in Ethiopia is not a product of lack of capital development but a product of the historical misallocation of the world's resources that capitalism engenders. There is no guarantee that with the further employment of capital large numbers of the population of the Third World countries would not join the ranks of the unemployed, and therefore fit to receive only 'relief aid' rather than productive work.

The demand for the new international economic order is a product of the failure of the existing order to meet the basic needs of Third World peoples. The old order has failed, and the new order refuses yet to be born. The increasing demand for the 'South' to unite in order collectively to dissociate themselves from the 'North' is political recognition of the fact that the North's system is exploitative and self-serving.

It is in this context that the question of delinking is posed. The bourgeois (whether 'Marxist' or non-Marxist) analysts' argument that there is a redemption for the Third World countries within the existing international capitalist system has already been invalidated by practical experience.

But to break away from the system, as we have shown, is not simply a matter of a rupture from the international capitalist system in a physical or geographic sense. But, as the historical examples of the Soviet Union and China show, it entails a complex process of struggle between contending classes.

Even where socialism has scored victories, and the working classes have gained control over the state and the means of production, the battle between socialism and capitalism is not yet over. While there are forces in the society that command individual appropriation of social wealth, there is always a possibility, even under socialism, for certain classes to arise which could convert individual appropriation into private ownership (as a class) of the means of production. When this happens the forces of capitalism can reassert themselves both at the level of the economy and at the level of the state.

In Zimbabwe and Uganda, far from being 'delinked' from the international capitalist system, we are witnessing the continued domination of international capital in production and exchange. In Zimbabwe a historically marginalized peasantry is being increasingly brought into commodity production. In Uganda, while international capital desperately tries to hold on to commodity production, and to influence the outcome of factional conflicts within the *petit bourgeois* intermediary classes, there are signs that large sections of the population are becoming both economically and geographically marginalized. This does not create the basis for socialist production in these areas, but it does create an opportunity for the people collectively to organize themselves to engage in production without the iron hand of capital. In the short run, imperialism will try to thwart these initiatives of the people through a populist regime, and bring these 'delinked' areas back into the fold; what will happen in the long run remains to be seen.

Notes

1. D. G. Clarke, *Foreign Companies and International Investment in Zimbabwe*, Harare, Mambo Press, 1980, p. 1.

2. Colin Stoneman, 'Foreign Capital in Zimbabwe', UNCTAD, 1979.

3. The Economic Intelligence Unit, 'Zimbabwe's First Five Years', November 1981.

4. D. G. Clarke, op. cit., p. 79.

5. André Astrow, *Zimbabwe: A Revolution that Lost its Way?*, London, Zed Press, 1983, p. 155.

6. Ibid., pp. 173–83.

7. Ibid., p. 1.

8. R. C. Riddell, 'The Interaction between the public and private sector roles in national development in Zimbabwe'. *Issues and Opinions*, Vol. 1, No. 3, August 1983.

9. Theresa Chimombe, 'Monetary Policy and the Planning Process in Zimbabwe'. Paper presented at the Conference on Economic Policies and Planning under Crisis Conditions in Developing Countries, Harare, September 1985.

10. ZANU(PF) Department of the Commissariat and Culture, *Zimbabwe: at 5 Years of Independence*, Nehanda Publishers, Harare.

11. Much of the material for this section is based on D. W. Nabudere, *Imperialism and Revolution in Uganda*, London, Onyx Press, 1980.

12. Richard Muscat (ed.), *A Short History of the Democratic Party*, Rome, Foundation for African Development, 1984, p. 13.

13. Uganda Government, *The First Five-Year Development Plan, 1961/62–1965/66*, Entebbe.

14. Uganda Government, *Work for Progress: Uganda's Second Five-Year Plan, 1966–71*, Entebbe, p. 16.

15. I. Gershenberg, *Commercial Banking in Uganda: A Prescription for Economic Development*, Kampala, 1972, p. 21.

16. Ibid.

17. The Uganda People's Congress, The Common Man's Charter, 1969.

18. Ibid.

19. D. W. Nabudere, op. cit., p. 295.

20. Quoted in ibid., p. 309.

7. Burkina Faso: August 1983 – The Beginning of Delinking?

Talata Kafandi*

Introduction

In modern Burkina, dependence on the world economic system manifests itself essentially at three levels: financial dependence – which shows itself in the fact that development is financed by a massive inflow of foreign, particularly public, capital; food dependence – which is growing year by year; and the scale of migration to nearby capitalist countries (Ivory Coast and Gabon in particular) – which confirms Burkina's acceptance of its role as supplier of cheap labour assigned to it by the world economic system.

In such circumstances, for Burkina, the policy of delinking necessarily involves first going through the stage of building an independent and self-sufficient national economy. Concretely, this means implementing a policy of growth based above all on: the quest for self-sufficiency in basic consumer items (food items) and basic production goods (technical equipment, agricultural inputs etc.); the elimination of financial and commercial dependence through a policy of national accumulation based on popular savings; the promotion of small and medium labour-intensive industry; covering basic social costs (basic social and economic infrastructure including schools, medical centres and housing) by collective investment (human investment).

In short, at this stage what is fundamentally needed is to give the national economy a new impetus based on satisfying the basic needs of the popular masses (particularly the peasants). This means a self-reliant development dynamic pursued as a means of endeavouring gradually but irreversibly to make the national economy fully integrated in its functions of production, distribution and consumption.

In order to carry through this new development policy successfully, the National Council of the Revolution chose to make agriculture the motor of national economic growth. This strategic choice has nothing in common with the priority given to the rural sector in classic development plans.

In order to appreciate the task already accomplished and have a clear idea of the obstacles still to be overcome in order to move forward, a look at the impact

* Translated by A. M. Berrett

of colonization and neocolonial policies is necessary. This will make it possible to have a clearer understanding of the processes that led to the revolutionary option of 4 August 1983.

The impact of colonial rule and neocolonial economic policies

In addition to the collapse of the Mossi social fabric (disruption of kinship relations, weakening of the power of the elders, decline of cultural and religious values) the feudalization of traditional chieftaincy emerges as the key feature of this impact.

Here as everywhere, the French demonstrated special contempt for the Mossi's traditional political organization. This anachronistic prejudice soon got them into trouble. For without the Mossi chiefs, any undertaking that failed to take account of their (the chiefs') interests was inevitably doomed to failure. André de Beauminy, an administrator in Upper Volta, made the following observation on this point:

> Not without reason, we followed the rule of regarding the great black chiefs as exploiters of their peoples, and this caused us to introduce and to maintain a policy aimed at reducing their authority. Later on we were compelled to abandon this policy in the face of discouraging results. During the past few years we have restored power and prestige to the Mogho Naba and to his vassals, the Mossi chiefs. (E. P. Skinner, *The Mossi of the Upper Volta*, p. 162).

An official report also stated:

> Certainly, the maintenance of their [the chiefs] authority and prestige is indispensable, and the local administration is firmly resolved not only to preserve it but even to strengthen it. Henceforth, however, this authority and prestige will be upheld on the basis of principles and methods better suited to the new order of things which has been established.

What this means is that having failed to exclude the chiefs from the colonial system they were establishing, the French sought rather to integrate them into that system. In 1924, the amount appropriated for the salaries of chiefs was increased from 86,000 to 190,000 CFA francs, not to mention the commission they collected from taxes which amounted to 163,260 CFA francs in the same year. By choosing to grant exorbitant privileges to chiefs, the colonial administration was by the same token choosing to neglect the interests of the peasant masses: the Mossi chiefs, strengthened by these privileges, pressed down all the harder on the peasants.

Taking advantage of the creation of common lands they grabbed the rich valley lands and coerced the peasants to perform forced labour using the prerogatives granted them by the colonial administration. The chiefs exploited the peasants outrageously. Before long the tribute paid to chiefs no longer derived from the customary laws in force in precolonial society but rather from a right that the chief exercised over the individual and his property. Such a process clearly shows a trend towards the feudalization of Mossi chieftaincy.

Migration

Mossi migration can be divided into two distinct phases: the first, of 'uncontrolled' migrations, between 1900 and 1925, and a second phase of 'controlled' migrations (1925–60).

By 'uncontrolled' migrations we mean the situation where individuals freely and with no organization move from one country to another. The origin of this migration lay in the relative proletarianization of Mossi peasants. Excessive taxes (which were out of all proportion to their meagre incomes) ruined Mossi peasants. They sold everything and they sold it cheap: animals, craft products (cotton goods, jewellery etc.). Crushed under the burden of taxes, they even sold their reserve stocks of food. Having sold everything, and faced with the choice between paying the tax or disappearing, the Mossi were reduced to selling the sole resource they had left – their labour power; they flocked to the Gold Coast to sell their labour. This manpower drain began in 1904, and from that date, about 100,000 Mossi workers crossed the frontier each year to go to Ghana. In addition to excessive taxes, two other factors precipitated and intensified Mossi migration. First, there was the forced labour system. Not only were the Mossi compelled to perform forced labour but they had to provide labour for the plantations in the Ivory Coast. This situation became increasingly unbearable for the Mossi as the colonial development of the Ivory Coast continued apace. The colonial administration in Upper Volta, working hand in glove with private Ivorian companies, sank so low as to divert young men regularly recruited for military service to the Ivorian plantations. In his book *Genèse de la Haute Volta*, Albert Balima confirms:

> In other words, under cover of a vague governmental decision, the massive recruitments of conscripts were not transferred to the barracks to be sent on to the front, but instead were placed in the hands of the Public Works Department or, worse yet, sent to the plantations of the ubiquitous colons of the Ivory Coast.

Second, conscription drained the country of its best men; several thousand Mossi and Voltaics were sent to the front in 1939. At the beginning of the war, the French exploited the Mossi's warrior tradition and, in 1940, says Balima, Mogho Naba Naba Kom II (1905–42) himself handed over to General Barraud, who had come to recruit 10,000 soldiers, his two eldest sons as a gesture of solidarity with France. But the whole population soon became mistrustful. Recruitment had become destructive and few of those leaving for the front returned.

Faced with such a situation, popular resistance soon appeared. Many young men and adults fled to Ghana, while those who had chosen to remain deliberately mutilated themselves to become unfit for any service (as soldier or worker).

Uncontrolled emigration, almost entirely to the Gold Coast, did not suit the private colonial companies. Steps were therefore taken to regulate emigration in such a way as to divert the flow towards the Ivory Coast and in 1925, a law was promulgated to this end. This law laid down that recruitment of workers must be carried out under the supervision of the administration. This law should be seen as the end-result of a long conflict between the authorities and the private trading companies. It marked a temporary victory of the authorities; but only temporarily, because in 1933 the Territory of Upper Volta was suppressed.

This suppression meant victory for the private companies since it ratified the position of Upper Volta as a labour reserve. A few years later, however, in 1946, forced labour was abolished. This marked the end of a conflict between foreign capitalist companies and emerging local capitalism. The economic report for 1960 refers to this migration:

> In Ghana, quite a large number have settled down permanently and taken jobs in the police (640 Voltaics), the army, the railways or long-distance trade, especially in cattle. Many have bought or established farms.
>
> There are 100,000 temporary Voltaic sojourners, three-quarters of whom are Mossi. Most of them make at least two stays; 15% are accompanied by their wives. Primary migrants generally leave with no set goal, not knowing what sort of work they will get; they change jobs frequently and then settle down to one particular occupation.
>
> Work on farms, especially food farms is preferred; this is best suited to share-cropping. Work in the mines and woodcutting are the most unpopular jobs. People take them when there is no farm work.
>
> The fate of the Voltaics in the Ivory Coast is perhaps less favourable and their protection is less well assured than in Ghana. On this point, it is to be hoped that the abolition of the SIAMO, and the take-over of recruitment and supervision of employment by the two states will improve the situation.
>
> Whatever the case, most towns in central and lower Ivory Coast have a core of Voltaics permanently settled around the oldest immigrant, who may be a trader or a planter or both. As municipal councillors or simply as leading figures, some play an important role in their adopted town.
>
> When it is possible to identify and assess this migration, and know how many men and what goods are involved in it, people will be surprised by the strength of this expansion of the Burkinabe peoples and their role in the economic and social evolution of the African bloc . . .

Meanwhile, the least one can say is that the price for Upper Volta of such a drain of working-age men was virtually total economic stagnation.

The socio-economic impact

The socio-economic changes that occurred are those that usually appear when a traditional economy comes into contact with the modern type of capitalist economy: monetarization of the traditional economy, development of commodity relations, appearance of the profit motive, birth of a trading stratum, decline of traditional activities (notably crafts).

In the case of Upper Volta, however, the following observations are in order. First, monetarization was not solely the product of the development of commodity relations; to some extent, it arose in part from the imposition of the head tax. Originally, the unit of exchange was the cowrie, but the colonial administration refused to accept it in payment. People were therefore forced to obtain francs by any means, notably by selling their labour power in neighbouring countries. Second, the colonial policy of making Upper Volta a labour reserve led to very little development of the country.

Upper Volta paid a high price for being forced to contribute its labour power to the development of neighbouring countries. Clearly, this situation explains why, on the eve of independence (1960), Upper Volta was the most economically backward country in West Africa.

The failure of neocolonial development policy

Following independence in 1960, the French Aid and Cooperation Fund (FAC) entrusted the Société pour le Développement Economique et Social (SEDES) with the task of proposing to the government of Upper Volta, which accepted it, the broad outlines of a long-term development policy.

It starts from the rather obvious observation that Upper Volta is an underdeveloped country, that is, a country whose level of development has not yet reached that attained, for example, by France, the United States or Japan. One indicator of underdevelopment is a low level of gross investment as a percentage of Gross Domestic Product (GDP). How, then, in these conditions can the social and economic development of the country be assured? Or, more precisely, how can the economic take-off of the country within 15 years be ensured? The SEDES experts saw only one possible solution: 'To make a considerable increase in the level of investment so as to raise it from 10% in 1960 to 26% in 1975.'

But at the same time they recognized that such a growth of investment presupposes that the country has adequate local financing capacity. Given that, the principal objective of 'development' policy would consist in mobilizing the nation's domestic resources and every possible external source, with the aim of reaching the investment rate of 26% seen as a necessary and sufficient condition for economic take-off.

Implementation of this policy would naturally run up against two constraints seen as absolute: technological constraints and external factors (contributions and outlets).

This leads to the proposal for the implementation of a growth policy that would make it possible to raise Upper Volta's import capacity to its maximum level, this import capacity being itself a function of the country's export capacity on the one hand, and on the other, of the external contribution in terms of private and public capital. But Upper Volta has no means of acting on this latter constraint.

Consequently, in the first stages of the history of its development Upper Volta had to make the maximum effort to export what it could in the conditions of competition imposed on it by the international market. In other words, in resource allocation policy, priority had to go to export crops (cotton, groundnuts, shea-nuts, cattle, sesame). In doing so, the international division of labour was accepted and with it the price system of the international market.

And because, in order to produce more and at competitive prices, modern equipment is needed, Upper Volta had to import technology. Import capacity is thus linked to export capacity and vice versa. Given that each limits the other, it means that recourse to external aid was unavoidable. In other words, the development dynamic was exclusively external.

On the basis of the philosophy thus outlined, the fundamental target was set of doubling production in 15 years of planning. Theoretically, and according to the hypotheses adopted, the various indicative orders of magnitude of growth between 1960 and 1975 would move as follows (1960 = 100):

Table 7.1
Economic Growth 1960–75

	1960	*1975*
Gross Domestic Product (GDP)	100	246
External contribution	100	171
Net investment	100	618
Amortization	100	333
Final Domestic Consumption	100	185

To achieve such results would involve a marked improvement in the people's standard of living at the same time as making possible the country's economic take-off.

To be able to attain the global target of doubling production in 15 years, the authorities were to adopt three five-year development plans.

Results of neocolonial development policy
Analysis of the recent economic evolution of Burkina clearly shows that overall, the development policy pursued following independence (1960–75) quite clearly failed. Today, the Burkinabe economy has the following features: deeper integration into the world economic system; greater disarticulation of productive structures; increasing exhaustion of the state budget; and great regional and social disparities.

Deeper integration into the world economic system: is reflected in increased extraversion of the national economy, seen in the following features:
a) the chronic trade deficit which rose from almost 10 billion in 1972 to slightly more than 95 billion CFA francs in 1982 (*Annuaire statistique du Burkina 1984*). At the same time, the rate of cover of imports by exports fell from 37% in 1972 to only 16% in 1982;
b) the deficit on services estimated at 19 billion CFA francs or about 98% of export receipts in the same year;
c) the limited current balance deficit, limited thanks to flows of unrequited transfers (income repatriated by nationals residing abroad), foreign shares in national enterprises, drawings on long-term borowings;
d) increase in the proportion of cereal imports in total foodstuff imports (51% in 1982 as against 22% in 1972). In volume terms these proportions rose from 35% in 1972 to 71% in 1982;

e) significance and persistence of external participation in investment financing (80% of plan investment over the period 1972–82).

Disarticulation of productive structures: Analysis of the productive structures shows both the importance (41% of GDP over the period 1972–82) and the backward character of the agricultural sector. Although it benefited from major investments over the period under review (25% of total investments), this sector continues to be inward-looking and quite unable to produce the bare minimum needed to provide for the people's subsistence.

After a phase of rapid expansion in the first half of the 1970s, the industry sector abruptly fell back into stagnation and blockage after 1977. These difficulties have to do essentially with: a) the fact that industrial activity is very highly dependent on the outside world; b) very high production costs due to rising import costs; and c) the smallness of the domestic market.

This premature blockage of the industrial sector naturally led to an impressive number of failures among enterprises, which in turn led to a marked diminution in the contribution of manufacturing industry to GDP (10% in 1982 as against 14% in 1972).

The decline in productive activities led to a revival in the fortunes of unproductive activities (commerce, services). Thus over the period the proportion of commerce and the hotel trade in GDP rose from 12% to 16% while administration doubled its share (13% in 1982 as against 6.6% in 1972).

The combination of these sectoral imbalances led to a marked slowdown in national economic activity. Over the period 1972–82, GDP grew at about 1–2% per annum as against a rate of population increase of slightly over 2% per annum.

Overall, the period saw an unprecedented deterioration of the national economic situation, accompanied by acute budgetary tensions arising largely from: a) the rapid increase in the public debt (25% per annum on average since 1977); b) the ever-increasing burden of administrative expenditure on personnel and equipment (70% on average of annual budgetary expenditure); c) the marked rise in national counterpart expenditure in the realization of projects.

If this trend were to continue the state budget would eventually be wholly taken up with recurrent expenditure, thus reducing state participation in the financing of investment to zero.

Regional and social disparities: In 1982, current national income was estimated to be 400 billion CFA francs (INSD 1984), or about 62,000 CFA francs per capita (US$ 210). All things being equal, this was one of the lowest incomes in Africa. According to the same source (INSD 1984) Gross Domestic Product in the same year was about 350 billion CFA francs.

This gap arose essentially from: a) surpluses of resources transferred by nationals settled abroad, notably in the Ivory Coast and Gabon (in 1982, these surpluses amounted to 41 billion CFA francs); and b) aid received from the rest of the world.

At the same time, per capita national income in the rural areas was estimated to be some 25,000 CFA francs as against 400,000 CFA francs in the urban areas. In other words, an urban dweller had a monetary income equal to 16 times that of a peasant.

The deterioration of the economic situation had serious consequences for the social situation. Thus, in 1982, there was only one doctor for 48,000 inhabitants and one bed for 1,200 inhabitants, while the school enrolment ratio was estimated to be 19%, as against the average school enrolment ratio in Africa of 78%.

To conclude, it is quite clear that neocolonial development policy was a failure.

Political aspects of the delinking process

The colonial and post-colonial history of Upper Volta was dominated first by the traditional chieftaincy and then by the trade unions. These two forces have been behind every profound political change that has occurred in the country.

The so-called traditional chieftaincy

History says that the elites who today make up the traditional chieftaincy are the descendants of warriors from Gambaga in northern Ghana who conquered most of the present-day territory and founded the Mossi kingdom there. Thanks to its efficient political and military organization, the Mossi kingdom victoriously resisted attacks by its neighbours as well as Muslim penetration. Not until the end of the 19th century (1893) did the Mossi state finally succumb under attacks from the barbarous French soldiers led by captains Voulet and Chanoine.

Although conquered by force of arms, the Mossi chiefs were able to adapt to the new colonial political order. They reorganized and in 1935 obtained a legal statute and thenceforth became the principal auxiliaries of the colonial administration.

Above all, in 1932, with the dismantling of Upper Volta and its division between French Sudan and the Ivory Coast, the political influence of the traditional chiefs revived; in 1947, pressure from the Mossi traditional chief led to the reunion and restoration of Upper Volta. Buoyed up by this success, the traditional chiefs openly participated in the political struggles for liberation that marked the country from 1945 to 1960, through the creation of a political party, the Union for the Defence of the Interests of Upper Volta (UDIHV). All went well until, in 1958, the Paramount Chief of the Mossi, fearing that Upper Volta might be swallowed up in the Mali Federation, ordered his warriors to march on the Territorial Assembly where the deputies were debating the question.

This action – which moreover was simply an act of intimidation – explains why the Voltaic authorities performed an about-turn: after signing the act creating the Mali Federation, they changed their minds at the last moment and joined the Community. After numerous twists and turns, during the course of which, thanks to the support of the chiefs, the African Democratic Rally (RDA) party absorbed the other parties (Voltaic Democratic Movement, Social Party for the Emancipation of the Masses), Upper Volta gained its independence with a two party-system: the RDA and the African Regrouping Party (PRA).

Contrary to all expectations, however, the first acts of the first government headed by Maurice Yaméogo were to shake the power of the traditional chiefs: he abolished payments to chiefs (benefits won since 1934) and, in place of customary laws, introduced universal suffrage for the election of chiefs. Suddenly deprived of both their economic livelihood and their traditional political power, the traditional chiefs, in order to survive, had to dig up the war axes against Maurice Yaméogo's government.

Five years later (January 1966) the traditional chiefs had the opportunity to make Maurice Yaméogo pay for what they had seen as an act of betrayal towards them.

The role of trade unions and political parties (1960–83)

In 1960, when Upper Volta became independent, there were practically no trade unions, because services or industries that might form the basis for the creation of trade unions were virtually absent.

But President Maurice Yaméogo's decision to introduce a one-party (the RDA) state, led to the creation of many trade unions, under the direct or indirect cover of official or underground political parties. All these corporatist-type trade unions (teachers, nurses, civil servants etc.) gradually came together in larger federations or unions: National Union of Teachers, Trade Union of Voltaic Workers (USTV), Voltaic Organization of Free Trade Unions (OVSL), National Union of Human and Animal Health Workers (SYNTSHA), African Confederation of Believing Workers (CATC), General Union of Voltaic Students (UGEV).

Generally inspired and supported by other political parties now forced underground (the USTV by the PRA, the National Union of Teachers by the National Liberation Movement (MLN) and the African Independence Party (PAI), the CATC by the traditionalist wing of the RDA and the UGEV by the MLN and the PAI), these unions fought side by side in the struggle against President Maurice Yaméogo's regime, which they saw as being more and more despotic.

When, in December 1965, the government decided to reduce civil servants' salaries by 10% it gave the unions the chance to embark on a trial of strength with the regime and its single party, the RDA. The traditional chiefs, to avenge the affront they had suffered in 1960, also threw their weight into the scales. On 3 January 1966, after several days of popular demonstrations in the streets of Ouagadougou, Maurice Yaméogo capitulated.

The Chief of Staff, Major Sangoulé Lamizana, acceded to the call from the demonstrators and took power. He first formed a Provisional Military Government (GMP) and later a Government of National Union including soldiers, representatives of political parties and representatives of some trade unions. This Government of National Union assisted by a Consultative Council of representatives of all social forces (notably the chiefs and trade unions) presided over the country's political affairs until 1970.

The year 1970 saw the advent of the Second Republic. A Constitutional Government still presided over by Sangoulé Lamizana (now a general) was established. The peculiarity of this constitutional regime was that President Lamizana had not personally taken part in elections. The adoption of the referendum that endorsed the institutions of the future Second Republic was deemed automatically to have made him President of this Second Republic; an RDA Prime Minister (the RDA being the majority in the legislative elections) was appointed. The ruling team was highly heterogeneous and this rapidly led to the development of politicking both inside and outside. In particular, the opposition parties and the trade unions were frustrated by the fact that the RDA they had driven out in 1966 was back again with the reins of power. This situation produced a wave of strikes and popular demonstrations leading to a complete blockage of constitutional life. In February 1974, the President himself carried out a *coup d'état*, dissolved the National Assembly and formed a Government of National Renewal (GRN I).

With the aim of settling the problem of political instability once and for all, the military officers who were members of the government pushed President Lamizana into institutionalizing military rule through the creation of a political movement called the National Movement for Renewal (MNR).

The political parties and trade unions, seeing the potential danger, with one group fearing their permanent elimination from the political stage and the other the questioning of the democratic freedoms and other social gains that they had won so dearly, once again combined their forces against those whom they now considered usurpers. An indefinite strike, launched in December 1975, led to the fall of the Government of National Renewal (GRN I). To resolve the crisis President Lamizana was obliged to form a new Government of National Renewal (GRN II) and promise a rapid return to normal constitutional rule.

Between 1970 and 1975, the political and trade union situation in Upper Volta was profoundly transformed. On the trade union side, there was, on the one hand, the birth of the Voltaic Trade Union Confederation (CSV), closely linked (in terms of leadership) to the PAI and, on the other, the break-up of the General Union of Voltaic Students (UGEV). Following this break-up the student movement escaped from the control of the MLN and came under that of the PAI and the Voltaic Revolutionary Communist Party (PCRV). At the same time, the Patriotic League for Development (LIPAD) was formed, led, in fact, by the PAI. These changes reflected a clear desire to radicalize the struggle against neocolonialism and its local agents. In these circumstances, in 1978, the Third Republic came into being following fully democratic elections that saw the candidate of the National Union for the Defence of Democracy force President Lamizana into a run-off, despite the fact that he had the backing of the RDA. The results of this first round of the elections contained two lessons.

The first was, that in addition to democratic freedoms the people wanted some expression of nationalism that had been lacking all through the 12-year rule of President Lamizana. The second was, that the Voltaic people as a whole, after so many vicissitudes, wanted at last to be governed by someone capable of imposing an adequate line on national political affairs. Whatever the case, the presidential elections having once again resulted in victory for the RDA, the struggles resumed, this time more bitterly and with more explicitly political goals. In November 1980, following a month-long strike launched by the National Union of Teachers, which was close to the MLN, a military *coup d'état* brought Colonel Saye Zerbo to power. This time, it was not the most senior officer in the highest rank who took power, in accordance with the rules of the game that had hitherto prevailed in the Higher Council of the Voltaic Armed Forces (CSFAV). This breach of the rules opened the way for every tendency to manifest itself within the army.

Colonel Saye Zerbo formed a coalition government in which soldiers were heavily represented but which included several civilian representatives of the RDA opposition. Colonel Saye Zerbo's government, initially strongly supported by the population at large in the hope that it would at last put an end to inter-group struggles, ran into its first problems in late 1981: internal divisions, conflicts with the trade unions, notably with the Voltaic Trade Union Confederation (CSV), appearance of political tendencies within the army, complete confusion of the political parties etc.

It was in these conditions that in November 1982, Army Medical Major Jean-Baptiste Ouédraogo overthrew Colonel Saye Zerbo and took power and formed a government with a majority of civilians and a soldier (Captain Sankara) as Prime Minister.

Just as under Colonel Saye Zerbo, partisan struggles soon surfaced in the new team: on the one side, President Jean-Baptiste Ouédraogo, supported by most of the parties and trade unions because he himself advocated a return to constitutional rule and, on the other, Prime Minister Sankara backed by the CSV, the PAI and the student organizations.

The President emerged victorious from the first clash. The post of Prime Minister was abolished and Sankara was thrown into prison for a few days. Faced with this, the opposition began to crystallize, first in the form of tracts and street demonstrations, then in armed clashes in the capital. The outcome was quickly favourable to Captain Sankara. On 4 August 1983, Captain Thomas Sankara and a group of progressive officers strongly backed by the CSV and the LIPAD-PAI took power.

The new team immediately set up a National Council of the Revolution (CNR) and proclaimed a Popular Democratic Republic. It quickly became clear that with the revolution of 4 August 1983, Upper Volta had joined the ranks of progressive revolutionary countries in sub-Saharan Africa, such as Benin, Ethiopia and Ghana.

In conclusion, it is clear that all through the political changes that occurred in Upper Volta (1966, 1970, 1974, 1975, 1980 and 1983) the action of the trade unions was always decisive.

Initial attempts to disengage from the West or the beginnings of Arab–Burkinabe co-operation

Co-operation between Upper Volta (now Burkina) and the Arab countries began with the advent of the Lamizana regime. But this co-operation really took off particularly during the 1970s and in the light of political and economic events (drought in the Sahel, world oil crisis).

Thus, over the period 1975–82, Arab countries' commitments (including the Maghreb countries) totalled some US$218 million (or some 72 billion CFA francs) of which 135 million were allocated to the industry and energy sector; the economic infrastructure sector came second with US$33 million. But commitments to rural development (agriculture, cattle farming and water resources) and human resources (education, health, social welfare), considered to be priority sectors, totalled only some US$33 million.

Trade relations were almost non-existent. Over the period 1975–82, Burkina's imports from Arab countries totalled some 765 million CFA francs as against exports to them of some 22 million. These flows represented 1.4% and 1.8% of Burkina's imports and exports respectively over the same period.

The advent of the RDP (Popular Democratic Revolution) in 1983 marked a new stage in the history of relations between Burkina and the Arab countries. After August 1983 Arab–Burkinabe relations developed strongly, notably with Libya and Algeria, as a result of a convergence of views on many political issues. This warming of bilateral relations, which affected all areas of national life (cultural, political, economic, financial and military), was accompanied by a marked decline in co-operation with the specialized inter-Arab agencies (BID, BADEA, OPEC and other national or international Funds).

What has been the result of this co-operation? From the beginning of the great drought of 1973, Burkina had recourse directly to Arab aid, thinking not only that this aid could enable it to deal with the catastrophic effects of the drought (famine and desertification notably) but, above all, that it could constitute an alternative similar to North–South co-operation.

These hopes were soon disappointed, as, contrary to all expectations, it was realized that co-operation with Arab countries was almost exactly the same as co-operation with the developed countries: long and complex procedures, humiliating preconditions, burdensome technical assistance etc. It was realized that: emergency aid (food aid, balance of payments support) soon overshadowed aid for productive investment (study on Arab–Burkinabe co-operation); that preference for financing went, in the last analysis, to financially profitable projects rather than to projects to provide basic collective social infrastructure (agricultural production infrastructure, health programmes, socio-cultural infrastructure); and that commercial exchanges developed one-sidedly to Burkina's disadvantage, leading, as in the case of North–South relations, to a chronic balance of payments deficit.

Apart from these drawbacks, it must, however, be acknowledged that co-operation with the Arab countries enabled Burkina to go a long way towards meeting its needs for finance, which are of course enormous. Furthermore, in terms of quality, aid from Arab countries, by supplementing Western aid in some sectors, undeniably enabled Burkina to strengthen its decision-making capacity in the area of the choice of projects to finance (for example, the Kompienga hydro-electrical project, finance for which was ensured only by the presence of Arab funders).

To conclude, it can be said that, overall, co-operation with Arab countries is really simply an extension of North–South co-operation. It thus failed to play the role that the Burkinabe side had a right to expect, that is, to be able to contribute to strengthening the country's policy of real independence.

This relatively meagre, indeed very meagre, balance-sheet of Arab–Burkinabe co-operation shows once again that when South–South co-operation develops within the economic system, it is inevitably subject to the capitalist market's law of value (prices, incomes, profit, competitiveness etc.).

Thus, the fundamental question remains: nation-building or trans-nationalization?

The fundamental options

The assertion of national independence

The present authorities in Burkina Faso are very conscious of the fact that a true break with the mechanisms of imperialist domination demands the adoption of an original national path of development. They pointed out in their 'Political orientation speech' of 2 October 1983 (p. 23) that:

> The various revolutions that the world has seen are not all alike. Each one has its own authentic character which distinguishes it from the others. Our revolution, the August revolution, is no exception. It takes account of the peculiar features of our country, its level of development and its subjection to the world imperialist capitalist system.

These authorities went on to observe that:

> It is a revolution in a small, land-locked country at a time when, at the international level, the revolutionary movement is withering day by day with no visible hope of it being formed into a homogeneous bloc capable of encouraging and giving practical support to young revolutionary movements. (DOP, p. 23)

After setting out these considerations on the peculiarities of the country, it is stated that the August revolution's 'primary tasks are to liquidate imperialist domination and exploitation, and cleanse the countryside of all social, economic and cultural obstacles that keep it in a backward state.' This is what gives it its democratic character.

The August revolution, it goes on to say, 'is an anti-imperialist revolution, but it is unfolding within the framework of the limits of a bourgeois economic and social order' (DOP, p. 24), which is, however, not seen as overly troublesome since the class analysis underpinning the August revolution suggests that 'the Voltaic bourgeoisie is not a single, homogeneous, reactionary and anti-revolutionary mass' (DOP, p. 24), but that it has the 'undesirable' characteristic of being incapable of 'revolutionizing society' as the bourgeoisie did in European countries in the 1780s, that is, at a time when the bourgeoisie was still a rising class.

These last two comments seem to justify the appeal launched to 'economic operators', that is, entrepreneurs in trade, industry and construction above all, for them to participate in the success of the agrarian reform by investing in agriculture.

This whole process, intended to lead to economic independence, was entrusted to the vigilance of the CNR which guaranteed the inviolability of the fundamental option, that is, the struggle against imperialism and its domestic agents who are: 1) the pre-4 August 1983 state bourgeoisie; 2) the comprador bourgeoisie; and 3) the middle bourgeoisie; the social base of the August revolution being made up of the peasantry, the working class and the *petit bourgeoisie*.

The quest for economic autonomy

Burkina Faso's economic autonomy means first of all food self-sufficiency through the development of agriculture and the production of staple foods. On the eve of the revolution, the country depended for food on imported products which accounted for 25% of total imports.

Currently, production of food crops is at a level of 185 kg/ha as against 244 in 1975 and far more in 1960. This shows the importance of modernizing a very backward, low productivity agriculture: agriculture on average supplies 45% of GDP by volume with a very stable economically active population equal to 85% of the total economically active population. Yet it continues to rely almost entirely on human energy for ploughing, uses little fertilizer and remains extensively over very poor soils, and finally faces ever-worsening climatic conditions.

Economic autonomy in the sense meant by the new rulers of Burkina Faso implies the quest for means to be 'self-reliant'. Thus, in tandem with an immense effort to tap savings (forced or voluntary) towards investments such as those of the PPD (Popular Development Programme), there has been massive resort to human investment, currently the country's sole major resource. The forms of mobilization are intended to be as democratic as possible in so far as development operations are intended to be increasingly identified and implemented by the popular masses themselves.

This philosophy of action for true self-sufficiency is summed up in the PPD, a two-year investment programme that aims to demonstrate that the nation possesses the means to promote its own economic and social development, comprising hard work, organization of the popular masses and use of the country's admittedly limited natural resources in order to build up a minimum of infrastructure in the country at minimum cost.

Prerequisites for economic autonomy

This concern touches a favourable chord among the authorities in Burkina Faso. The type of industrialization must aim to provide the broad popular masses with basic products so that from the outset there is a broad market for industrial products, at least in terms of the number of consumers.

The quest for an incomes policy, that will make it possible to sustain the economic activity to be embarked upon, seems to be only at the drafting stage, apart from the firm belief that a better agricultural pricing policy will make possible a redistribution of national income in favour of the peasantry, thus achieving the aim of extending the market, and at the same time, protect it against a demand for imported goods that is seen as emanating almost exclusively from the bourgeoisie and the *petit bourgeoisie*.

The reorientation of agricultural production towards food crops shows that priority is being given to the domestic market, but this option is hardly consistent with the intention of setting up an industrial sector fuelled downstream by agricultural products, since it is hard to see why peasants would suddenly become consumers of industrially processed products that they are consuming quite happily without any industrial processing, especially if nothing happens to alter their food and cultural habits etc.

Mastering technology

The whole PPD is an illustration of what the CNR sees as the true acquisition of technology by the popular masses.

From the construction of buildings in mud, in the framework of 4 August housing estates for example, to the building of reservoirs through human investment, by way of vaccination centres built of local materials, the CNR has sought to give the masses evidence of just what they can achieve and the uselessness of sophisticated and poorly mastered techniques. There is thus a real determination to demystify imported technology in the eyes of the masses. At the same time, however, the CNR planned to promote access to developed-country technology by giving priority to training and technical and scientific research.

The guidelines issued by the CNR for the preparation of the 1986–90 five-year plan spell out this determination to seek technological mastery that was already explicit in the DOP, which stated that, as regards the agricultural sector, 'the CNR will harbour no illusions about huge sophisticated projects. On the contrary, lots of small achievements in the agricultural system will turn the country into one big field, an endless series of farms' (DOP, p. 38).

The same idea of 'small achievements' prevails in the area of industrialization through the establishment of small-scale agro-industrial units designed to provide the peasants with 'year-round markets for their produce'.

In short:

> The reforms in this area aim at gradually establishing effective control by the people of Upper Volta over the channels of production and distribution. For without genuine mastery of these channels, it is practically impossible to build an independent economy in the service of the people (DOP, p. 40).

Implementation of a new economic growth policy
The driving force of the economy in the revolutionary process in Burkina Faso is agriculture, therefore industry could play only an auxiliary role in the development of agriculture, both upstream and downstream.

The agrarian reform, which is the vital prerequisite for raising agricultural productivity, aims to:

> Increase labour productivity through better organization of the peasants and the introduction of modern agricultural techniques in the countryside; develop a diversified agriculture, together with regional specialization; abolish all the fetters that are part of the traditional socio-economic structures oppressing the peasants; finally, make agriculture the lever for developing industry.

It will be observed that this last objective of the agrarian reform implies going against what so far has generally been accepted as the inward-looking strategy for an underdeveloped economy, that is, the primacy of industrialization over agriculture, agriculture being thought of as quite incapable of developing without being fully backed up by a viable and dynamic industrialization, extraverted though it be.

The choice made by the CNR implies that imports of agricultural inputs and equipment will continue and be stepped up for a period that might be quite lengthy, but which would end in a gradual reduction of imports of foodstuffs in favour of imports of industrial capital goods.

It should be noted that this strategy is very novel among actual attempts at delinking from the world economic system made by underdeveloped countries. The choice of agriculture as the motor of Burkina's development, despite the crushing burden of climatic and human constraints that stand in the way of winning successful control of this sector, seems to rest not only on observation of its importance in the GDP formation but also from the need to remove agriculture from its current extraversion and make it the key mechanism in the accumulation of national capital.

Implementation of the Popular Development Programme (PPD) provides the proof that the CNR wants to accumulate, in favour of agriculture, on the basis of available surpluses, both in the countryside and in the towns, by building socio-economic infrastructure through voluntary contributions and human investment, and compulsory levies on the incomes of the urban population (traders, middle and *petit bourgeoisie*).

Furthermore, it should be noted that this new growth strategy is taking shape in a system of planning that is also new, based on the organization of popular forums through which the masses identify their needs, formulate actions and propose the means to implement them.

Key role of base organizations
Escaping from the grip of imperialism requires collective discipline in order to be able to deal with subversive activities, whether internal or external.

It is in this framework that must be seen the creation of Committees for the

Defence of the Revolution (CDRs) as the spearhead of the revolutionary movement, with twin goals: to ensure the armed defence and the ideological defence of the revolution, and to act as cadres for the organization of the popular masses throughout the country:

> to wage the merciless struggle to transform this country into a prosperous and radiant country, a country where the people are the sole masters of the material and spiritual wealth of the nation. (DOP, p. 41)

The Popular Development Programme (PPD) and implementation of the 4 August 1983 fundamental options

In order to achieve the fundamental objectives of economic independence and autonomy as set out in the Political Orientation Speech of 2 October 1983, the National Council of the Revolution chose to rely first on the nation's own resources, that is to rely first and foremost on the labour of the popular masses. But the masses' hard work can be effective only if it is integrated into a framework of action carefully worked out in both time and space.

It is in this spirit that a Popular Development Programme (1984–85) was conceived and drawn up. The PPD is a set of sectoral investment programmes at national and regional levels whose realization is designed to make it possible, in the short term, to meet partly or totally the needs of the rural and urban toiling masses through:

– a marked improvement in food crop production;
– an increase in the availability of drinking water especially in the rural areas;
– selected urban improvements (building of popular housing estates);
– increasing the amount of socio-economic infrastructure (schools, health posts and social centres, sports and cultural centres).

Beyond the socio-economic objectives thus pursued, implementation of the PPD aims essentially at political objectives:

– to show that at all levels of economic and social achievements, Burkina can and must rely on its own resources;
– to prove at the same time that in the specific context of Burkina, the masses' work effort remains above all the determining factor in the achievement of further social advance;
– to endeavour to raise the level of the toiling masses' political awareness and their spirit of initiative.

The financing required to carry out the PPD amounted to some 160,692 million CFA francs, of which 31,237 million would come from national resources and 129,455 million from external resources. The explanation for this imbalance between domestic and external resources is that the CNR did not want to put an immediate end to the classic development programmes still underway on 4 August 1983.

With regard to the base programme strictly so-called (that is the programme initiated by the masses themselves at the level of the country's various provinces) it can be observed that: domestic resources cover 75% of the total cost of this programme; and human investment accounts for 46%. The sectoral allocation of total financing is as follows:

rural development sector:	36,438 million
industry and service sector:	7,375 million
economic infrastructure sector:	87,757 million
human resources sector:	15,303 million

Thus whether in the distribution of financing by source of finance or in the sectoral allocation of this financing, it can be seen that both are in line with the CNR's political and economic options. But the major problem, as will be seen below, is the national capacity to sustain this effort effectively.

Paradoxically, this sector contributes a large proportion of export receipts (receipts from the exploitation of agricultural and animal products represented on average 90% of total annual export receipts over the period 1975–82) whereas it is not even able to provide for the population's food self-sufficiency. The explanation for this distortion is the neocolonial nature of development policies that consistently gave priority to export products (groundnuts, cotton, cattle, vegetables and fruits) at the expense of food crops (particularly cereals).

As for the industrial sector, as has also been stressed above, the new industries (import-substitution industries) very soon fell into a situation of premature stagnation and blockage. Thus this sector's production stagnated and even declined in some cases over the period 1975–82.

Overall, the Burkinabe economy is an essentially rural economy that is regressing and has no possibility in the short term of producing from its own resources those resources necessary to ensure the country's autonomous development. In this sense, the national economic situation currently poses a major obstacle to the success of the national delinking policy embarked on since 1983.

Regarding social obstacles, these are mainly due to the mentality of the vast majority of peasants (95% of the total population). Ignorance, illiteracy, working conditions and age-old cultural habits mean that they find hard to grasp both the ideology of class struggle and the hegemonic policies of the imperialist powers. This reality is also perceived by the CNR which proclaims (DOP, p. 24) that among the tasks of the revolution is: '. . . to cleanse the countryside of all social, economic and cultural obstacles that keep it in a backward state'.

To win the masses over fully to the objective of the Popular and Democratic Revolution will necessarily take a long time. Socially, it needs also to be stressed that the government's budgetary austerity measures have sometimes led to tensions between the government and the trade unions which look on powerlessly as their influence over the mass organizations slips away to the benefit of the Committees for the Defence of the Revolution (CDRs).

Burkina Faso's delinking policy: obstacles and prospects

Obstacles

Obstacles to the delinking policy embarked on by Burkina since 4 August 1983 are both domestic and external.

Domestically, they are essentially political and social. In the framework of the achievement of 'honour, dignity, true independence and progress' (DOP, p. 5) that the National Council of the Revolution has set since 4 August 1983, it naturally encountered opposition from reactionary forces (the state, the commercial, and the middle bourgeoisie) who seek to retain the privileges they had held for the 23 years of colonial and neocolonial Upper Volta. These reactionary forces continue to plan plots and sabotage in order to recover their 'lost kingdom'.

On top of this reactionary opposition there are ideological disagreements over the exact nature of the Popular and Democratic Revolution: is it a Popular and Democratic Revolution or a National Popular and Democratic Revolution? Furthermore, differences began to surface between the CNR and the LIPAD-PAI over, it seems, questions of revolutionary praxis. These disagreements inevitably hamper the homogenization of the struggle at this stage. The economic obstacles, as we have seen, are a reflection of the Burkinabe economy's continued domination by rural production activities (traditional agriculture and herding).

As regards external obstacles (in addition to the ceaseless destabilizing activities of international imperialism) the Popular and Democratic Revolution has to face the hostility of Burkina's immediate neighbours who fear that the Burkinabe experience would prove to be contagious in the sub-region. On a wider level, it must be acknowledged that the 4 August 1983 revolution occurred at a time when the cohesion of the international revolutionary movement was going through a very hard time. The National Council of the Revolution (CNR) is fully aware of this situation and stresses in the DOP (p. 23):

> It is a revolution in a small, land-locked country at a time when, at the international level, the revolutionary movement is withering day by day with no visible hope of it being formed into a homogeneous bloc capable of encouraging and giving practical support to young revolutionary movements.

This set of political, economic and social facts weighs heavily on the delinking policy embarked upon in Burkina since August 1983. The DOP acknowledges that the 4 August revolution must take account of the 'special features of the country, its level of development, and its subjection to the world imperialist capitalist system' and goes so far as to specify that 'our revolution, characterized thus, while it is an anti-imperialist revolution, is nevertheless unfolding within the framework of the limits of the bourgeois economic and social order.' (DOP, p. 24)

Do all these blocking factors increase the risks of a possible tightening of links of dependence with the world economic system? The question remains open. What is certain is, that if all the trends observed over the period 1975–82 had continued there would eventually have been a serious dislocation of the national economy. Per capita income would eventually have been reduced to zero. In the plausible hypothesis of an annual decline of 12% in the value of money, the 1990 GDP in 1990 francs would have been 270 billion as against 378 billion in 1983; an overall fall of 27% in seven years, an annual fall of some 4%. Given a rate of population increase of 2.1% per capita over the period, that would be equivalent to a fall of per capita GDP of 6.1% p.a. on average; such a fall would halve GDP in seven years.

Furthermore, analysis of economic forecasts shows that, in real terms, by 1990 per capita income would be barely half that of 1983.

Such a situation would make it impossible for the country to restore the people's standard of living without a massive inflow of foreign capital. In other words, every new investment effort necessarily leads to a greater burden on the external public debt and hence enhanced dependence on the world economic system. The country would thus fall back into the vicious circle of dependence/underdevelopment/dependence with the main function of being a permanent provider of cheap labour for the system's periphery.

Prospects

The National Council of the Revolution's Political Orientation Speech of 2 October 1983, clearly set out the two fundamental options that would guide its action in the political, economic and social domains: 'to build a democratic and popular society, and to build an independent, self-reliant and planned economy'.

Building a democratic and popular society is indeed a fundamental political objective, the achievement of which involves profound economic, social and human transformations. Hence, the urgent necessity to construct an independent, self-sufficient and planned national economy, this type of economy alone seen as capable of creating new socio-economic relations to serve as the basis for building a democratic and popular society within which the people (the working class, the *petit bourgeoisie*, the peasantry and the lumpen-proletariat) alone exercise all power. Such, in a few words are the ideological and political foundations of Burkina's policy of independence.

But the precise content of this option in terms of the current context of the political and economic situation needs to be spelled out.

If the political obstacles listed above appear relatively easy to remove, the same is not true of the economic obstacles. Theoretically, any self-reliant development policy implies control by the country of: (a) natural resources; (b) mobilization and use of the economic surpluses resulting from the exploitation of those natural resources; and (c) the technological base.

The end-result of the delinking policy means: expropriation of foreign capital; nationalization of industries and commercial activities in the hands of compradors; and breaking the bonds of financial, monetary and commercial dependence. Given the prevailing socio-economic conditions described above, to take this path immediately would manifestly mean heading for marginalization and failure.

The National Council of the Revolution understood this very clearly, which is why it preferred to embark on a policy of relative and gradual delinking by initially attacking the key aspects of dependence.

In making such an option, what is required is: to concentrate the bulk of investment and modernization efforts in the agriculture and herding sector and particularly in food crop production; to promote all agricultural production by creating or converting industries using local agricultural products; to reshape the national market in such a way as to give pride of place to the consumption of local agricultural and agro-industrial products; and to mobilize the surpluses engendered by the agricultural sector as a whole to promote the development of other sectors.

These prospects of the Burkinabe revolution, however, face two major handicaps. First, there is the problem of the low capacity for national accumulation and effective control of the accumulation process by the rural masses. As we have seen, Burkina is a Sahelian country without strategic mineral resources, and no agricultural potential sufficient for it to secure the financial resources necessary for its development. Its financial resources arise essentially from agriculture and herding, activities which are still at a semi-artisanal stage.

On top of these handicaps there is the virtual non-existence of public savings, because national budgetary receipts are made up almost entirely of customs dues and taxes. Private savings are also insignificant. In 1983, the marginal propensity to consume reached 92% of GDP and 80% of National Income. This can be traced to the low level of per capita income (57,000 CFA francs in 1983), and explains why, during the 1970s, the potential for saving and accumulation remained very limited (about 30 billion CFA francs per annum on average). Furthermore, the volume of bank deposits, after rising steeply after 1975 (+ 17% per annum), fell sharply after 1980 to barely 1% of GDP as against 3% for the earlier period.

This tendency for the national capacity for accumulation to weaken inevitably had repercussions on investment. After a rapid rise in the early 1970s, the global volume of investment fell continuously after 1976, leading to a reduction of its share in GDP formation. Thus, while the investment ratio rose from 16% to 22% between 1970 and 1976, it fell back to only 15% in 1983.

But beyond this problem of the national capacity for accumulation the fundamental question is undeniably that of the popular masses' control of this accumulation. In other words, must the state be a direct, active partner in the effort at national accumulation or, on the contrary, should the preponderant role fall on the popular masses?

Experience has shown that delinking policies in Africa have generally ended in failure because of this fundamental question. That means that the success of Burkina's delinking policy will depend, in the last analysis, on the role given to the popular masses.

The second handicap is of course Burkina's isolation.

Isolated in the midst of countries totally opposed to any revolution, the Burkinabe revolution must, if it wants to succeed, become part of a wider policy of collective autonomy, bringing together several countries around this ideal of national independence. That is the only path that will surely enable it to avoid marginalization and failure. The Accra–Ouagadougou axis created after 4 August 1983 is indeed a minimum base for a policy of collective autonomy, but it must be recognized that the economic problems experienced by both sides seriously limit its scope.

Ghana's repeated resort in the last two years to the IMF proves that, given the conditions generally attached to Fund help.

Bibliography

1. *Planification et Développement en Haute-Volta*, pp. 45–63, University of Paris, 1980.

2. *Discours d'Orientation Politique* (DOP), pp. 5–24, Conseil National de la Révolution, Ouagadougou, October 1983.

3. *Programme Populaire de Développement*, Ministère de la Planification et du Développement Populaire, Burkina Faso, October 1984.

4. *Coopération Arabo-Burkinabè*, FTM/UNITAR, Kafando Talata, October 1985.

5. Notes sur le concept de Déconnexion [Delinking], Samir Amin, Third World Forum, Dakar.

8. Ghana Under the PNDC: Delinking or Structural Adjustment?

Kwame A. Ninsin

Introduction

Delinking, as the ultimate solution to the vicious cycle of underdevelopment, seems increasingly to engage the attention of Third World radical intellectuals as a result of the permanent crisis of Third World economies and the futility of attempts to reform the existing international economic order.[1] The effect of past IMF adjustment policies on the economies of Latin America, and their implication for Africa under the current wave of similar policies has sharpened anxieties about the future. It seems clear that many more countries are slipping ineluctably into the neocolonial trap rather than building up the capacity for independent national development. At the same time, the deepening crisis of Third World economies appears to be whipping up revolutionary pressures which are challenging the neocolonial model of development and increasingly opening up the possibility for an alternative option out of the crisis.

The focus of this chapter is on Ghana's politics of development, especially as the country's new leaders have opened a new frontier of relationship with the IMF and the World Bank. The consequences of the current model of development, which is a blueprint of IMF adjustment policies and programmes, will be appraised, and the potential of this model to create the momentum for either consolidating the neocolonial position of the country, or overcoming the crisis and for propelling a process of development independent of the capitalist world economy, will be examined.

The world economy of which Ghana is part is dominated by the law of capitalist accumulation (the capitalist law of value). Colonialism was a period of incorporation of African economies generally into this world system. They stand in a dialectical relationship to the rest of the world economy, and their participation in it has had the effect of what Gunder Frank calls the development of under-development.[2] Samir Amin argues that the solution to the current crisis of underdevelopment would be a rupture of this dialectical relationship such that national development would not be subject to the law of value of capitalism. Instead the 'imperatives of "globalization"' would be replaced by the imperatives of a popular based law of value.[3] Essentially, therefore, delinking is the process of negating the dictatorship of capitalist law of value through a rupture of the structural links that ensure such determination.

Amin has a point when he says that delinking connotes 'a national and popular development which can lead to socialism'; but that the first may not necessarily lead to socialism but to the progressive development of inequality in the distribution of wealth within the structure of social ownership of the means of production.[4] Given the resilience of the capitalist law of value, however, a point cogently argued by Tandon,[5] there is a real prospect of collapse for a delinking movement that lacks a firm socialist, as against a mere popular, content. This danger places the first possibility in Amin's concept of delinking in almost the same family as the 'bourgeois Marxists' who argue that it is possible to realize autonomous national development on the strength of national capital acting in opposition to international capital. The limitation imposed on this option by the capitalist law of value is graphically illustrated by the current balance of payments and debt crisis of the so-called Newly Industrialized Countries (NICs).

In our view, therefore, delinking, whether in its national or international variant, calls for a complete rupture with the global economy and the assumption of an independent, national and socialist posture in economic decisions and planning such that a country which has opted for this will not be subservient to the commercial, financial and technological ties which it may find prudent to establish with the world's capitalist economies. To this extent I would argue that delinking demands the revolutionary reorganization of the political and economic life of society with a view to establishing the hegemony of the popular forces. This is a necessary precondition to delinking.

Political and economic context

On 31 December 1981, the civilian regime of the People's National Party (PNP) was overthrown in a *coup d'état* and replaced by the Provisional National Defence Council (PNDC) led by Flight-Lieutenant J. J. Rawlings. Rawlings' return into national politics seems to have been precipitated by the PNP government's apparent failure to take measures to strengthen the national economy, in particular its productive sector. Prior to this (in the third quarter of 1979), the Armed Forces Revolutionary Council (AFRC) had intervened in Ghanaian politics to arrest the rapid destruction of the economy through the conscious misallocation of resources to the unproductive sector and for the benefit of idlers. To that extent, steps were taken to impose summary justice on those who had committed grave economic crimes during the rule of the Supreme Military Council (SMC), and others were instituted to eliminate the opportunistic business practices, including checking the worst excesses of corruption and profiteering. On the whole, the thrust of these policies 'could only have been in favour of a more stable and regulated pattern of capital accumulation and to the advantage of both indigenous and foreign enterprise . . . through the reallocation of resources and opportunities' from the speculative section of the commercial *petit bourgeoisie* to the more 'productive' sectors of the economy.[6] When Rawlings himself had the advantage of hindsight to justify the handover of power to the PNP he said rather perceptively:

> When we handed over [power] in September 1979 we did so . . . in the belief that the conditions which compelled us to intervene directly in the political process would be removed by the incoming Government and that the initiative which we had begun during our short stay under the AFRC would be continued. These were that realistic steps would be taken to bring some measure of sanity into the economy; [among them would be to] bring prices down to the level at which the mass of our people can afford . . . and end the rampant speculation and the general privatisation of government property, and the political corruption and moral decay which prevailed in the country. We had also hoped that the incoming administration would stick to the norms and practices of parliamentary democracy which at the time we did all in our power to install, nurture, and protect. Instead it continued the system which rewarded cheats, rogues and speculators and punished hardworking men and women.[7]

This primary concern of the AFRC with correcting the distortions and anarchy of the Ghanaian economy can be understood only in the context of the country's prevailing political and economic conditions. The period 1966–79 had seen quite significant changes in both the political and economic realms of society. Prior to these developments, Kwame Nkrumah's government of the Convention People's Party had attempted, through an extraordinary development programme, to contend with the colonial basis of the Ghanaian economy. This commitment was articulated in the Party's *Seven Year Development Programme*, in which the CPP showed a clear resolve to carry out a policy of building state capitalism in competition with private capital – both foreign and local. This was seen as a necessary step toward socialism.[8] The consolidation of state capital was seen as the essential instrument in ensuring this transition. In the words of President Nkrumah 'State enterprises are the main economic pillars on which we expect to build our socialist state'.[9]

This economic direction had a strong political content and, above all, justification. The CPP had come to power on a wave of populist support, and its mass base comprised mainly poor, small and middle peasant cocoa farmers,[10] artisans, urban workers, elementary school leavers, the unemployed, small-property owners, clerks, teachers and intellectuals of poor origin.[11] By the early 1960s this heterogeneous ensemble of class forces found the independence vision of economic well-being receding further into an unattainable future. The CPP, as a mass party, began to experience a crisis of legitimacy, credibility and survival. But it was also clear that the global economy's power over a weakling like Ghana's, was becoming graphically manifest in a worsening balance of payments crisis, worsening terms of trade[12] and a declining standard of living.[13] Complementary to this external assault was the growing assertiveness of the national bourgeoisie in both the political and economic sectors. It was in its resolve to address these emerging economic and political crises that the CPP opted for a militant anti-imperialist posture in its political and economic policies.

Towards its socialist aspirations the regime realized definite gains. It could, for example, check the consolidation of the hegemony of international and local capitals. By 1966 gross manufacturing output from state enterprises was 10% more than that of wholly Ghanaian private enterprises. Similarly, the share of foreign private enterprises in gross manufacturing output had declined from 63.3%; and that of joint state–private enterprises had risen from 7.1% to 12.7% State capitalism was clearly poised for a major struggle with international and local private capitals.

The growing strength of the state sector, however, could not effectively undermine the total hegemony of the global economy of capitalism. The result is that despite the tremendous advances made by the CPP government in confronting international capital, and in increasing the aggregate domestic capital investments during the period, the structural disequilibrium of the economy persisted.[14] The effects of this disequilibrium were, the debt crisis, gradually creeping to the fore; the persistent balance of payments side by side with the denationalization of capital through invisible and visible multilateral links with the global economy; rapacious inflation; inefficient industrial enterprises which, apart from being merely import-substituting systems, were also heavily dependent on foreign inputs. In fact, at the time of the fall of the CPP government the economic scene generally was far from healthy.[15]

This crisis provided the opportunity for international and local private capitalist interests to unite to overthrow the CPP government in February 1966. That event marked the beginning of an unprecedented drive, since colonial times, to strengthen the neocolonial foundations of the Ghanaian economy and society. From 1966 onwards, therefore, the solution to Ghana's economic crisis has been sought in neo-classical economic policies: devaluation, trade deregulation and price increases for all commodities, including the price of bank credits; wage freeze and labour retrenchments; and a general cut-back on public sector expenditures. It is precisely during this period that the foundations of the neocolonial economy were shaken by economic crises. This period of a little over one decade has also witnessed the total devastation of the Ghanaian economy; the worst labour unrests in the country's history also occurred during this period. And it is remarkable that the working-class struggle should make significant advances in terms of organization and articulation of working-class and national interests.[16]

The coming to power of the AFRC on 4 June 1979 and of the PNDC (both under Flight-Lieutenant Rawlings' leadership) could be understood only against this background of economic and political turmoil. As the quotation from Rawlings[17] emphasizes, the military uprising of 1979 was motivated by the need to stop the dangerous drift towards a 'civil war',[18] and he had personally hoped that the new constitutionally elected (in August 1979) regime of the People's National Party (PNP) would act swiftly to stabilize the explosive political and economic situation. But events following the assumption of office of the PNP government did not reverse the situation, but rather exacerbated it.

By the 1980–81 period it had become clear that the PNP government was not implementing the appropriate policy package to restore health to the economy. The productive sectors, especially those engaged in production for export, continued to do poorly. Ghana's share of world cocoa production, for example, had reached the disastrous level of 15.4% by 1981. This apart, the country's terms of trade were still unfavourable. The big deficit on current account (of Ghanaian cedi, ¢202.7 million) recorded in 1980 continued into 1981. For the first half of 1981 alone a deficit of ¢23.2 million was recorded – showing an increase of about ¢7 million over that of the previous year. There was also evidence of continued misallocation of resources. The dramatic growth in money supply for example, did not arise mainly from excessive government spending (82% as against 25%) the bulk of which was financed by the central bank. The commercial sector had also resumed its rapid expansion which had been temporarily halted by the intervention of the AFRC in 1979. These and smuggling contributed immensely to the rapid expansion in money supply which rose from 40.3% in July 1980 to 51.1% in June 1981. According to the *Quarterly Economic Review* (1981) of the Ghana Commercial Bank, this unhealthy development began towards the end of 1979; that is, with the coming to power of the PNP government. Inflation galloped, reaching 122.4% in July 1980. One year later it showed a slight drop – to 118%. In these circumstances, those who monopolized goods that were increasingly in short supply and who also commanded millions of cedis, benefited from that state of anarchy; the *Quarterly Economic Review* (1981) commented: 'The immediate future of the economy still looks bleak . . .'[19]

The political crisis had also not been resolved by the return to constitutional rule and the restoration of the paraphernalia of liberal democratic institutions, ideas, norms and practices. Workers and progressive organizations responded to the damaging social effect of the economic crisis with sustained and widespread political agitation and open denunciation of the government. It was clear that parliamentary (liberal) democracy had failed to open the domains of power to the popular masses as a way of giving public policy a popular content. Its only justification, it seems, is that it was appropriate for promoting bourgeois rule and alienating the masses from the instruments of rule as well as from the material means of labour and of life. Signs of this crisis of bourgeois political arrangements were reflected in the 18 June 1979 election results; only 35.9% of the 5,059,982 registered voters actually voted. But the bourgeoisie remained unconvinced of its implications, which would have been obvious to the bourgeoisie of the stable democracies of the West. Only when workers and progressive organizations intensified their attacks on the state and PNP government did the bourgeoisie take steps to unite in self-defence. It was in this situation of crisis and uncertainty for the bourgeois order that the PNDC ousted the PNP government on 31 December 1981.

Mass mobilization: its politics and ideology

The PNDC correctly comprehended the dual character of the crisis: political and economic; and that the first arose from the second. First, the nature of bourgeois rule excludes the masses even from active participation in political decision-making. Public policy therefore is a summary affirmation of the interest of the national bourgeoisie. Secondly, because of the bourgeoisie's weakness at the periphery, it is unable to implement its own ideology to provide the necessary normative framework for legitimation, and to secure for itself an effective moral basis upon which to extract necessary obedience. This is compounded by its material poverty which also weakens its political capacity to make material concessions to the broad masses of the people whenever necessary. More especially, it is unable to provide the barest minimum of material security for the masses. The crisis of the state at the periphery therefore stems partly from its inability to provide a sound material basis and justification for demanding political obligation from members of the political community. The result is widespread cynicism, and withdrawal of active support for political regimes and institutions.

Upon assuming office, therefore, the PNDC's first priority was to resolve the political crisis. This it did by disorganizing then reconstituting bourgeois institutions of rule to incorporate the masses. To provide a credible basis for this reorganization the masses had to be mobilized in a way radically different from anything the country had experienced. The aim of persistent calls on the masses during 1982 to form defence committees in work-places and residential areas was to achieve this. By this means, new commitments and a new and practical sense of involvement and identification among the masses would be developed. The emphasis was on the people becoming 'part of the decision-making process of this country' irrespective of their position or rank within the social structure.[20] It is true that there was talk of revolution. For instance in his 31 December 1981 speech, the *coup*'s leader (Flt-Lt. Rawlings) had declared: 'I ask for nothing less than a revolution'. In the same vein, he was careful to affirm the 'fundamental legitimacy of the PDC's in the Revolution';[21] because they constituted 'the democratic bedrock of the new people's power that the revolution is building'. They were regarded as 'organs through which the oppressed must organise and educate themselves and mobilise . . . to destroy oppressive power relations and institutions . . .'[22]

Notwithstanding these declarations of radical mass mobilization and the praxis that followed there was compelling evidence that the essence of the defence committees fell short of the revolutionary. It increasingly became clear that they were meant to enhance the parameters of the political arena for mass participation. This became evident as the masses accepted the challenge of self-assertion and organized themselves into defence committees to struggle against the existing 'oppressive power relations and institutions', lifestyles and practices. This immediately carried to a new pitch the muted contradictions in the social structure. The national bourgeoisie mobilized the entire state and non-state institutions for political struggle against that sudden onslaught on the political and economic structures of bourgeois rule being staged by the masses.

After barely one year of stout defence of the masses in their confrontation with the bourgeoisie the PNDC rapidly withdrew further state support from them.[23] By the middle of 1983 the regime was openly castigating defence committees and humiliating their militants for wanton excesses. Their vanguard group of left-wing and 'progressive' organizations were also rebuked for infantilism, flunkeyism and adventurism; and new policy guidelines were quickly announced to open up membership of the defence committees to every Ghanaian, irrespective of social class. And in December 1984 the leading organs of the defence committees and other new working-class organs within the management structures of public industrial enterprises were dissolved and replaced with what the TUC dismissed as 'hollow concessions to workers' demand for participation in the management of industry.'[24] In the confusion and disillusionment that followed, a leading of government defence committee spokesman found it necessary to define the revolution to mean that:

> The ordinary people, persons who were deprived of a say in political affairs, who hitherto were inactive [in politics] . . . ought to be drawn to the forefront of political activity. Here, one is talking about democracy. We want a society which is based on social justice, in which though there are people in authority, though there is a stratified society, those at the bottom are brought together in a way that those who are supposed to originally take decisions for and on behalf of the people are given a clue as to what the mass of other people have to say as part of the decision-making process.[25]

It should be emphasized that the government's sudden crackdown on the defence committee militants and leaders of left-wing and progressive organizations was in response to a further deterioration in the Ghanaian economy. For international capitalist interests had teamed up with the national bourgeoisie to deny the PNDC new trade and credit facilities at a time when these were most needed to stop any further damage to the economy. This counter-offensive may be taken as having signalled to the new regime the limits of mass mobilization. In retrospect, however, it must be observed that the CPP regime's response to such an imperialist offensive was the direct opposite. Rather than succumb it assumed a militant anti-imperialist stand backed by militant internal mass politicization, and an emphasis on building state capitalism as a means toward socialism. The options before the CPP were, therefore, clearly understood and a definite commitment made to oppose imperialism and attempt a movement toward socialism; and, in the process, create the necessary momentum toward delinking. For the PNDC to abandon its policy of militant mass mobilization could not, therefore, be taken as helpless acquiescence. It should rather be seen as a logical imperative stemming from bourgeois populism, which further reveals the inherent limitations of this strategy – especially in the periphery; that is, the inability of the bourgeoisie of the periphery (because of its material poverty) to initiate reforms as a pragmatic and prudent political response to an internal crisis. Indeed anything beyond symbolic reforms seems to threaten the fragility of its rule – what Anyang' Nyong'o calls 'hegemonic vacancy'.[26] As an excuse it proclaims the doctrine of the primacy of economics over politics and hence the need to rehabilitate the economy and produce wealth before sharing. The PNDC therefore rapidly deradicalized the politics of the masses and turned its attention fully to the ailing economy.

Economic crisis and response

The deepening of the economic crisis clearly defined the dialectically related options of adjustment back into the world economy and delinking. It also exposed the nature of the relationship between Ghana's economic, political and social structures and the world economy; by so doing the implications of those options were clearly defined. Adjusting into the world economy meant continuing to sustain the capitalist economy of the periphery together with the total superstructural political apparatus. This option immediately imposes a mandatory accommodation with international capital. On the other hand, delinking, as argued above, means to rupture the economic and other links with international capital for the purpose of creating a new structural basis and impetus for autonomous national development. This calls for a radical restructuring of the old social and political relations.

Meanwhile, the national bourgeoisie still dominated not only vital economic establishments such as the Bank of Ghana and the Ministry of Finance and Economic Planning, but also controlled the National Economic Review Commission, the State Commission for Economic Co-operation, and even the PNDC's own secretariat. Those it could not control, such as the National Defence Committee (the national command centre of the defence committees) had been effectively excluded from the centre of decision-making. With the bourgeoisie still entrenched in the bureaucratic centres of state power it was possible to intensify negotiations with the IMF with a view to restoring the confidence of international capital in the Ghanaian economy. The government's Economic Recovery Programme was the product of that renewed confidence: 'With the launching of that programme, international financial institutions and business interests which had previously lost faith in the Ghanaian economy began to renew their interests.'[27] The government was convinced of the need to stop the down-turn in the economy, but it also considered that the only way to accomplish this was to:

> Stimulate production – particularly in the foreign exchange earning sector of the economy – by providing it adequate financial incentives in the form of bonuses for foreign exchange earnings from legal exports . . . [and imposing] taxes or surcharges on all users of foreign exchange.[28]

This was necessary to discourage such unproductive but highly lucrative activities as currency speculation, smuggling and retail trading, while rewarding productive economic activity. The failure of the PNP government to arrest further deterioration of the economy obliged the PNDC to assume that responsibility. Thus, for Chairman Rawlings, the stiff monetary and fiscal measures that his government has been implementing since 1983 are 'the only viable option open to us'.[29]

The impression is created that the government responded to the economic crisis in an independent way[30] – that is, the 'viable options open to us' have been determined on government's own initiative. Some measure of independent assessment and propositions on optimum models of economic stabilization and rehabilitation policy could not be ruled out; this is the task of the economic bureaucracy which the national bourgeoisie dominates. But it is also on record that the structure and direction of what has now become the Economic Recovery Programme (ERP) were carefully worked out by a World Bank Mission, that was in Accra from 4 November 1982,[31] and whose determination of the underlying causes and prescribed solutions have remained the policy framework for the Ghana government since April 1983. The Economic Recovery Programme must therefore be seen as a package of economic policies and programmes that was the product of consensus between the PNDC, IMF and World Bank 'experts'.

For example, the World Bank Mission identified two factors which, in its view, accounted for the country's economic crisis:

> 1) The key weakness of past policies was the combination of virtually absolute protection with an overvalued exchange rate and grossly inadequate export incentives. This system led to misallocation of resources and robbed Ghana's industry of the stimulus of expanding markets and bracing competition.[32]
>
> 2) [the failure of past governments] to take maximum advantage of [Ghana's] natural ability to produce mining, timber and agricultural products . . .[33]

In the end the government itself agreed but only with a hesitant recognition of the external factor. It explained:

> The reasons for this poor performance are of both internal and external origin. A series of past policy decisions and actions had a cumulative adverse effect on the economy. These included: the maintenance of a fixed and highly overvalued exchange rate that discouraged exports and produced huge profits for traders of imported goods; large deficits in the Government's budgets which resulted in inflationary pressures which further distorted effective exchange rates; the imposition of price controls at the manufacturing stage which discouraged production, while deriving excessive profits to the unregulated small-scale trading sector; misallocation and use of import licences which created further inefficiencies and denied critical inputs and equipment to high priority areas.

The external factors were said to include 'The sharp increase in petroleum prices in 1979, followed by a world recession and declining export prices [which] created a major deterioration in the terms of trade.'[34] Having attained this remarkable consensus it was inevitable that among other things the ERP should aim 'at realigning relative prices in favour of the productive sectors (particularly cocoa, timber and mining), improving the financial position of the public sector and encouraging expanded private investments.'[35] From 1983 onwards the hub of economic policy would be staggered devaluations and the rehabilitation of the export sector, mainly cocoa, timber and mining.

Economic adjustments

The current crisis of the world economy has produced quite distinct modifications in the organization of production. Namely, it has led to the global reorganization of production, and new financial and monetary policies rather than new productive investments and the rationalization of production. The up-shot is the internationalization of capital[36] and consequentially the greater integration of Third World countries into the world economy, with devastating effects. For African countries this global crisis has meant not only deteriorating terms of trade. More especially, it has forced a return to that neocolonial situation of dangerous dependence on raw material production and export, because the Africa region generally is discounted as a profitable investment area and therefore has not benefited from the globalization (relocation) of production currently in process. The strengthening of the structural links with African countries has rather taken the form of a determined campaign to confirm the role of such countries in the international division of labour as raw material producers and exporters,[37] because the current global crisis seems to have accentuated the advanced capitalist economies' need for raw materials. I would therefore regard this as the underlying motive for interest the industrialized capitalist countries are showing in Third World countries. Leaders of Third World countries have also been receptive to the West's campaign that to develop an export market for those products (raw materials) for which their respective countries enjoy the greatest comparative advantage on the world market is of benefit to them. They have therefore actively collaborated in strengthening the neocolonial foundations of their respective economies.

The PNDC seems to be no exception! Its Economic Recovery Programme has been tailored to meet the imperatives of the world economy rather than to facilitate a break with it. It is also, in part, a response to the demands of the national bourgeoisie. The main features of the programme may be stated as follows:

1) continuous adjustment in the exchange rate of the nation's currency to the American dollar;

2) drastic reduction in government spending, including removing subsidies for commodities and social services, and retrenchment of labour in the public sector;

3) deregulation of internal and external trade, and promoting natural competition in the market;

4) privatization of public sector enterprises;

5) promotion of export of primary commodities – those in which the country

enjoys the greatest comparative advantage in the IDL; for example cocoa, timber and minerals.

Since 1983, when the Economic Recovery Programme was announced for a phased implementation, the trend has clearly shown an accelerated movement to strengthen the country's neocolonial position in the world economy as a raw material producer and exporter. For example, between April 1983 and December 1985 the government devalued the currency by more than 2,300%. It was the regime's understanding that 'The problems of declining production, foreign exchange crisis, income distribution and budgetary deficits . . . *can all be traced back more or less to this over-valuation of the national currency*'.[38] Devaluation is therefore seen as a central policy instrument for adjusting the economy back on to a growth path.

As part of the recovery package special attention is paid to the cocoa, timber and mining industries, which form the officially designated 'export oriented sector' of the economy. To back-up this sector there is also considerable emphasis on rehabilitating the physical infrastructure, because, 'it has become clear that obsolete roads, railways and ports are causing a bottleneck in evacuating export goods (particularly, timber and minerals)'.[39] In consonance with these, the distribution of capital resources during the three-year period (under two options of a base and higher case) provides for the highest amount (almost 62–65%) of total resources to be invested in fuel, power and crude oil, and on rehabilitating the physical infrastructure; and 30–32% is earmarked primarily for the importation of raw materials and other vital inputs and to revive the export sector (which has 12.3–12.6%), and for the 'other productive sectors' of agriculture and manufacturing (with 18.8–20.2%); the social sector receives a mere 4.6–4.7%. Naturally, this latter sector is regarded as wasteful and unproductive.[40]

Concomitant with these major policy components are policies and programmes designed to strengthen the private sector and liberalize trade, based on the long-held view of the efficiency of private-sector management and market forces. To complete the return to a free market economy, subsidies for public sector enterprises are being withdrawn, allegedly to enhance competitiveness on the market; this has affected the provision of health services, education, water and electricity, also the District Councils which themselves must now pay their employees' salaries. Government is also dismantling import restrictions and reducing excessive tariffs on imported goods. In other words, the Ghana government has embarked on a policy of making the economy safe and profitable for private capital by opening it up more fully to both local foreign capital. The questions raised by this adjustment programme are, is the ultimate goal to delink the economy? and, is this a feasible option? These questions will be dealt with presently.

The politics of economic adjustment

Those aspects of politics that have gone into the formulation and implementation of similar adjustment programmes in Ghana have been brilliantly dealt with by Hutchful.[41] What is clear from Hutchful's article is the determination of Western creditor nation–governments and multilateral financial institutions to secure a programme of austerity that is beneficial to the interest of capital, particularly international capital. It is too early for a total picture of the extent of the political manoeuvres that have shaped, and continue to influence, current adjustment programmes in the country, but the little evidence available is compelling enough.

During the 12 months of official vacillation (1982) about whether to collaborate with the IMF and the World Bank to work out and implement a regime of adjustment programmes and policies, the struggle over direction of government policy was triangular. The PNDC's role was to reconcile all the contradictory claims and where necessary contain whichever seemed irreconcilable. There were claims from the representatives of: i) the national bourgeoisies and other dominant groups such as chiefs and church leaders; ii) workers, left-wing and other progressive organizations who were concentrated in what later became the National Defence Committee, with representation also on the PNDC itself; and iii) Western creditor nation–governments and the IMF–World Bank group.

As a result of the dominant position enjoyed by the national bourgeoisie in both the old and new economic state bureaucracies it was not difficult for the representatives of Western donor country–governments and the two international agencies to achieve a consensus over appropriate policy options before the country; and of course the PNDC could not be said to have acted in a disinterested or neutral manner. It must have thought through the options before it acted; because as early as November 1982 Chairman Rawlings told the nation that his government was determined to pursue an orderly programme of economic recovery.[42] Even more revealing was his assurance to the nation that 'The measures announced in the 1983 Budget are the result of very careful analysis of the state of our economy. That is why it took a whole year to launch an Economic Recovery Programme'.[43] The deciding factor was the regime's inability to secure immediate agreement from all three parties on the principal elements in an economic recovery programme, and the justification for it.

As the positions of the representatives of local and international capital were reconciled the regime's major task was eased. The left and progressive organizations that were still recalcitrant could then be discredited and disorganized. Initially, the PNDC systematically closed existing lines of communication between itself and the left, in complete disregard of the loud protestations from left leaders.[44] Subsequently some of left and progressive organizations that had rallied to the support of the regime at the dawn of the Revolution were attacked and driven to the immediate periphery of state power; others disintegrated. The Defence Committees that had been promoted as organs of popular revolutionary power exclusive to the working masses were suddenly opened up to *all Ghanaians* irrespective of class position or political viewpoint. Their cadres were further subjected to persistent attacks until the Defence Committees were finally transformed into integral organs of the existing bourgeois state.

From 1984, (the second year of the Programme) the national bourgeoisie and their allies – chiefs, leaders of the Christian churches and of some professional associations – have been showering commendations on the government for initiating the Programme. Like the representatives of Western donor nation–governments and multilateral financial bodies, they have demonstrated a remarkable, but unfounded, enthusiasm for the success of the government's economic adjustment policies. Yet only some two years ago (1982–83) this same axis of national and international interests was unanimous in its opposition to the PNDC. Two examples will illustrate this political somersaulting. First, in a despatch titled 'Bishop rallies X'tians behind Government', to the *Ghanaian Times* (26 August 1985), Yvonne Mark-Hansen reported:

> Rt. Rev. Francis W. B. Thompson, Anglican Bishop of Accra, has charged Christians to throw their full weight behind the Government in its effort to reorganise the social and moral lives of Ghanaians . . .

But even more significant is the current trend whereby almost every spokesman of various groups of the national bourgeoisie gives the impression that the Economic Recovery Programme has the final solution to the nation's economic crisis. It has indeed become the god by which they swear and whose glory every Ghanaian is urged to proclaim. All Ghanaians are admonished to apply diligently their individual and collective labour to ensure its success. Such exhortations are deemed to relate equally to the payment of income tax, charging or paying the correct transport fare, and observing the highest level of environmental concern as to tree planting projects to conserve the nation's forests against their rapid destruction (which ironically has been exacerbated by the Programme's impetus for increased timber exports).

The second example is taken from the *People's Daily Graphic*, 20 September 1983:

> The Executive Director of the World Bank, Mr. Mourad Benachenhou, has arrived in Accra from Washington for a two-day consultative meeting with the government on the latest financial policy of the bank relating to Ghana's economic development. . . . The Executive Director praised Ghana for what he called 'a tremendous improvement in the country's economy'. He said everybody at the headquarters of the bank in Washington clearly appreciates the current state of Ghana's economy, adding that Ghana had proved itself capable of absorbing such assistance from credit.

The government's success in restoring the mutual trust and confidence of international and local capitalist interests in the Ghanaian economy in the context of the IDL accounts for its unusual, often excessive, show of confidence and determination. In particular this accounts for the government's relentless commitment to the pursuit of the measures outlined in the Programme in spite of the knowledge that the cost to Ghanaians is enormous. For, all said and done, it has succeeded in re-establishing the conditions necessary for the profitable operation of the two capitals by tactically mobilizing the masses for incorporation into bourgeoisie state political institutions and simultaneously undercutting the left and progressive organizations.

In contrast to this impression of overwhelming commendation and support is the anger, frustration and condemnation that has pervaded the occasional reactions from the left, progressive organizations and the labour movement. For instance in a statement issued on 22 January 1985 by the New Democratic Movement, the Catholic Graduates for Action and some individuals, the economic, social and political aspects of the Economic Recovery Programme were subjected to strong criticism. The following sums up the spirit of their statement:

> In short, instead of the official Recovery Programme, typical neo-colonial policies are being implemented on the orders of the IMF and the World Bank. . . . The objectives of economic transformation have been abandoned . . . both at the political and at the economic level, the commitment to the revolutionary transformation of our society which formed the basis of our support for the 31st December process, has been abandoned both in practice and in official speeches.[45]

The United Revolutionary Front, on the other hand, did not mince words in dismissing the Rawlings government as a 'sell-out'.[46] Later when the full social implications of the Programme touched the health services the Front again attacked the government for betraying the broad masses of the people.

The obvious implication of these contradictory reactions to the Programme is that the 'revolution' is not being made for all classes, but for the dominant class forces only, and for the benefit of local as well as international capital. It also suggests that public policy still lacks popular content, which may account for the deradicalization of the Defence Committees following the bitter political struggles of 1982–83.

Conclusion: prospects for delinking

We have emphasized that any successful delinking project should be a mass movement; only through a mass base can the popular masses, led by the working class, effectively rise to a hegemonic position and shape the content and direction of public policy in their favour. Granted that any such movement would have to move through various stages according to a country's historical situation, one might hypothesize that in the initial phase of a delinking movement the national bourgeoisie would join the masses in a national democratic front against international capital.

The foregoing discussion has touched on the process of radicalizing the Defence Committees after two years of mass onslaught on existing bourgeois political and economic institutions and privileges. By 1984 the emphasis was already shifting from their role as leading organs of industrial discipline and production.[47] and by the close of 1985 this metamorphosis was complete; the defence committees (now renamed CDRs) had become an integral part of bourgeois state political and economic institutions. With that development, the usual mass political upsurge collapsed. Currently the CDRs are better known as agents for promoting community involvement in a communal development effort. Meanwhile the instruments of political and economic power are firmly controlled by the PNDC on behalf of the national bourgeoisie with the active support of 'experts' and bureaucrats – both local and from the IMF–World Bank – within the economic bureaucracy, especially to ensure the success of the Economic Recovery Programme.

It is not possible for us to apply Amin's[48] delinking-adjustment comparative model of development. We could nonetheless gain an insight into the extent to which the social product is being disproportionately or democratically distributed, starting from the government's monetary and fiscal policies. The package of policies emphasizes devaluation and overall price increases for commodities and services, including an increase in the cost of bank loans, in order to achieve a reallocation of resources and benefits from the unproductive to the productive sectors. So far the policy of price rationalization has conferred increased incomes on peasant cocoa, coffee, shea-nut and maize farmers. For example, the price of cocoa which stands at ¢56,000 per ton, assures producers of about 66% of the 1970 price. This contrasts sharply with the 1983 price which was about 39% of the 1970 price. Nonetheless between 1970 and 1982 real incomes had fallen by more than 80%. It should also be noted that cocoa and other cash crop farmers carry a heavy tax burden; in 1985 cocoa farmers provided approximately 11% of total government revenue.

For unskilled and semi-skilled workers, real minimum wage is about 70% of the 1977 level even though in real terms this is twice what it was in 1980. Thus even in the light of recent salary increases the majority of wage earners receive poverty-level incomes which have been estimated at a threshold of ¢4,000–¢5,000 per month. Taken together with the general increase in the price of goods, and social as well as utility services, peasant farmers as well as wage and salary earners cannot be said to be doing well in terms of their share of the social product.

This leaves us with a brief evaluation of the Economic Recovery Programme as an instrument for defending and consolidating national capital generally against foreign capital. A recent official statement revealed that real GDP growth rate reached a target of 5.3 in 1985 following a real rise of 7.6% in 1984. Agriculture grew by 3.9%, and industry by 13.7%. At the same time inflation declined from 40% in 1984 to about 12% in 1985. These constitute a vast improvement on the previous record; but the constraints of the global economy still remain. Accordingly the country could increase its total foreign exchange earnings only marginally: from 45% in 1983–84 to 50% in 1985. The limiting factors have remained; namely deteriorating terms of trade, price instability in the world commodity market, low demand for primary exports of timber, minerals and cocoa, and, of course, the economy's low capacity to increase productivity in the critical export commodities.

These data raise a number of critical questions. The first concerns the dynamics of the recovery programme and its potential to succeed; the second deals with its capacity to then propel the economy beyond the limited objective of 'recovery' on to the path of dynamic and autonomous development and growth. First its potential for success: the emphasis on (i) an export sector dominated not by manufactured but primary commodities; and (ii) a massive infusion of aid, concessionary type official development aid particularly assumes a large measure of flexibility, openness and, above all, growth in the Western economies (Ghana's main trading partners and donor countries). This optimism is unfounded, the evidence points rather to the contrary. The persistent crisis in the world economy continues to manifest itself in the form of growing protectionist policies and budget deficits in the developed industrial economies. The structural problem that the recession has revealed to be inherent in the industrial economies has reversed any commitment to free trade, which means that protectionism will become a far more prominent feature of the industrial economies thereby imposing competing national restrictions on the free flow of international trade.[49]

Clearly, the current movement toward trade wars is restricted mainly to industrial goods – particularly steel, automobiles, textiles and clothing, and electronic equipment. But it also places at potentially grave competitive disadvantage all manufactured products from Third World countries – in particular textiles, but also plastics and even semi-processed goods. With respect to the latter, for instance, EEC Countries are known to be invoking Article 115 of the Treaty of Rome which enables them to temporarily deny access to goods already available in another member country and to impose restrictions on trade with Third World countries particularly to diminish textile imports.[50] Recently under the EEC–ACP conventions even such processed and semi-processed primary commodities as wood and timber products do not escape these barriers.

This trend toward non-tariff trade restrictions inhibits any effort to realize the full potential for growth in Third World economies, especially in those sectors where a high comparative advantage applies. For Ghana this danger is real in the cocoa, mining and timber industries where the country still exports mainly unprocessed, but also processed or semi-processed products (cocoa and timber). The country's real earnings from exports are thus affected, which limits its ability to import vitally needed consumer and industrial items, as well as pay its external debts.

It is important to emphasize that the recession in the world economy has had two additional and equally significant effects on Third World economies: 1) worsening trade terms; and 2) lower capital inflows. The first emanates directly from sluggish demand for primary products which then depresses world market price levels. The second is the result of growing budget deficits, particularly in the industrialized West. This has led to a decline in savings (as a proportion of world income) available for productive investments both at home and abroad. There is therefore an aggressive competition for the small amount of savings available for such investments, with all its attendant fears of insecurity, and so on.[51] According to some observers, even such limited savings are being withdrawn from 'productive investments in favour of financial investments and speculation [while the] remaining productive investments [are being applied] to rationalization rather than expansion'.[52]

These trends in the world economy are already showing negative effects on Ghana's economic recovery programme. The government's 1984 Report (para. 84–85) states:

> Partly because of the unfavourable international market conditions for some of Ghana's export commodities and partly because of the slow response of production to increased inputs and export incentives, projections of export earnings for 1985 and 1986 have been revised downward as compared to the targets set in the original Economic Recovery Programme.

The reason is that 'aggregate exports during 1985–86 will be running $259 million lower than the original targets'. Accordingly, the government's own contribution to financing the Programme has had to be reduced from $3,605 million (69%) to $2,015 million (49%). Overall the Programme has been cut back from the original level of $5,300 million to $4,150 million.

Low export earnings are only part of the problem. The other major constraint is in two parts: i) the slow rate of disbursing promised aid; and ii) the low level of official development aid (ODA) Ghana is receiving. In 1984, only $305 million against the planned $419 million was disbursed to finance the Programme. That raised the undisbursed balance to $498 million by the end of 1984. In the circumstance it is doubtful whether increased disbursements to propel the Programme into full motion can be expected in subsequent years. But if this were possible the government's greatest need is for ODA rather than non-concessional loans, yet the inflow of this type of aid has been quite low. In 1982 ODA to Ghana was only $11.6 per capita compared with the average of $21.4 for all low income countries of sub-Saharan Africa; in 1983 it was still low ($150 million). This level appears to have increased in 1984, but contributions were from only a few sources, mainly multilateral agencies ($293 million) and not donor nation–governments (bilateral sources) which contributed only $20 million (para. 88).

So far the IMF has been a major source of funding since 1983, but after 1985 this ceases (para. 89), leaving the problem of capital inflow unresolved. It also leaves Ghana without an independent source of its own, given the depressed global market situation for its major export commodities. This leaves the government two options: i) non-concessional sources of lending with the usually high interest rates and shorter repayment periods; and ii) scaling-down whatever programme of economic expansion the government may have.

None of these looks propitious. Concerning the first, there is the real danger of exacerbating what is already a heavy debt burden. The effect on the country's development and growth potential will be disastrous. According to the government Report, 'Ghana's debt service payments have been pre-empting an unusually high proportion of the country's export earnings' (para.

89). In 1985 this is expected to take up the greater part of the country's export earnings (para. 59). Thereafter it is likely to be in the region of 66%. Due to this debt service problem 'net official inflows are less than half of the gross official inflows'. Net official inflows as a percentage of gross official inflows are: 1984 = 45; 1986 = 50; 1984–86 = 46 (para. 89). With sluggish exports, and recession in the world economy it is unlikely that Ghana will be able to realize more from its exports to finance her development programmes and also pay its debts, which means that the debt burden may be a permanent fetter on development and growth; and further, that the country must continue to export more and raise fresh loans in a futile endeavour to pay its debt. This future seems less than bright for Ghana's economy because:

> Ghana's debt service ratio for government and government guaranteed debt climbs from 44 percent in 1984 to 61 percent in 1986 but falls to 52 percent by 1988. Excluding arrears, but including the IMF the burden will fall to 47 percent. More than half of the burden in 1988 is on account of the IMF repurchases and charges. It is not clear at this stage whether a new Fund arrangement on extended terms will be possible to reduce net transfers to the Fund in the 1986–88 period. The need for such an arrangement cannot, however, be over-stated since Ghana has little flexibility on its other obligations. . . . Since both payment arrears and Fund obligations nearly come to an end by 1990 (unless, of course, there is another Fund programme), the projected debt service ratio by that year drops sharply to 29 percent. The sensitivity of these projections to actual export performance is easily illustrated. If exports turn out as projected in the low scenario, by 1988, debt service including Fund obligations would amount to 56 percent, some 9 percentage points above the presently projected level.[53]

In spite of its circumlocutory description of the debt problem, this World Bank Report's message still remains unobscure: the debt problem has a strong tendency to remain unresolved; and this leaves economic recovery and growth in the freezers of economic planners and political wizards. Above all, it means that the country will remain a net capital exporter at the expense of national development. For example, the PNDC government had to make cash payments between 1983 and 1984 which, plus 'valuation adjustments' reduced the country's large external arrears from $601 million in 1983 to $287 million by April 1984 (para. 58). This drain on aggregate national wealth should be recognized as one of the severest obstacles to national development and consolidation of national sovereignty.

The continued growth in nominal and real interest rates on international capital markets further compounds the problem of external debt and economic recovery. Yet this trend on the capital market is likely to persist as it is, in fact, a product of the insecurity in the economic environment (mainly inflationary pressures) compounded by political risks currently prevailing in the world economy. Fishlow summarizes the implication of high interest rates for a weak economy such as Ghana's:

The higher the cost, the greater the transfer of income abroad and the lower [the] national income. Interest payments must be made at the expense of other applications of resources. Countries are poorer as a consequence.[54]

When the appreciation of the dollar is also taken into account then the net transfers of capital from debtor countries become politically suicidal and socially unacceptable.

The negative implications of the debt problem become clearer if assessed in terms of its impact on a country's potential for development. As Wolf[55] points out, 'all debt represents a deferred claim on goods (read: a debtor's capital assets) and must ultimately be repaid by the transfer of goods from debtors to creditors . . . The transfer of goods must take the form of a real trade surplus.' Debt, therefore, has its own logic that compels the debtor country–government to push the need to export to absurd limits in order to create a trade surplus to pay off its debt. But such an expected trade surplus may be a false one – imposed by bilateral and multilateral creditor bodies. This is to say that instead of the expected mutual adjustment by both creditors and debtors[56] it has often implied an external adjustment by debtors only. It is this that ensures a reduced trade deficit for debtors (without a similar reduction in trade surplus for creditors) in order only to facilitate the expected transfer of resources from debtor to creditor.

In Ghana, closing the trade deficit gap has implied a reduction in imports, in government spending generally (public sector deficit) and an indirect tax on every user of foreign exchange (including the private sector) through a chain of devaluations of the local currency. The doubtful performance of the principal export sectors as a result of both internal and external constraints has already been noted; the poor production performance of manufacturing enterprises, some of which do export their products should also be noted.[57] Therefore, although the government remarked that in 1985 'imports are projected to rise sharply by 39 per cent in value (33 per cent in volume) over the 1984 level', at the same time, the limitation on imports is acknowledged: 'The import estimates . . . are . . . lower than the aggregate of needs estimated by the relevant Ministries.'[58] But even these conservative estimates seem to have sustained the trade deficit and obliged government to expect additional external loans to finance it.[59] Shortage of consumer goods and industrial raw materials, spare parts and machinery will inevitably persist, however concealed or occasional it may be. This situation, as acknowledged by the 1984 Report, was partly responsible for the poor performance in manufacturing (para. 71). In this way both present and future production is lost, as has been the case, and that imposes additional fetters on Ghana's capacity for industrial growth. It also neutralizes its capacity to adapt foreign technology to local conditions and needs and thereby lay the foundation for an independent economic development and growth.

As already argued, the reported growth of over 6% in the GNP recorded in 1984 was accounted for mainly by improvements in local food production. In that case one could argue (also in the light of the poor performance of the critical export sectors) that the adjustment policies have actually stimulated a limited growth response in the major sectors of the economy. In the light of these poor results government is likely to find it increasingly impossible to relax restrictions on public sector spending, move away from more austerity measures, and embark on a progressive reduction in the country's excessive dependence on imports. For example, the PNDC has embarked on a policy of extensive retrenchment of labour from the public sector, and of not embarking 'on new investments, but rather to raise the capacity utilization of existing investments' (para. 60). This includes manufacturing, in which recovery has been rather sluggish (para. 86). The truth of the matter is that the money is just not there (para. 29), yet government finds itself committed. Hence, 'The broad policies and programmes outlined in the Economic Recovery Programme will be maintained.'

Despite the fact that since 1966 Ghana has made no headway with the IMF–World Bank programme of structural adjustments, the present regime has deemed it necessary to implement an 'advanced version' of this package. The question now is, why do regimes persist in the face of overwhelming historical evidence of the futility of conventional wisdom? According to Fishlow,[60] regimes become committed to such policy prescriptions because they want to be able to pay their debt to avoid a situation in which a default would disrupt trade with traditional partners and also cut off the 'net capital flows they need and expect in the future'. This is a genuine fear which in the Ghanaian case is fully buttressed by the experience gained during the early years of the NRC/SMC regime.[61] There is also the immediate experience of the PNDC government itself when, through a greater part of the 1982–83 period, Western trading partners (including neighbouring Nigeria) as well as bilateral and multilateral creditor bodies placed a *de facto* embargo on all trade and related transactions with the country.

This explanation, however, does not sufficiently address the material and ideological pressures that shape the conduct not only of regimes but also of the dominant classes. These pressures emanate from both the world economy and the social structure of the Third World country concerned. In the first instance the current world economic crisis has unleashed a fresh onslaught on Third World countries in a bid by the West to secure a firm control over all major sources of raw materials, especially strategic minerals. This also means keeping such countries within the world capitalist economy, which leads to the second tendency. The bourgeois classes of Third World countries are compelled by the crisis of accumulation unleashed by the global crisis to make demands that coincide with those held by the bourgeoisies of the advanced capitalist countries. That is, they demand greater liberalization of international trade in order to reconstruct their economies along capitalist lines that constitute the essence of the New International Economic Order.[62] The various accords signed between the EEC–ACP countries are a classic example of this collaboration between the bourgeoisies of the capitalist countries and their counterparts in the Third World countries.

This attitude of the bourgeoisies of Third World countries stems from the fact that they have become 'compradorized'. That is, they have shed their nationalist–patriotic outlook on the ideological basis upon which they have based their successive attempts to implement the bourgeois project in their countries since independence.[63] The recurrence of the global crisis with its devastating effect on capital accumulation in Third World countries therefore automatically induces a process of mutual policy adjustments (on the part of bilateral–multilateral bodies in the world economy on one hand and Third World bourgeoisies and their political representatives on the other) to modify the existing IDL for their mutual benefit. But for Third World countries, such structural adjustments mean a further neocolonization – as exporters of raw material products. Under the Stabex scheme of the Lomé Convention II signed between the EEC–ACP countries, for example, it is more beneficial for an African country to export fruits or palm oil to Europe than to another Third World country. The emphasis is on the export of primary commodities. Under Ghana's Economic Recovery Programme this has meant a growing emphasis on the export of cocoa, timber and minerals to enable it to pay foreign debts, which are nonetheless growing daily. This is why the country has been committing a greater percentage of its export earnings to debt settlement obligations and thereby become a net exporter of capital since the 1960s.[64]

Because this situation represents a conjuncture of global and national forces, successive regimes have always inclined toward creating a congenial political climate to support their policies of collaboration with international capital. In this regard, it should be recalled that the PNDC's primary task during the 1982–83 period was to establish '*the economic, social and political conditions [necessary] for the launching of a three year Medium-Term Plan in 1984*' (my emphasis). Thus by the end of 1984 the Defence Committees, which had become the leading organs in the masses' struggles for political and economic democracy, had been deradicalized and brought effectively under the control of the old state apparatus. Its cadres, on the other hand, had been rebuked and demoralized.[65]

The re-establishment of appropriate political conditions also represented the conjuncture of expectations of leading agents of international and local capital. The World Bank's 1984 report on Ghana[66] specifically demanded that the activities of the Defence Committees should be restrained. This 'command' was based on the conviction that the contribution of the private sector toward ensuring the success of the Economic Recovery Programme depended on whether the regime would be able to foster a favourable 'general political and social milieu . . . [therefore] while the People's Defence Committees (PDCs) and Workers Defence Committees (WDCs) can play useful roles in increasing productivity their exuberance and misplaced enthusiasm may have the potential of causing unintended harm in the economy and interfering with the efforts the Government is making towards economic recovery.' The heart of the matter is bluntly that the interests of labour and capital are irreconcilable. The triumph or resurgence of one requires the defeat or subjugation of the other. Under the PNDC's Economic Recovery Programme labour has to be suppressed.

This World Bank Report clearly indicates that donor governments and agencies demanded the establishment of this political and other conditions as prerequisites for any form of assistance. For example, the Bank had insisted that though the government had made determined efforts to improve private sector confidence in the economy the signals to this sector still remained contradictory and unclear. Among other demands aimed at clearing such doubts were that, as part of its liberalization policies, the regime should clarify the role, functions and limitations of the WDCs, with wide publicity. Initially the donor governments and agencies which were part of the Consultative Group meeting held in Paris in 1983 (after 13 years' break) were sceptical about the government's ability to meet those requirements. To confound that scepticism the government had to take additional measures – in particular, to foster a congenial political environment for capital. Once these conditions had been met the government's Economic Recovery Programme received the IMF's full backing for one year, ending 30 June 1984. Initially, however, the deep-seated doubts of bilateral donors at the time accounted for the low pledges of aid and also slow disbursement of pledged aid during the first year of the Programme. Even IMF officials first wanted to be assured that the regime had met 'the fund's performance criteria . . .'

It is remarkable that the Fund and Bank officials should make such demands on the PNDC; because Fund officials had been in Ghana from July 1982 and worked closely with government officials to produce the Economic Recovery Programme – 'a programme of far-reaching reforms which was unveiled with the 1983 budget in April 1983'. Evidently, the settlement of a framework for structural adjustment merely sets the stage for bilateral and multilateral agencies to continue to influence the formulation and implementation of a country's policies and programmes.

What then are the implications of the Economic Recovery Programme for delinking the Ghanaian economy from the IDL? It would appear from the foregoing analysis that the prospects for remaining within, or opting out of, the IDL are a function of the balance of political forces in any particular society as well as the dominant ideological tendencies within the organs of state, especially government. Where the state merely functions to reinforce the existing dominant ideological and class dispositions that find co-operation and co-optation within the existing IDL beneficial, the painful process of delinking becomes immediately impossible. Conversely, where it becomes a catalyst for dissolving the existing social structure and facilitating the emergence of a new constellation of class forces that confirm socialism into a position of political dominance, it becomes feasible to wage a determined struggle against international capital's hegemony. Delinking then becomes a practical possibility.

In Ghana since 1982 the trend seems to emphasize a congruence of the dominant ideological viewpoint in government on one hand and the dominant ideological tendencies in the Ghanaian social structure on the other. Two primary strands in the policies and programmes of the PNDC underscore this: i) the prominent role the regime has conferred on foreign private capital and the private sector as the principal engine of economic recovery and growth; and ii) the rapid pace at which the Defence Committees were neutralized as the decisive political weapon in the struggle of the masses against exploitation and political subjugation. The resurgence of the private sector to a position of dominance has occurred not only on the independent political initiative of the national bourgeoisies, but become possible through the active and open intervention of international capital through the mediation of the state, IMF and the World Bank. The emphasis on free enterprise, free market, increased credit and other incentives to the private sector is part of a grand policy package designed to enhance private accumulation through exorbitant profit. It is this that immediately renders labour assertiveness and the general upsurge of the masses (which is becoming a principal feature of Ghanaian politics) entirely incompatible with the dominance of capital.

In short, the policies and programmes being implemented by the PNDC government with the active support of bilateral and multilateral donor agencies perpetuate and deepen the exploitation of the working masses. The mass dismissals of labour, the poverty-line wages and salaries, withdrawal of subsidies on a wide range of social services, deregulation of commodity prices, and so on are merely specific ramifications of the profound level of exploitation taking place. This degradation of labour is also evidence of the importance the regime attaches to labour generally; that is, as an inconsequential factor in production. Any regime that does not value labour as a critical factor of production cannot expect to develop society successfully. For a low regard for labour not only exacerbates the problems of unemployment and under-employment, but also, inevitably affects the level of technical and scientific development of society generally. In the event of such unmitigated depression in scientific and technical development the impetus for autonomous development is automatically suppressed, thus probably delaying society's development indefinitely.

Epilogue

The future of the Ghanaian economy and society is bleak, even on the basis of IMF projections. The IMF's revised annual *World Economic Outlook* predicted that the cumulative Third World debt would rise from $943 billion to $990 billion in 1987. The potential success of an economic development model based on the strength of primary commodity exports is also unlikely according to this publication's projections. The prediction for Third World non-oil commodity prices, except for coffee, remains low; and the terms of trade for developing countries will worsen. Cocoa prices on the London commodity market for the last week of April 1986 were the lowest in 30 months and this tendency is likely to persist while demand continues to be low. All this makes the future rather ominous given the additional facts that real interest rates and inflation in the industrial economies may continue their upward swing; and that recession and protectionism are likely to remain major features of the world economy. The

IMF-sponsored structural adjustment policies and programmes being implemented by the Ghanaian government are therefore likely to perpetuate the neocolonial foundations of its economy.

Ghana's Economic Recovery Programme therefore exposes once more the IMF's neocolonial role in so far as this institution operates globally to recycle new credits from Third World countries to the industrialized West, and in so far as it seeks through its various policies to make the Third World safe for multilateral capital. The worsening of the global crisis and breakdown of attempts to reform the international economic order may as well promise, as Frank predicts,[67] a great new popular beginning toward delinking.

Notes

1. Frank, A. G., 'Rhetoric and Reality of the New International Economic Order' in H. Addo, (ed.) *Transforming the World Economy?* London, Hodder & Stoughton, 1984, pp. 165–203.

2. Frank, A. G., *Capitalism and Under-development in Latin America*, New York, Monthly Review Press, 1967.

3. 'A Note On the Concept of Delinking'. *International Foundation For Development Alternative* (Dossier 50) November/December, (1985), p. 38.

4. Ibid.

5. Tandon, Yash, 'Some Theoretical Aspects of the Delinking Debate and the Experience of Zimbabwe and Uganda in this context' mimeo, 1985.

6. Hansen, E. & Collins, P., 'The Army, the State, and the "Rawlings Revolution" in Ghana' mimeo. Department of Political Science, University of Ghana, Legon, (n.d.) p. 11.

7. Radio & Television Broadcast to the Nation on Thursday 29 July 1982 in *A Revolutionary Journey*. (Selected Speeches of Flt-Lt. J. J. Rawlings) Vol. 1, Accra, Information Services Department.

8. Ghana, *Seven Year Development Plan*, Accra, SPC, (n.d.), p. 3.

9. Ghana, *National Assembly Debates*, Accra, SPC. Vol. 38, Col. 10.

10. Beckman, Bjorn, *Organising the Farmers*, Uppsala, Scandinavian Institute of African Studies, 1976, discusses structure of this peasant constituency and their organization's politics; and Owusu, Maxwell, *Uses and Abuses of Political Power*, Chicago, University of Chicago Press, 1970, provides a case study from the Agona Swedru area of the Central Region.

11. Austin, Dennis, *Politics in Ghana*, London, Oxford University Press, 1964, is still a useful resource on the social basis of the CPP.

12. For a discussion of these see Krassowski, A., *Development and The Debt Trap*, London, ODI, 1974.

13. For instance by 1966 the real incomes received by salaried workers and farmers were far below compared to 1950s levels. See Ewusi, K., *Economic Inequality In Ghana*, Accra, CODESRIA, 1977, pp. 28, 51.

14. Szereszewski, R., 'The Macro-Economic Structure', in Birmingham, W. and others, *A Study of Contemporary Ghana*. Vol. 1 (The Ghana Economy), London, George Allen & Unwin, 1966.

15. Bank of Ghana (1966). *Report of the Board for the Financial Year Ended 30 June*.

16. Ninsin, Kwame, A., *Political Struggles in Ghana*, Accra, Tornado Publications. Forthcoming, Chs 2–4.

17. *A Revolutionary Journey*, op. cit.

18. This point was underscored again during Chairman Rawlings' *Easter Broadcast* Accra, 1986.

19. See also Central Bureau of Statistics, *Economic Survey 1981*, Accra, State Publishing Corporation, 1984.

20. *A Revolutionary Journey*, 1981, op. cit.

21. Speech delivered at a May Day Rally, 1982, in ibid.

22. Address Delivered at the Hogbetsetso Festival at Anloga, 1982, in ibid.

23. Ninsin, Kwame A., *Ghanaian Politics After 1981: Revolution or Evolution?*, Accra, Tornaso Publications. Forthcoming.

24. Ghana Trades Union Congress: 'Memorandum to the PNDC–Position Paper on Present National Situation', Accra, 12 February 1985.

25. Akrasi-Sarpong, Y., 'Building PDCs into Organs of Popular Power', *People's Daily Graphic*, 1984, p. 3.

26. Anyang' Nyong'o, Peter, 'State and Society in Africa', *Africa Development*, Vol. VIII, No. 3, 1983.

27. Radio & Television Broadcast to the Nation on the 1983 Budget Statement 2 May 1983, in *Forging Ahead* (Selected Speeches of Flt-Lt. J. J. Rawlings), Vol. 2, Accra, Information Services Dept. (n.d.) p. 19.

28. Ibid., pp. 17–18.

29. Ibid., p. 16.

30. Flt-Lt. J. J. Rawlings, Chairman of the PNDC. Speech Delivered at a Workers' Solidarity Rally in Accra, 25 November 1982.

31. See various *Background Papers*. Prepared for the *Ghana: Policies and Programs for Adjustment Report*. No. 4702-GH issued on 3 October 1983.

32. Ibid., 'Manufacturing Sector', para. 90.

33. Ibid., p. 1.

34. Economic Recovery Programme, November 1983, para. 26–7.

35. Republic of Ghana: *Economic Recovery Programme, 1984–86. Review of Progress in 1984 and Goals for 1985, 1986*. Report Prepared by the Government of Ghana for the Second Meeting of the Consultative Group for Ghana, Paris, December 1984, Accra, November 1984, para. 33.

36. Lipiets, A., (1985) 'The World Crisis: the Globalisation of the General Crisis of Fordism'. *Institute of Development Studies Bulletin*, April, Vol. 16, No. 2, pp. 7–9.

37. The most recent elaboration of this trend is contained in World Bank, *Accelerated Development in Sub-Sahara Africa: An Agenda for Action* (The Berg Report), Washington D.C., 1981.

38. *Economic Recovery Programme*, November 1983 para. 63 (my emphasis).

39. *Economic Recovery Programme*, November 1984 para. 86.

40. *Economic Recovery Programme*, November 1983 Vol. 1.

41. Hutchful, E., 'International Debt Renegotiation: Ghana's Experience'. *Africa Development* Vol. 9, No. 2, 1984.

42. Speech delivered at a Workers' Rally in Accra, 25 November 1982.

43. Radio & Television Broadcast on the 1983 Budget in *Forging Ahead*.

44. See n. 23 above.

45. 'Statement on the Political and Economic Situation of Ghana', Accra, 22 January 1985.

46. 'Press Statement on The Third Anniversary of the 31 December Coup', Accra, n.d.

47. Jonah, Kwesi, 'Rawlings Revolution: Two Years After'. *Journal of African Marxists*, 1984, No. 5, pp. 25–31.

48. Amin, Samir, (1984) in Addo, H., (ed.) *Transferring the World Economy?* London: Hodder & Stoughton, in association with the United Nations University.

49. For a discussion of this new protectionism see Shultz, S., 'New Protectionism: Forms and Consequences in the Industrial Sector'. *Economics* (Tubingen, FRG) Vol. 31, pp. 7025, and Frank, A. G., 'Rhetoric and Reality of the New International Economic Order' in Addo, H. (ed.), op. cit., pp. 165–203.

50. Shultz, S., op. cit. p. 11.

51. Wolf, M., 'Two Faces of a Coin: International Trade and Debt'. *Institute of Development Studies Bulletin*, Vol. 16, No. 1, p. 10, January 1985.

52. Trobel, F. et al., 'Changing Patterns of World Market Integration of Third World Countries' Paper Presented at the Seventh International Colloquium on the World Economy, Dakar 20–22 May, 1985.

53. World Bank, *Ghana: Towards Structural Adjustment*. Vol. 1 (The Main Report). Report No. 5854-GH 7 October 1985, p. 94.

54. Fishlow, A., 'The Debt Crisis: Round Two Ahead', in Feinberg, R. and Kallab, V. (eds), *Adjustment Crisis in the Third World*, New Brunswick & London, Transaction Books, 1984, p. 45.

55. Wolf, M., op. cit. p. 9.

56. Ibid., p. 9.

57. *Economic Recovery Programme*. November 1984 para. 71.

58. Ibid., para. 44.

59. See for instance the speech by Addo, J. S. (Governor of the Bank of Ghana) delivered at the inauguration of the National Planning Committee of INDUTECH 1986 (Accra, 30 July 1985).

60. Fishlow, A., op. cit. p. 58.

61. The NRC/SMC regime repudiated (on 5 February 1972) all the country's bad debt of $94 million owed to British creditors, and unilaterally rescheduled the so-called good ones which amounted to $200 million in suppliers' credit on IDA terms; also rejected outright the moratorium interests that had accumulated from previous debt settlement agreements. For a detailed account of the politics of Ghana's debt resettlement negotiations, see Hutchful, op. cit.

62. See Frank in Addo, H., op. cit.

63. Amin, Samir., 'Self-reliance and the New International Economic Order' in Addo, H., op. cit. pp. 212–13.

9. Structural Adjustment or Delinking: The Question Posed

Azzam Mahjoub*

The Ghanaian case study concludes our presentation of various African experiences. Throughout the analyses we have attempted to interpret the specific features of the attempts at 'positive' adjustment, positive in the sense both of redistributing power to the nation-state and the popular classes and challenging the relationship to the capitalist world economic system. Our method of interpretation was organized around the concepts of adjustment, readjustment, internal and external delinking; these are the key concepts at the centre of the theoretical underpinnings of our investigation. As foreshadowed in our introduction we shall now provide the theoretical analysis necessary to spell out the problematic at the base of our method of interpretation that, so far, has remained implicit.

The theoretical clarifications will deal with the key concepts that make up the underlying schema, that is, adjustment and delinking. The basic proposition is that the concepts of adjustment and delinking refer to three theoretical areas, those of capital, of capitalist world accumulation and of transition and building socialism.

It is the law of value that brings these three areas together to form the theoretical site at which they converge and overlap; this is the second main proposition. In other words, as has hitherto been assumed, the law of value is at the centre of the theoretical field or benchmark to which the adjustment–delinking problematic refers, a field or benchmark with three dimensions: capital, worldwide accumulation and socialist transition.

The law of value and capital

What is the law of value? The answer lies in the theoretical area of capital:

> Every child knows that a nation which ceased to work, I will not say for a year, but even for a few weeks, would perish. Every child knows, too, that the masses of products corresponding to the different needs require different and quantitatively determined masses of the total labour of society. That this *necessity* of the *distribution* of social labour in definite proportions

* Translated by A. M. Berrett

cannot possibly be done away with by a *particular form* of social production but can only change the *form* in which it *appears*, is self-evident. No natural laws can be done away with. What can change, in historically different circumstances, is only the *form* in which these laws operate. And the form in which this proportional distribution of labour operates, in a state of society where the interconnection of social labour is manifested in the *private exchange* of the individual products of labour, is precisely the *exchange value* of these products.

Science consists precisely in demonstrating *how* the law of value operates.[1]

The law of value is thus a historical social form of the necessary law of the distribution of social labour. It both regulates the distribution of social labour and expresses particular social relations of production. It accounts for the particular social forms acquired by the products of labour in a commodity economy. The regulatory function of the law of value, as the proportional distribution of social labour, is carried out indirectly through the intermediary of the market and the exchange of commodities.[2]

How can that be?

In manufacturing, the *iron law of proportionality* subjects definite numbers of workers to definite functions, but chance and the arbitrary play their unregulated game in the distribution of producers and their means of production among the various branches of social labour. It is true that the various spheres of production have a constant tendency to return to equilibrium . . .[3]

This tendency towards equilibrium at the heart of the law of value works through the movement of market prices. In other words, the law of value determines the movement by which the necessary adjustments (within production and circulation) and the distribution of social labour are effected. This movement is that of market prices. Through the shifts and fluctuations of market prices that it determines, the law of value imposes the social equilibrium of production. 'The law of value acts here exclusively as an immanent law, as a blind natural law; it imposes the social equilibrium of production in the midst of that production's accidental fluctuations.'[4]

Thus the law of value presides over the movement of market prices, through which the proportional distribution (equilibrium of social production) of social labour is effected. Through its action, the law of value meets two requirements: 1) the determination of the magnitude of the mean social labour that needs to be expended for the production of each type of commodity; and 2) the quantitative distribution of the social labour necessary for the production of the various types of use-values proportional to quantitatively defined needs.

These two requirements, which are at the heart of the law of value, are realized through competition in the market where 'chance and the arbitrary play their unregulated game'. Through its action and through the movement of market prices that it determines, the law of value ensures a double sanction, in relation to: a) the expenditure of labour (individual value) compared to the expenditure of necessary social labour (social value or market value); b) the total expenditure of the mean social labour effectively expended in the production of a use-value compared to the extent of social need.[5]

Thus, in short, the law of value is the abstract theoretical concept of the movement through which the division and distribution of social labour between branches is accomplished.

In the framework of a simple commodity economy, this distribution is accomplished in such a way that all branches acquire equal values for the same expenditure of a quantity of labour. In other words, a definite quantity of labour (of equal intensity and quality) brings in a roughly equal value to the various producers in the various branches. This distribution is regulated by the mechanisms of market prices, and these prices revolve around the social value or market value corresponding to the mean quantity of labour socially necessary.[6] The magnitude of this social value is determined by the level of development of the productive forces. Differences in productivity between the various units of production of a given branch mean that the individual values may be different from the social value; the latter will impose itself on all, and sanctions them both positively and negatively, producing flows and counterflows of social labour.

Market value enables a commodity produced in different technical conditions (different productivities) to have only a single market value, which will eliminate the variety of conditions of production (positive or negative sanctions) while being the result of this latter. The magnitude of social value is thus directly related to labour productivity, and changes in labour productivity thus affect the magnitude of social value and hence the market price and thus influence the distribution of labour. Given the variations in productivity it is obvious that in the event of a quantitative preponderance of production units producing in the best conditions, the market value which will impose itself, and around which the market price will gravitate, will be determined by this higher productivity labour.

It is, then, this social value or market value that is the centre around which market prices revolve; it is the same as the market price only on condition that the quantity of commodities available on the market corresponds to the quantum of social need. Thus, the conditions prevailing on the market, supply and demand, determine the gaps between market prices and market values, the latter remaining the centres around which the fluctuations of supply and demand cause the market prices to vary.

In other words, the law of value stipulates that commodities are exchanged not according to relative prices proportional to their value, but according to market prices revolving around a certain mean level represented by the market value. In the framework of capitalism this stabilizer takes in the norm of the equalization of profit rates. Under capitalism, commodities are not exchanged simply as such (products of the labour of simple commodity producers) but as the products of capitals which claim to share in the total mass of surplus values according to their size, equal shares for equal size. It is here that the concept of the price of production comes in.

> What we have said here of market value also holds for the price of production . . . The price of production is regulated in each sphere . . . But it is again the centre around which the daily market prices revolve, and at which they are balanced out in definite periods.[7]

Thus the law of value operates here through the price of production, and this latter corresponds to the tendency towards equilibrium in the distribution of capital and hence of social labour among the various branches. In other words, here the distribution of labour is primarily governed by the distribution of capital. The basic principal of the distribution of capital is, as we have stressed, that *capitals of equal values engaged in different productive processes bring in the same profit.*

$$\frac{r_1}{C_1} = \frac{r_2}{C_2} = r \qquad \begin{array}{l} r = \text{rate of profit} \\ C = \text{capital engaged} \end{array}$$

On the basis of *freedom of competition*, the tendency towards the formation of a uniform rate of profit through transfers of capital (with different organic compositions) makes it possible to achieve a balance between the branches. The price of production indicates the mean price through which precisely this equilibrium is established, that is the ending of transfers from one branch to another. The price of production constitutes the specific instrument in capitalism, based on freedom of competition, that enables it to equalize profits through transfers of capital and thus obtain the spontaneous (*post facto*) distribution of productive forces.[8] The alignment of the various rates of profit on the general rate is an end-product; it is made possible and effective thanks to the movement of capitals and that of course assumes competition and mobility.

In conclusion, this theoretical digression enables us to grasp that the law of value[9] is the law that governs the system of price formation, the system by whose movement adjustments and readjustments in the distribution of capitals and productive forces are effected. The concept of social value (which in the capitalist mode of production includes the norm of the equalization of rates of profit) is central; the magnitude of this social value is directly related to the productivity of social labour.

Such then is the first theoretical area to which the law of value refers.

Our second area is constituted by the Capitalist World Economic System (CWES) and hence by the theory of worldwide capitalist accumulation.

Law of value, capitalist world economic system and world capitalist accumulation

Our argument contains three main hypotheses:

1) there is a World Economic System that is becoming all-embracing and its process of formation and expansion is and remains fundamentally polarizing and reproductive of unequal development;

2) the basic law that governs the process of accumulation within the CWES is the expression of the law of value operating increasingly predominantly at the level of the CWES as a whole;

3) the law of value as it operates today at the world level, while it is all the time tending to homogenize the space in which it acts, maintains and reproduces the bases of the unequal distribution of productive forces worldwide.

The basic premise is the existence of a totality called the CWES that came into being in the late 16th–early 17th centuries; it started from Europe and gradually extended and developed, tending to cover the whole world. Thus the dominant tendency today is towards complete freedom of movement of the factors of production and hence the total realization of the law of value.

Put differently, the process by which the world system was formed and expanded, 'the commoditization of the world', is at the same time a process of ceaseless enlargement of the area in which the law of value operates. The strong tendency, predominant today, is towards the pre-eminence of international values. The basic principle of the law of value is in action worldwide: *a simple unit of labour time of the same intensity provides here and everywhere the same quantity of value.*

Of course, different quantities of commodities of the same type, produced by different countries at the same time, possess different national values (given differences in the conditions of production and unequal distribution of productive forces worldwide) nevertheless, the tendency is towards the formation of a world social (or market) value, the centre around which market prices revolve.

Thus, our first premise signifies that the CWES is a process that is 'totalizing',[10] that is, that the dominant tendency today is towards the constitution of a single space where value is created and realized. Our present world thus constitutes a single social space structured by capitalist relations of production, in which the law of value operates. This process of totalization of the CWES is often called transnationalization.[11] Productive systems and exchange flows cross national boundaries and obey logics that go beyond those of nations and are predominantly global. Seen from this viewpoint, transnational firms are seen as active agents of this process.

All contemporary societies are integrated to varying degrees into the CWES in the process of becoming worldwide. From its origins, this integration has occurred on a base that produces and reproduces unequal development and hence the polarization of centres and peripheries.

Thus the CWES designates a dynamic historical totality constituted on the basis of the creation and maintenance of the inequality and polarization of productive forces between countries. Whence the contradictory tendency that exists within the dynamic of the CWES towards homogenization of the world space and reproduction of heterogeneity and inequality between centres and peripheries.

How does the law of value operating worldwide create and reproduce this dual dynamic of homogenization/heterogenization?

The controversy over unequal exchange

Arghiri Emmanuel's thesis of unequal exchange constitutes a first response, which is in fact a particular interpretation of the functioning of the worldwide law of value. What does this thesis argue?

The world market is dominated by a definite law of price formation, a modified form of expression of the law of value, the modification being due to the immobility of labour. Thus, the law of unequal exchange is the modified expression of the law of value operating worldwide. Unequal prices of labour and unequal rates of surplus value, serving originally in the formation of a system of prices of production, involve unequal exchange.[12] At the heart of the modified functioning of the law of value then, lies unequal development, the unequal distribution of productive forces, in short the unequal international division of labour.

Thus the law of value (or the law of the formation of prices of production) operates through unequal exchange and the latter manifests itself in a movement to distribute value (surplus value) towards the countries of the centre (at a high rate of surplus value) from the countries in the periphery (at a lower rate of surplus value) producing and reproducing an unequal and polarized distribution of productive forces.

The law of unequal exchange is thus *one* interpretation of the functioning of the worldwide law of value. Can the law of value be reduced to the law of unequal exchange? The answer to that question opens up other theoretical possibilities.

To start with we have, as already suggested, a whole called the CWES with the pre-eminence of *international values*; that means that (notwithstanding the social relations of production within which they are produced) all products, because they are intended for the world market, are world commodities with a single value (social value or market value);[13] in addition, the strong hypothesis here is that this world social value (or price of production) is that obtained in conditions of production that reduce it to the minimum. Thus, given the increasing opening-up of each country to the world market, each country's system and movement of price formation is ever more predominantly marked by the functioning of the worldwide law of value.

Given the rather weak tendency towards the existence of truly specific products to be exchanged, the vast majority, if not all goods produced in the so-called countries of the periphery, are also produced in the centre, where different production conditions obtain. Thus the world system of price formation (governed by the law of value) is established in a world market where producers (from the centre and the periphery) produce in different conditions of productivity.

From this viewpoint, the *essential proposition* is that the world value (social market value or price of production) *will align itself on the value prevailing in the high productivity economies* (higher $\frac{C}{V}$).

Thus, the law of value, such as it governs worldwide price formation, implies world social values (that stabilize market prices) determined by the level of productive forces at the centre of the CWES. The law of value as it operates within the CWES is reflected in the real world by *adjustment* of the system of relative prices of the periphery to that existing and dominant worldwide, a system determined by the level (and the structure of distribution) of productivity within the economies of the centre.

Here a new proposition is in order: adjustment to the CWES via the law of value (system of world prices) produces and reproduces the unequal distribution of productive forces worldwide.

In practice, the law of value as it operates within the CWES, governs the formation of a system of worldwide prices, and through that of a system of distribution of productive forces (flows, counterflows, transfer, adjustments, readjustments) such that a tendency develops to the relative homogenization of levels of productivity within the different spheres in the centre (whence a tendency to a relative homogenization in the system of rewarding labour and capital). Given the differences in levels of productivity, and in the structure of distribution of productivity within various branches in the periphery, *adjustment* to the system of world prices (via the action of the law of value) tends to maintain and even deepen the unequal development of productive forces between branches (agriculture and industry) and to reproduce the growing heterogeneity in the rewards of capital and labour.

In fact, the system of world prices, to which the periphery adjusts, because it reflects the level (and structure of distribution) of productivity, constitutes the structural economic space within which unequal development between centre and periphery, and within the periphery between branches (notably agriculture and industry) is reproduced.

The law of value, as it governs the world system of formation of relative prices, constitutes in effect the frame of reference of what is known as 'economic rationality'. Rationality signifies, in fact, the interdiction 'objectified' by reference to true pricing (truth of the law of value in fact) on gradually liquidating sectoral and social disparities[14] in terms of productivity and in terms of the reward to producers in the various spheres (notably agriculture and industry); these disparities constitute the essence of the manifestation of the law of unequal and polarized development within the CWES.

Adjustment to the CWES means acceptance of: a) submission to the functioning of the worldwide law of value. It involves recourse to the criteria of functioning of production units, choice of projects for investment in which economic and financial profitability is established by reference to the law of value, that is, to the system of world prices; b) the *de facto* impossibility of embarking in the periphery on economic programmes that challenge the dominated subordinated position within the international division of labour, the international division of labour being nothing but the expression of the unequal development of productive forces resulting from the action of value.[15] Whence the decisive importance given to external exchanges and comparative advantage.

Adjustment to the CWES, that is, adjustment to the system of world prices governed by the law of value, thus presupposes acceptance of/submission to the global functioning of the CWES. Socio-politically, this assumes a particular class structure and distribution of power.

We have emphasized that the law of value assumes a social form, that is, that it manifests itself and acts in the framework of a particular configuration of relations of production and hence of classes and class alliances. The law of value, such as it operates, and to whose action the producer in the periphery adjusts himself rather than being subjected to it, presupposes the dominance[16] of capitalist relations of production; it is the effect of these relations and of the class and political power systems that correspond to them.

The law of value operates in capitalism on the basis of class relations based on an unequal distribution of the means of production (concentration of capitals, land and so on) and the creaming-off of the surplus (surplus value) to the benefit of the dominant classes.

In this relationship the law of value such as it operates worldwide brings into play the dual principle of adjustment and the existence/domination of exploiting classes.

This principle, that is, adjustment to the CWES through acceptance/submission to the functioning of the law of value presupposes the presence and domination of exploiting classes (to whose benefit the distribution of the means of production and the creaming-off of the surplus is done) is one allied to the dominant social forces in this CWES; just as domination of the exploiting classes presupposes adjustment to the CWES, that is acceptance of/submission to, the functioning of the law of value. This single principle signifies that adjustment to the CWES is a fact underlying two facets (one internal, one external); the two facets are the terms of a single reality.

This simple proposition is essential, as it underlies the dialectical nature of the processes of challenging the operative principle of adjustment,[17] *delinking*. Delinking is apprehended at this level as the voluntary and deliberate attempt to neutralize the effects and manifestations of the worldwide law of value; it is a matter, in fact, of transforming the socio-political forms that constitute the basis of its concrete historical expression.

It is only the form in which it [the law of value that distributes social labour][18] appears that can be changed. No natural laws can be done away with. What can change, in historically different circumstances, is only the form in which these laws operate.[19]

Delinking at this level thus does not signify the negation or suppression of the law of value, but the conscious alteration of the ways in which this law acts and manifests itself, and does so on the basis of a transformation of social class relations that constitute the socio-historical form of the law of value.

Thus, the final proposition is that delinking takes on a fundamentally political dimension involving the replacement of old social forms, and class relations and alliances, by new forms of social relations and alliances.

This last proposition opens up the third theoretical area to which the law of value refers, that of the socialist transition.

Law of value and building of socialism

At the historically concrete level, this area covers several so-called socialist experiences inaugurated by the Bolshevik revolution. Initially, then, there were attempts to transform the social system and the establishment of new class alliances designed to promote another type of development of productive forces than the one that had prevailed hitherto, and resulting from adjustment to the CWES.

These various experiences (however we judge their scope and historical limits) concern us from the viewpoint of the theoretical framework of our problematic of delinking. Here and there, conscious and deliberate (or imposed) processes initiated by 'anti-systemic' social forces (a worker–peasant alliance) have been launched to modify (not negate) in concrete historical situations the form in which the law of value operates. On the basis first of a transformation in the appropriation of the means of production, and a new class configuration, a type of development of productive forces tending to negate the active principle of adjustment to the CWES was embarked upon.

For the theoretical issues that concern us here, we want to stay with certain aspects of the debates of the 1930s in the Soviet Union, as they are revealing on the articulation between the law of value and the building of socialism.

Broadly, and staying with the main points of the controversy between Preobrazhensky and Bukharin, we would like to bring out the theoretical and political cleavages centred precisely on the interpretation of the functioning/modification of the law of value.

Simplifying, Preobrazhensky argued that the law of value, as the law of the distribution of social labour through commodity exchange is subordinated to what he calls the law of primitive socialist accumulation; this latter constitutes the basic regulatory principle that modifies the law of value. Primitive socialist accumulation underlies the necessity, through various mechanisms, including the price system, of the forced contribution from the peasantry.

This is a conscious and deliberate non-equivalence in favour of industry (and the towns), the sole condition required by the radical modification of inter-sectoral relations and the acceleration of the development of productive forces. Preobrazhensky's viewpoint thus stipulates, *de facto*, the break-up of the alliance of popular classes (proletariat–peasantry).

In short, the modification of the law of value under the effect of the so-called law of prior socialist accumulation is a political act breaking the system of alliances that emerged from the 1917 revolution. On this basis a redistribution of productive forces (labour and means of production) would be effected in the form of a forced contribution from the peasantry.

Bukharin's reasoning is that proportionality in the division of social labour cannot be biased. The deliberate breach in the non-respect of proportions leads to imbalances and disturbances. If the law of value is a law of the distribution of labour *ex post facto* and (through the vicissitudes of the market), the Plan, while respecting the principle of compensation for expenditure incurred, *anticipates*, which, in a spontaneous context of regulation is done after the event. The law of value is respected as a whole but its action is now 'rationalized' through anticipation thanks to the Plan; which deprives it of its immanent character that imposes itself through sanctions and catastrophes.

Bukharin is, as a result, more respectful of the need to preserve and consolidate the alliance between the proletariat and the peasantry. How far might this viewpoint be more similar to the Maoist model as it was summarized by Mao in the *Ten Major Relationships* popularized by the principle *walk on two legs*? The ten major relationships particularly stress the need to establish a fair relationship between heavy industry, on the one hand, and light industry and agriculture, on the other, whence the requirement to readjust the proportions in investment in favour of these latter:

> In the circumstances of China, accumulation through agriculture and light industry is more significant . . .
>
> The Soviet Union has adopted measures which squeeze the peasants very hard . . . Our policies towards the peasants differ . . . Our agricultural tax has always been relatively low. In the exchange of industrial and agricultural products we follow a policy of . . . *exchanging equal or roughly equal value.* The state buys agricultural products at standard prices while the peasants suffer no loss, and, what is more, our purchase prices are gradually being raised. In supplying the peasants with manufactured goods we follow a policy of larger sales with a small profit and of stabilizing or appropriately reducing their prices.

The Maoist model thus underlies the introduction of an original *specific content* of the law of value. The social form which presides over its new content is expressed at the political level by the nature of the social class alliance between the working class and the peasantry. Exchanges between town and countryside, between industry and agriculture tend to be made on a basis of equivalence or rough equivalence.

In other words, the basic principle of the law of value is thus: one unit of labour time (of the same intensity) provides the same quantity of value wherever it may be. Taking account of working conditions (time-span and intensity), and *disregarding qualitative differences and hence differences of productivity*[20] we shall take one year to be that unit. The expenditure of mean social labour in industry and agriculture during one year claims the same quantity of value (or almost), leading to exchange at equal or roughly equal prices.

This, then, is one way in which social labour, productive forces and incomes are distributed that modifies the classical content of the law of value. Through this conscious modification the perverse effect of adjustment to the CWES (adjustment to the system of world prices) is negated, the effect that produces and reproduces heterogeneity in the distribution of productivities and rewards between sectors, notably agriculture and industry.

Here, a different rationality is at work, one based initially on the demand for effective solidarity between workers in the towns and peasants in the countryside, a rationality that underpins a development that will gradually overcome the historical backwardness and gradually negate the effects of worldwide unequal and polarized development.

Delinking is simply the *political* implementation (the demand for a popular alliance) of an alternative rationality involving, through equal or roughly equal exchange between unequally developed sectors (different productivities), a distribution of productive forces tending to the negation of this structural inequality and homogenization in the distribution of productivities and rewards (especially between agriculture and industry).[21]

Conclusion

So far we have tried to place the adjustment–delinking problematic in relation to three areas in which the law of value converges and overlaps. One key idea has been argued throughout – that adjustment to the CWES maintains and reproduces unequal and polarized development. Adjustment to the CWES is, however, not synonymous with the absolute negation of growth; but we have argued that this growth through adjustment is perverse, in the precise sense of unequal growth, reproducing and deepening the heterogeneity and sectoral and social disparities while rendering the external positions even more fragile, that is, making the drawbacks of adjustment even more evident. Through growth and adjustment the shaping of the societies of the periphery by external constraints is reproduced in new forms.

Growth through adjustment[22] is in fact an *ideological* justification of a growth realized in favour of a minority that imposes its development, to make its class domination permanent.

We have, furthermore, argued that delinking from the CWES is consubstantial with socio-political readjustments (a new alliance of the popular classes) giving the direct producers themselves a dominant position in political and economic processes. This is a new distribution of political and economic powers in favour of the popular classes to embark on a development leading to nation-building. Thus, delinking refers to the gradual establishment of a new social system (popular participation, more equal relations of distribution and so on) making popular nation-building possible.

If delinking is the logical product of unequal development, it is not, however, the ineluctable and irreversible product of it. Because the new social space that it creates is traversed by the arena of social classes locked in struggle, it is an open space. Delinking can open the way to real social advances.

But real history is not a straight line on which every advance is irreversible . . . Delinking can open up a new social order (of liberty and equality) . . . That is a possibility and not a necessity.

The different historical experiences that we have analysed here have shown that, generally, attempts at socio-political adjustment in the form of a redistribution of political and economic powers have been rather limited and for the most part reversible; in addition, submission to the active principle of adjustment to the CWES has been only slightly attenuated (or not attenuated at all) by the acquisition of spaces of relative autonomy relative to the CWES. The spaces acquired in precise historical contexts, at best made it possible to renegotiate the classic forms of integration into the international division of labour. These spaces proved to be fragile and all the more limited by internal class relations marked by the *de facto* exclusion of the popular classes.

Notes

1. Marx, K., *Lettres à Kugelman*, Paris, Editions Sociales-Classiques du marxisme, p. 103.
2. The (capitalist) commodity economy only becomes social through the process of exchange. The link between the independent autonomous private producers is expressed through commodity exchange of the products of their labour. The law of value establishes the social linkage between autonomous commodity producers.
3. Marx, K., op. cit.
4. Marx, K., *Capital*, Book 3, vol. 8, (Editions Sociales) p. 252.
5. 'Even if an individual article, or definite quality of one kind of commodity may contain simply the social labour required to produce it, and as far as this aspect is concerned the inherent value of this commodity represents more than the necessary labour, yet, if the commodity in question is produced on a scale that exceeds the social labour than it actually contains'. K. Marx, *Capital*, London, Penguin, 1981, commodities in question then represents on the market a much smaller quantity of social labour than it actually contains'. K. Marx, *Capital* (London: Penguin, 1981) vol. I, p. 288.
6. This is work carried out with the average degree of skill and intensity, in conditions which are normal in relation to a given social environment.
7. Marx, K., *Capital*, vol. I, p. 280. Here the law of value acts as the law forming prices of production. This transformation results from the double separation between capitals and capital and labour in the capitalist mode of production.
8. While competition transfers capitals from less profitable branches to more profitable ones, it leads to changes in productive combinations and hence to a new distribution of productive forces, labour forces and means of production.
9. Or the law of the formation of prices of production.
10. Notably over the last three decades.
11. The vogue term to describe this reality is worldwide *interdependence*.
12. What does the law of value of unequal exchange say exactly?

Regardless of any alteration in prices resulting from imperfect competition on the commodity market, unequal exchange is the proportion between equilibrium prices that is established through the equalization of profits between regions in which the role of surplus value is 'institutionally' different. The term institutionally means that these rates are, for whatever reason, safeguarded from competitive equalization on the factors market and are independent of relative prices. A. Emmanuel, *Unequal Exchange*, (NLB) pp. 61–4.

13. Because wage goods are also more and more becoming world commodities (even if they are produced in a pre-capitalist framework), the tendency is towards the constitution of a single value of labour. However, given the constellation of

numerous historical facts (mode of penetration of capitalism and mode of articulation between the CMP and other modes of production that have been subordinated but not destroyed) the *prices of labour are different*.

14. At the level of the disaggregation of the national economy into a dozen branches, the $\frac{C}{V}$ (organic composition of capital) varies from 1 to 4 in the centre for an average profit rate of 15–20%, productivities vary from 1 to 2. In the periphery, the range of $\frac{C}{V}$ is 1 to 35, and that of productivities 1 to 10. 'It is this feature that accounts for the sectoral differences in remuneration and constitutes the principal aspect of inequality in income distribution in the Third World.' (Samir Amin, *Développement inégal*, Paris, Editions de Minuit, p. 189).

These gaps are at the heart of the structural qualitative differences between centre and periphery. In terms of income distribution, Samir Amin (*La déconnexion*, Paris, Maspero, 1986) provides the following indications

	Centre	Periphery
Rate of surplus value = shares, profits, wages	$\frac{40}{60}$	$\frac{40}{60}$
Wage-earning population Total population	75–80%	= 30% maximum
Share of income of		
25% of the population*	10%	5%
50% of the population	25%	12%
75% of the population	50%	35%

In the periphery, broadly,

$\frac{1}{3}$ of the (urban) population receives – $\frac{2}{3}$

$\frac{2}{3}$ of the (rural) population receives – $\frac{1}{3}$

* the poorest.

15. It should not be forgotten that the law of value is a historical social form of the distribution of social labour, of productive forces.

16. Dominance, in the sense too, of the subordination of other pre-capitalist types of relations.

17. This refers back to the notions of internal delinking and external delinking.

18. Parenthesis added.

19. Marx, K., op. cit.

20. As regards productivity, it must be pointed out that labour is said to be more productive when over a single unit of time it produces more use-values but not value. What meaning then can be given to the comparison between x use-values of a good i and y use-values of another good j produced over the same unit of time?

21. Although critical evaluation of Soviet- or Maoist-type models is not the central concern of this book, we must point out that many analysts tend to argue the idea of imposed, not voluntary, delinkings, imposed by the destabilization of the dominant forces of the CWES. In addition, it is strongly argued that the delinkings achieved in both the Soviet Union and China are reversible. The effects of adjustment to the CWES (via the law of value) have never been finally neutralized, whence the strong tendency towards reintegration into the CWES as partners more or less openly accepting the principle of adjustment to the CWES.

22. The ideological expression of growth through adjustment is transmitted growth.

Index